HARVARD BOYS

HARVARD BOYS

A Father and Son's Adventures
Playing Minor League Baseball

JOHN WOLFF & RICK WOLFF

SKYHORSE PUBLISHING

Jackie Robinson once observed that a life is not important except in the impact it has on other lives.

That philosophy certainly personifies Bob and Jane Wolff, Patty Wolff, and John D. Rapoport. Without their support, our dreams would have never been fulfilled.

CONTENTS

PREFACE

What you're about to read is a true story. Every word of it.

Now, I know that writers and television and movie producers say that all the time. But in this case, all that you're about to read really did happen. As Casey Stengel used to say, "You could look it up!"

Here's one for starters. In 1972, when I was a junior at Harvard University, I was drafted by the Detroit Tigers. I was a low draft choice (33rd round), mainly because I was a six-foot, 165-pound, righty-hitting second baseman with little power. The book on me was that I could run well, had excellent hands and range at second, and was determined to do well. On the down side, I didn't hit many balls over the fence. (I always preferred to be called a "gap hitter" as opposed to being labeled as a "Punch-and-Judy".) Overall, I was projected to be a .250 hitter if I could beat out some bunts and get a few lucky hops on the grounders I hit through the infield.

Now fast forward to 2006. My son John, also a second baseman, is also drafted after his junior year at Harvard—no, not by Detroit, but by their division rival, the Chicago White Sox. John was also a low draft choice (47th round). True, John is bigger than I was (he's six feet, two inches, 185 pounds), and hits lefty. Yes, he has excellent hands and a better arm than I ever did; but I was quicker on the bases whereas he's a better pure hitter.

There are other similarities as well. Neither one of us got much playing time at Harvard. (Though over the last several years, ironically, a few ballplayers who rode the bench at Harvard ended up signing up pro contracts. I'll let you draw your own conclusions about the Harvard coaching staff.) In our summers away from college, both John and I developed into league All-Stars in the highly competitive Atlantic Collegiate Baseball League (ACBL), a wooden-bat league that serves as a major showcase for pro prospects. In the ACBL, I was fortunate enough to have played for Al Goldis, a solid baseball man who played in the Reds' farm system and who went on to become a highly respected major league scout. During his stint in the ACBL, John had the good fortune to play for Dan Gray, a former star catcher in the Dodgers' organization and now a highly respected baseball coach and instructor.

John and I both took off our last semester from college to go to spring training. We both returned to Cambridge, Massachusetts, the following fall, finished our last semester, and graduated. But it did raise some eyebrows to some on campus when I took off my last semester from Harvard, and apparently John went through the same experience.

You have to understand (and if you're a baseball fan, you certainly will) that John and I both share a deep and lasting passion for playing baseball—a passion that I inherited from my dad, Bob Wolff, the legendary sportscaster who was inducted into the Broadcasters' wing of the National Baseball Hall of Fame in Cooperstown in 1995. The game has been a major theme in my life from the day I was born, and I'm certain that the Wolff baseball-based DNA was then passed on from me to my son. Or more precisely, from father to son to grandson. Sounds like the perfect double play combination.

I went to my first Florida spring training in late February, 1973. In those days, long before cell phones and the Internet had been invented, long distance phone calls home from Lakeland, Florida (home of the Tigers' spring training base) to Scarsdale, New York (where my family was), were not only extremely expensive, but you often had to wait in line to use the one pay phone in the minor league camp. As a result, I spent a lot of time writing letters longhand to my family.

Those letters, which documented my daily experiences as a minor league player, were kept by my mom and dad. One thing led to another, and—thanks to the encouragement of New York sports columnist Phil Pepe, editor Zander Hollander, and my dad—those letters morphed into a book with the provocative title, *What's a Nice Harvard Boy Like You Doing in the Bushes?* The book, published in diary form by Prentice-Hall, captured my two full years as a pro player, including my spring training experiences, my first year in Anderson, South Carolina, and then my second season in Clinton, Iowa.

Now, back to the present. John signs with the White Sox and reports to their spring training facility in Tucson, Arizona. Hmmmm. Another generation of Harvard baseball player about to embark on a career in pro ball. It didn't take too much of a creative leap to suggest to my son that he, too, keep a diary of his pro career.

Of course, there are differences between then and now. John went to spring training in Arizona, and I went to spring training in Florida. John wrote his diary home via e-mail, while I wrote my letters in longhand and had to mail them with a stamp. But in the end, the differences were few. What was more striking to me were the amazing parallels between my experiences in chasing my major league dream in the 1970's, and John's own chase some thirty years later. As I pored through his e-mails on a daily basis, I found myself reliving the same highs and lows—the daily ups and downs of professional baseball—feelings I hadn't thought about since I was in my early twenties.

I had almost forgotten that, unlike most professions, where successes and failures are mostly mixed together, baseball is a very definitive world—where a 2-for-4 day at the ballpark lets you stand a little taller and smile a little easier, whereas the misery of an 0-for-4 (a collar, in baseball parlance) can humble you in so many awful ways. That's just the way baseball is.

Indeed, that is what is so timeless about this game. As this book will reveal, minor league baseball still revolves around the same universal dream, whether you played in the 1970s or today

— *Rick Wolff*
Armonk, NY

EDITOR'S NOTE

Harvard Boys is John's diary of his first year in professional baseball. His entries come first in this book, followed by his dad's responses and reflections in italics.

HARVARD BOYS

MARCH

WELCOME TO SPRING TRAINING, ROOKIE.

March 6, 2006
Tucson, Arizona

I stepped outside the airport in Tucson. The sun was shining, there wasn't a cloud in the sky, and the temperature was a spectacular eighty-five degrees.

Just five hours earlier, I had left my home in New York where it was overcast, snowy, and downright cold.

Welcome to baseball weather!

The Chicago White Sox clubhouse manager Dan Flood picked me up at the airport along with three other young players who had just arrived. As we sat silently on the bus on our way to the hotel, we all sized each other up, thinking to ourselves, "I bet that guy is pretty good, but he's got nothing on me." Maybe that's just hopeful thinking, but to me, baseball has to be played with a sense of arrogance and cockiness. If you don't have that inner confidence then you might as well hang up the spikes before you even step in the batter's box.

As we cruised down the flat Arizona highway, I recall being amazed by the beautiful mountains in the distance surrounding the city of Tucson. I also kept looking for signs of green foliage, but the only color I could see along the way were in the different kinds of brown cactus that flanked the roadway. Arizona looked so different to me that it was almost intimidating. There were seemingly very few living things—just a lot of rocks, sand, and dirt. In truth, a lot of nothing. I take that back; there was a lot of sunshine.

I guess one of the more experienced players on the bus noticed that I was starting to get uncomfortable with the scenery, and he blurted out, "Yeah man. I hope you like it hot. They say it's a dry heat but I think that's B.S. It's like sitting in your oven at 120 degrees."

I laughed and introduced myself. Ryan McCarthy had been a top draft choice out of UCLA and had played Class A ball the year before for the White Sox in Kannapolis, North Carolina. Over the next few months, I would find out that Ryan was considered to be one of the star shortstops in the White Sox organization. But before I knew any of this, he was the first player I met in Arizona and also one of the nicest guys around camp. Ryan was a true Southern Californian ballplayer with his style of play and also his general laid-back and friendly attitude. He had spiked-up dark hair and dressed like a surfer. Growing up in the Northeast, I've always been somewhat jealous that I didn't have the style sense to dress like a true vintage surfer. I'm more of a collared shirt, blue jeans, and top-siders (aka boat shoes) kind of guy. Basically, I'm not a particularly radical or intriguing dresser. However, if you were to visit the Harvard campus you'd quickly notice that I fit in perfectly. There are a lot of collared shirts at Harvard. Some guys even wear pink ones.

On the ball field, everyone wears his uniform a certain way. Pants down, socks up, wristbands, no wristbands, jewelry, metal spikes, plastic spikes, eye black, sunglasses, and many other ways to express "who you are" on the field. Some organizations force players to always wear their pants up and to use only a certain type of sunglasses (the

Gargoyles brand is very common). Certain organizations do this at the minor league levels (A to AAA) in order to promote uniformity and the idea that everyone is equal, even though that is not true whatsoever. Once you make it to the big leagues you can wear your uniform any way you want. Fortunately, the White Sox didn't have these strict rules and the players had a lot more flair and personality in how they dressed.

It's always fun to note what the players wear off the field. For example, a player who dresses with great style on the field may dress like a total slob when he's away from the field. Ryan McCarthy, as I would soon find out, was not only a good dresser on the street, but also on the field. It was pretty clear that Ryan had been around for a few years and was well-liked by the organization. Unfortunately, I heard a week later that Ryan's throwing shoulder had been bothering him for a while and he had gone through an MRI. The results showed he had torn his labrum and needed surgery. He left spring training to have surgery and then was sent home to rehab. He ended up missing the rest of the season.

In truth, I wanted to ask Ryan a million questions on the bus, but I tried to act like I'd been through this routine before— which, of course, I hadn't. We pulled up to the Riverpark Inn off of Interstate 10 near the University of Arizona and I was eager to unpack and grab some food. The Riverpark, although not very big, was a very nice hotel by minor league standards. It had a Bennigan's restaurant, a sunny patio, tennis courts, a pool, and cable television. It all felt pretty good, except that as the days wore on, I began to discover that hot water, electricity, and air conditioning were not always guaranteed.

In any event, the clerk at the front desk told me that my roommate, Dustin Shafer, had not checked in yet. I went to my room, unpacked, got some take out from Bennigan's, and relaxed. Shafer (aka "Shafedog") didn't show up until later that evening, when he strolled into our room with a big country smile on his face and a couple of suitcases. Shafer was from Kentucky and had already played a year or two with the White Sox as an infielder/ outfielder. A big, strong, tattooed, blond-haired kid drafted out of junior college, Shafedog gave me a big handshake and then started making phone calls to all his old buddies, who were having some beers across the way. It's good to be a veteran in spring training.

After having a few beers with Shafer and his old teammates, I finally crawled into bed and tried to get some sleep, because physicals were scheduled for 6:00 A.M. sharp the next day. Shafer got back to the room and hopped on his computer. I was relaxing on my bed. "Hey Wolffman, you ready for this nonsense tomorrow? Just think, a full month of slave labor with no pay."

Whoa! No pay? I thought we were professionals. That sucks. Turns out that we wouldn't see our first paycheck until sometime in April, after we've made a team. Meanwhile, our hotel and food are supplied by the White Sox. But despite this disappointing news, I couldn't understand why Shafedog wasn't excited about spring training. As for me, I could barely sleep that night.

But Shafedog explained to me that the best part of spring is the beginning—when you see your buddies from last season—and also the end, when you break camp to start the season. The part in between, he said, quickly gets boring. Real boring.

That being said, as you might imagine, I was still very excited to get to the field and experience spring training for myself. Hey, my first day on the job as a pro!

. . .

I can recall arriving at my first spring training in 1973. I also recall the sudden and revitalizing instant warmth of stepping out of the airport in sunny Florida after leaving the cold, cold climate of New York City. Baseball is indeed a warm weather sport—it always has been, and always will be. I also recall checking into the spring training facilities in Lakeland, Florida. "Tigertown" had its own dorm for minor league players—Fetzer Hall—and the accommodations, although a bit spartan, were clean and neat. My roommate was an outfielder from, I believe, the Midwest. Nice guy, but as I recall, he snored.

Like John, I couldn't wait to get going the next day. It was like Christmas morning in the beginning of March!

March 7, 2006
Tucson, Arizona
I woke up at 5:00 A.M. It felt as though my head had just hit the pillow, but it was already time to be getting up. I showered, shaved, and then grabbed a bit of what passed as breakfast from a big, temporary tent that had been put up behind the Riverpark Inn for the minor leaguers. I quickly learned that the ballplayers staying in the hotel were not allowed to enjoy the hotel's nice breakfast buffet. Instead, we had to go to the tent, where they would serve us what could best be described as some highly questionable meals. I was

not a fan of the tent's cuisine, although I learned to force the food down in an effort to keep my energy going throughout the day.

In short, the food was a joke. It was barely edible. As a result, I began buying a lot of energy bars from the local Circle K store and occasionally tried to sneak into Bennigan's for some real eggs and toast. I always made sure to dress up when I went into Bennigan's so that the hotel staff would think that I was a regular guest in the hotel, and not a baseball player (the hotel offered a free breakfast to its real guests, but not to the baseball players.) If I got caught, which happened on occasion, I would have to pay for my breakfast. Hey, I wasn't proud of this charade, but remember—we don't get paid in spring training, the tent food was terrible, and I needed to get some food in my system.

A shuttle bus took players to the ballpark, which is about ten minutes away from the hotel. I grabbed a shuttle along with a bunch of other players, eager to get to the ballpark. But mind you, there were literally dozens and dozens of young ballplayers reporting to camp. The White Sox minor league facility is located out beyond the major league field in Tucson, and I soon realized that my first major task as a pro ballplayer would be to try to find my locker in this massive clubhouse. There was row after row of open lockers! And it was total mayhem. Hundreds of hulking ballplayers, yapping in either English or Spanish, wearing the same gear, swarmed in the room all at once trying to organize their baseball equipment. Everyone was clad in their team-issued White Sox black mesh shorts and their grey shirts that said just "White Sox Baseball."

Trust me, this never happened at Harvard. And the worst part about this scene in Tucson was that I couldn't find my White Sox shorts and shirt. Everyone was supposed to wear these clothes for the physical exam. But, because I couldn't find mine, I had to wear the only shorts and t-shirt I had in my bag. And as luck would have it, my shorts were bright orange—and my tee shirt was Harvard crimson.

Not only was I a fashion nightmare, but I stuck out like a sore thumb amid a sea of grey and black White Sox shirts and shorts. Imagine showing up on your very first day of work looking like you just escaped from the circus! I thought to myself that this might not be the best way to start off my career with the Sox.

However, to my surprise and undying relief, all the doctors and medical examiners thought my get-up was hilarious. I even tried to play along by making jokes about myself with them—that somebody had put me up to this. The Harvard Baseball shirt was a walking punch line. Everyone offered their lame Harvard or Ivy League joke and I forced an awkward early morning smile.

Fortunately, I had some unexpected support. As it turns out, Dr. Bernie Bach, who serves as the orthopedic surgeon for the White Sox, apparently had given all of the trainers and medical staff a heads-up to look out for me. (Dr. Bach's son, David, was a very talented baseball player and teammate of mine at Harvard.) I appreciated Dr. Bach's efforts, because I got a very warm welcome from the staff.

But enough of the funny stuff. The physical turned out to be the most intensive examination I had ever experienced. The doctors told me that I had 20/13 vision, which is excellent, but then the EKG examiner told me to bring my card to the head physician immediately. While I was waiting on line to show the physician my card I noticed that in big block letters it said: "NOTE: ABNORMAL HEART BEAT—HYPERTROPHY OF LEFT VENTRICLE."

I wasn't pre-med, and I'm certainly not a cardiologist, but I knew that the words *abnormal* and *hypertrophy* were not good things. All of a sudden I got very nervous that the team might not let me work out because of an abnormal heart beat. I gave the physician the form and he looked at me and smiled. He could tell I was anxious. He explained that in young athletes who are in good shape, sometimes the left ventricle is in fact bigger than usual. That's okay, he said, because it's in charge of pumping the blood throughout the body—so it is not really an abnormal heart beat. Quite the opposite, actually. The EKG is actually showing that I'm in pretty good shape. Interesting, and what a relief.

Our next chore was to run two 300-yard shuttles. We had to complete them both in under fifty-four seconds. I thought this wouldn't be much of a problem, but as I was running I realized that I was having a very hard time. I couldn't catch my breath! My throat was so dry that I could barely breathe. Then I realized that this is the dry Arizona air that everyone had been telling me about. All of a sudden, those little shuttle runs turned into quite a challenge. I survived, but many players couldn't finish. The penalty for failing the fitness test is long distance running in the mornings. Not fun. I was grateful to have passed.

• • •

Curiously, I don't recall much about undergoing any physical examinations, or for that matter, participating in any running sessions.

Back in my day, ballplayers still regarded spring training as a gentle way of guiding one's body back into shape after a long winter's hiatus.

But I will say this: If a new kid ever showed up on the first day of spring training wearing orange shorts and a red shirt, he'd never hear the end of it!

March 8, 2006
Tucson, Arizona

Today was my first day as a professional ballplayer.

I have to admit, it was pretty cool.

Understand that I've been doing my homework and reading up about the White Sox organization. Not just about the big leaguers, of course, but about the top prospects Chicago has throughout their minor league system. And as I made my way out to the minor league fields this morning under warm and gloriously blue skies, I was like a kid at his very first ball game.

All around me were the players I had read about for years, guys like Jim Thome, El Duque (Orlando Hernandez), Juan Uribe, Scott Podsednik, and on and on—all big leaguers up close and in person. They were all wearing crisp and clean Chicago White Sox uniforms, and I had to keep reminding myself that I was now one of their colleagues. Well, of course, they make a little more money than I do, and in truth, the major leaguers have nicer caps than the cheesy ones that the minor leaguers get. (I would later learn that the "cap hierarchy" was a good way to figure out who was on the fast track; only the best and brightest prospects warranted the fully-fitted White Sox caps—everybody else, like me, had the low-rent one-size-fits-all cap.)

I would later find out that these top prospects would get called up to play in a few major league spring training games, and that's where they would receive the "fancy" hats. These caps, of course, became treasured possessions, and the minor leaguers wore them like status symbols. By the way, it looks as though the White Sox do a good job at calling up a lot of minor league prospects in spring training to give them a taste of playing with the major leaguers. I hear that other organizations don't call up any minor leaguers, or call up only a very few at the end of spring training, when the veterans feel that they have had enough and are ready to start their season. But the White Sox would take it easy on their major league veterans and let them just play four or five innings, and then the minor leaguers would take over. This gives the major leaguers a break, and it gives the minor leaguers a thrill. Because of this philosophy, there were a lot of prospects walking around with nice hats. After a week or so I started to see some guys who I knew weren't top prospects walking around with nice hats, and I couldn't believe that they had been called up to play in the major league spring training games.

I finally asked my roommate, "Hey Shafedog, did Moreno get called up to a major league game?" Shafer answered flatly, "No, why?" I explained, "Well, he's got one of the nice hats on that they give to all minor leaguers who get called up." Shafer started to laugh, "Wolffman, they sell those stupid hats at the local mall for fifteen bucks. I'll buy you one later today if you want to seem important. Trust me though, I've tried it all before and it really doesn't make a difference. You are not going to fool anyone with a fancy cap." And so with that conversation I figured out that there are prospects and then there are "suspects," who buy hats at the mall. Any player who felt the need to buy a fancy hat at the mall was definitely not a prospect.

The first impression I had of the major leaguers, by the way, was that they are huge. I mean, I'm a pretty decent-sized guy at six-one, 185 pounds, but compared to guys like Thome, a mountain of a man, or even El Duque, I'm a mere mortal. The same goes for the vast majority of the minor leaguers as well. These are, generally speaking, very large people.

We really didn't do much in terms of actually playing ball today. There were no games. But we did exercise, throw a little bit, and strut around in the Arizona sun. It felt good to work the kinks out and to bask in the warm realization that I really am a professional baseball player.

• • •

The first thing I remember about spring training is that, unlike in high school or college ball, here you are surrounded by a veritable army of ballplayers—all of them decked out in similar uniforms (in my day, we all wore grey Detroit Tigers double knits, with a very inexpensive cap). But as noted, there were dozens of players! There weren't just two or three catchers in camp—there had to be at least fifteen! There weren't just a few middle infielders—there were at least thirty! There weren't a few left-handed pitchers—they were all lined up, at least two dozen deep!

And all of these guys, you could be sure, were superstars in high school, or junior college, or at four-year colleges. Some got big bucks just to sign their name to a contract. And most importantly, they could all play the game.

Psychologically, just to make sure I didn't feel like I was at the bottom of the heap, I remember always looking around for a player or two who I seemed to be better than. Fortunately, even on that first day, there were one or two (but not many!). I just remember hoping that whatever these coaches were looking for that, hopefully, I was making a good impression on them. Nobody wants to get cut on the very first day of spring training.

March 15, 2006
Tucson, Arizona

I've been here for about a week now, and life has settled into a daily rhythm. Up early, shower and shave, get some breakfast, and head out to the ballpark on the shuttle bus. The first few days have been filled with plyometric exercises, drills, infield and outfield practice, batting practice, and so on. We haven't played any games yet, but we are working hard and breaking a sweat. Of course, in the dry heat, any perspiration quickly dries up, and I have to keep reminding myself to drink plenty of water during the day, lest I dehydrate.

I'm feeling good, though. I'm taking ground balls at second, getting my swings in the batting cage, running the bases. The coaches seem pleased. So far, so good.

• • •

I remember spring training also falling into a predictable routine very quickly during the first week. You did your work, you made sure you had plenty of suntan lotion on your arms, neck, and ears, and you went about your business. In Tigertown in the 1970s, we used to get on the field around 8:30, do our drills until 11:30, have a very weak lunch (usually a bologna or cheese sandwich and a cup of thin soup), and then we'd play an intrasquad game in the afternoon. It wasn't necessarily exciting, but for kids like me who wanted to impress anyone who might have been watching, you tried to do everything you could at top speed.

March 16, 2006
Tucson, Arizona

One of the more nerve-racking drills that we do is a game called "27 Outs." The game is designed to improve and perfect our defensive abilities, positioning, and coverage.

The idea of the drill is fairly simple. You have every position filled defensively, and the coach places various runners on base. He then fungoes the ball anywhere on the field. Of course, our job defensively is to make the play, get an out, and if necessary, make the right cut-off throw. Neither physical errors nor mental mistakes are acceptable. And, of course, the objective is to achieve twenty-seven consecutive outs.

It may not sound all that tough, but trust me, when you get to twenty-two outs in a row only to blow a routine relay throw and have to reset the count back to zero under a broiling sun, people begin to lose their tempers in the field. And when that happens, the physical errors come. Oh, and to add to the pressure, the entire front office and coaching staff watches the game. Needless to say, this can be a bit intimidating for us rookies.

Yet, under the watchful eye of everyone important to my career,

I played a strong second base today, turning a few key double plays and handling some tough ground balls. After a couple hours of trying to complete the drill, we had twenty-six outs and our coach, former major league shortstop Rafael Santana, lofted a Texas leaguer into short center field. I couldn't get to it, and our very fast centerfielder seemed to be too deep to make a play. I thought we were going to be back at zero again when, out of nowhere, our centerfielder, Sean Smith, sprinted in and made an amazing diving catch to save the day. The entire team swarmed centerfield and piled on Smitty. All the coaches were laughing and loving every minute of it. So much so that they told us all to call it a day and hit the showers.

As you might imagine, Sean Smith didn't buy his fancy hat at the local mall. He played in a few major league spring training games and hit pretty well. He's well-built, speedy, and one of the most popular players in camp. He's one of the few guys who never forgets to say hello or to pat a fellow teammate on the back. Everyone knows he could be a major leaguer.

• • •

That's the funny thing about playing pro ball. You begin to learn intuitively how to evaluate talent, and at the same time, you begin to appreciate just how good these guys are. Sure, you know that the odds of any minor leaguer ever getting even a cup of coffee in the show are astronomical (by most accounts, only about ten percent of all minor leaguers ever spend one day in a big league uniform), but that's not the point. Professional baseball, even at the lowest rung of the minor leagues, is still an elite fraternity.

Day by day, you begin to get a better sense of why these guys were signed to pro contracts. Some guys are great outfielders with terrific speed. Others have cannon arms from behind the plate. Some pitchers have sharp curveballs. Whatever their talents are, you definitely begin to see them emerge—much in the same way that a scout or two must have seen those talents as well.

March 17, 2006
Tucson, Arizona

After all the physicals, defensive drills, and lectures, we finally played our first game today. It was just an intrasquad game, to be more precise, but it was real baseball, and everybody here was ready and raring to go.

I'm glad to report that my first hit as a pro came in my first at-bat. I was batting lefty against Steven Squires, a right-hander from Michigan whose dad had played many years for the big league White Sox. In any event, the first pitch I saw was a fastball, outside, and I took it for a ball. On his next offering, Squires threw me a two-seam fastball on the outside corner. I waited on it perfectly and laced it into leftfield over the third baseman's head. A solid, clean base hit.

Of course I always assumed that I would get a hit or two at some point during the course of spring training, but getting that first one—well, that was a pretty sweet feeling. Somehow, I felt my whole body relax a bit. I think I even smiled.

. . .

I remember early in spring training in 1973, for some reason they brought me over to Joker Marchant Stadium on a beautiful day to play in a scrimmage game. I was wearing the traditional grey Detroit double knits. I was number 89 in your scorecard—that's right, number 89. I remember coming to bat against a big, hard-throwing righty named Dave Lemanczyk.

I didn't know Dave from the man in the moon, but I figured he must have been something special because he was wearing the home white Tigers uniform, and his jersey had his name spelled out on the back. In any event, I forget the count, but I do recall lining a bullet to right center that was flagged down by the center fielder. And on my next at-bat, I walked, stole second, and eventually scored.

My performance, of course, was not exactly headline stuff. But I do recall that, somehow, I had made an impression. Apparently, the coaches and scouts who were in attendance were impressed by this low draft choice second baseman who had lined a shot off one of their top pitching prospects, and then walked and later scored. In other words, that one game in Marchant Stadium helped establish me as something of a real pro player as far as the Tigers were concerned. Dave Lemanczyk, of course, went on to have a wonderful career in the big leagues. I wonder if he ever remembered pitching against me in Marchant that day.

Now, I must confess that I don't recall my first real hit in my first spring training in Tigertown. Chances are it was either a seeing-eye grounder up the middle, or a bunt hit. But I do know this: When you're a rookie in your first spring training, you walk around on egg shells. You automatically assume that every action you take is being watched by a thousand sets of eyes from the coaches, scouts, and other players. In other words, you can't wait to do something positive to feel as though you belong. And when you get that first hit, especially a line drive hit, you start to feel as though you're beginning to earn your way into the pro baseball fraternity. Trust me, it's a nice feeling.

March 18, 2006
Tucson, Arizona

Hey, Dad, let the record show that my first extra base hit—a double—came off a lefty named Alex Woodson, who hails from Puerto Rico. He threw me a high, outside fastball, and I drilled a one-hopper off the wall down the leftfield line. Hey, this pro baseball might be a lot easier than I thought!

• • •

Ha-ha-ha! I guess John never read Bart Giamatti's famous essay about how baseball is a game that is "designed to break your heart." This is a game based upon failure, not success. As a pro player, you have to learn to live with the ups and downs every day, and trust me, there are a lot more valleys than peaks. Especially in the minors.

March 19, 2006
Tucson, Arizona

Today's events were more than a bit jarring.

Just as everybody seemed to be fitting in nicely, and we were all getting to know each other and enjoying the fun and camaraderie of being fellow pro ballplayers, suddenly and out of nowhere, twenty players were released.

It was quite a wake-up call. With the White Sox, you stroll into the clubhouse in the morning with your buddies to get changed to work out … but if you don't find your jersey in your locker, that means a plane ticket is waiting for you to take you home.

One morning you show up at the clubhouse and your uniform

is gone. That means goodbye. It is harsh. And it's just as brutal as it sounds.

My roommate, Dustin Shafer, was one of the guys who got released today. We exchanged a few words in the clubhouse, but I was eager to talk with him in more detail back at the hotel. But when I arrived back at our room from the ballpark this afternoon, Shafer's bed was neatly made and all of his stuff was gone. Just like that.

When a player gets released you don't really know what to say or do. Some guys get angry and throw stuff, break things, curse, and generally throw a fit. Other players will just sit quietly by their locker as if in shock waiting for people to come by and say they are sorry or offer some words of sympathy. These players are just waiting to tell anyone who will listen how badly they got screwed and why they are "too good" to be released.

Others may have tears in their eyes because it's just struck them that their lifelong dream is not going to come true. And other players just pack their things and walk out of the clubhouse before anyone even realizes they were let go.

It's that last group of players who I admire and respect. These are the guys who are surprised by getting released. It stings them but they don't voice their anger or let on that they're hurt. They pack up their stuff and say their goodbyes. They don't talk about getting screwed. Rather, they stay optimistic, and they even thank the coaches.

Shafer was kind of a mixed breed. Yes, he did come up to me in the clubhouse to say his goodbye but I really wished he had waited for me to get back to hotel to go out and have one last night of beers and partying.

In Shafer's case I can't really say we were best friends. However, we were about as good as friends as you can be with a complete stranger whom you just met and lived with for about two weeks. Shafer had struggled with his fair share of injuries over the past couple years in pro ball. These injuries didn't appear to be getting better and it frustrated him that he couldn't play up to his full potential.

I'll miss Shafer. He took good care of me. He had a cute older sister who worked in Tucson and she treated both of us to a few very nice meals after some tough days on the ball field. Remember, good food is hard to come by when you are not making any money.

I now have to switch rooms and live with a kid named Josh Morgan. A huge, good ol' country boy from Alabama, Josh was drafted out of the University of South Alabama. At least he's one of the friendliest kids in the White Sox organization. When I informed Josh that I had been assigned to move in with him he grinned and gave me a huge bear hug and said, "We are going to have so much fun!" I just smiled, somewhat sheepishly.

· · ·

The dark side of pro ball is getting released.

I don't know how all the other organizations give kids the bad news, but I recall in Tigertown that the word would come forth on the Fetzer Hall public address system. Seemingly at any time and out of nowhere, suddenly, a burly voice would blurt out, "Attention ... attention ... would the following players report immediately to the front office ... " And then a number of minor leaguers' names would be listed.

Trust me, everything came to a sudden stop when the P.A. system came on. Guys turned off the TV, guys stopped in their tracks, guys got off the phone, and so forth. You held your breath and said a prayer that your name wouldn't be called.

And if and when one of your closer buddies had his name called, you knew it was baseball's version of his walking that last mile. There just weren't any words to say. Yesterday, he was a pro ballplayer with dreams of getting to the big leagues. Today, he had been instantly transformed into another civilian, just another guy who would shed tears as he had to tell his family and closest friends that his dream wasn't going to happen.

March 20, 2006
Tucson, Arizona

One of the morning attractions is the ongoing commotion around the water cooler located in the far back area of the clubhouse. Every day, long before we head out to the field, the water cooler is clearly the most popular place to be. At first I just assumed that all the players were simply trying to stay hydrated for a long day on the field under the hot sun, but upon closer inspection it's evident that numerous pills and powders are being passed around.

No, they are not steroids or performance enhancing drugs. Rather, they are forms of hangover-eliminating potions and powders to help all the guys who partied a little too much the night before. The sad irony is, of course, that more often than not, it's the athletes who show up hungover who go on to blast home run after home run in batting practice and then run the fastest in the sprints.

Also, this morning I made a rookie mistake. I accidentally called hitting coach Nick "Cappy" Capra by the name of Kirk "Champy" Champion. Immediately, Cappy turned on me, took off his Oakley sunglasses and barked, "Are they just giving away diplomas at Harvard? Do I really look that short and fat to you? Champy is that lumpy little coach over there! You are as stupid as that Stanford kid, Donny Lucy."

I was a bit taken aback until Cappy finally smiled and patted me on the back. Now I know Cappy from Champy, and I won't make that mistake again.

You get a glimpse from this encounter that in baseball nicknames are very important. You never address anyone as "Coach" or "Mister," and most players and coaches have distinct nicknames. If you don't have a nickname, your name may turn from Matt to Matty, Don to Donny, John to Johnny, and so on. My nicknames have included Johnny Wolff, Wolffie, Wolffman, Wolffo, Johno, and of course the Spanish translation of *wolf*: el Lobo. Baseball is a small world and everyone is friends. These nicknames are a way of keeping everyone young and on good and equal terms. Some may find this tradition to be somewhat impolite, but it's flattering and accepted to call a coach by his nickname even if he may be thirty years older than you. For example, Nick Leyva will only answer to his nickname, Cuz.

· · ·

Baseball players and beer have gone hand-in-hand (no pun intended) since the game was invented. Some guys do think that they can handle a night of drinking followed by an early morning workout. But trust me, after a while, they all learn their limitations. Especially in spring training, where the days only get longer, dustier, and hotter.

March 21, 2006

Tucson, Arizona

Some random observations from today:

- With more than 130 players walking around in camp—most of whom don't know each other—any item in your locker, or near your locker, that is not clearly marked with your name or number or locked up in the safe, will most likely disappear in the amount of time it takes you to get a drink of water down the hall. It is amazing. There have even been nightmare stories about players stealing money from other players while they are out on the field. In fact, I heard a rumor that one time the instructors locked all the players in the clubhouse and didn't allow anyone to go home until someone confessed and coughed up the missing money. One player finally did, and he was released on the spot.

- Razor Shines, the AAA manager, has the coolest name in camp. By far. I haven't met the man yet, but with a name like that, there is a lot of coolness to live up to.

- Each morning, they post a list of White Sox minor league rosters: Charlotte, South Carolina (AAA); Birmingham, Alabama (AA); Winston-Salem, North Carolina (A); Kannapolis, North Carolina (A); Bristol, Virginia (Rookie); and Great Falls, Montana (Rookie). And of course, each day you have to check to see to which team you're reporting. The truth is, there are a lot of players here but only so many slots on the roster. My job is simple: to make sure that my name stays on one of those rosters.

Right now, my name usually appears on the Bristol or Great Falls roster. But sometimes, I find myself with the Kannapolis team. I have no idea why these moves are made, but I sure don't plan on asking anybody. All I know is that when camp breaks in a few weeks, I want to be on a team.

• • •

Even back with the Tigers, I recall the posting of the daily rosters quite well. And if you're not accustomed to them, they can be quite nerve-racking. Because if you do a little arithmetic, you will realize that the typical minor league team carries only twenty-three players. If the spring training rosters list, say, twenty-five or twenty-six players, then you can quickly figure out that somebody is going to get released. Even worse, as the big league camp starts to reassign spring training invitees back to the minor league camp, suddenly all of the posted rosters begin to slide down to a lower classification. That is, the kids who were on the AAA roster start to get pushed back to the AA roster, and the AA players get pushed back to A ball, and so on.

In short, it's a brutal form of musical chairs ... a domino effect ... and invariably, the kids who are at the lowest rung on the ladder are the ones who find themselves being let go. I haven't shared this information with John yet, because I'm hoping that even though he's currently on the lowest rung of the rosters, that since he's a first-year player the White Sox will want to see him for at least an entire year before making a decision on him. Giving any signed player at least a full year is the customary style in pro baseball. I do want to warn him, though, that more and more cuts will be made throughout the spring.

March 22, 2006

Tucson, Arizona

Juan Uribe, the starting shortstop for the White Sox, appears to have a lot of free time on his hands. For a good part of the day at the field he races his golf cart along with other major leaguers like El Duque and even Manager Ozzie Guillen. This probably doesn't happen in most spring training camps, but the White Sox just won the World Series a few months ago so everyone is in a fairly relaxed and happy mood. This morning as Uribe rounded a sharp turn near the minor league facility, he hit a patch of sand and almost wiped out into a pile of cactus. He decided to stop the racing and just take some batting practice, so he hopped off his cart and promptly began to blast baseballs 500 feet to all fields.

As noted, I have clearly begun to recognize that big league talent is, well, big league talent.

Also, the more time that I'm here, the more I'm noticing that there's a caste system in place here. That is, it's very easy to tell who the big time players and prospects are. There are two ways to tell: 1) Guys who wear White Sox fleeces over their jerseys and 2) guys who wear sunglasses on top of their hats. Both of these are dress violations, which are strictly enforced on every other minor leaguer. There are a rare few, however, who wear their fleeces over their jerseys and their sunglasses on top of their caps and no one gives them a hard time. But I'm not on that level yet.

A stroll through the minor league parking lot is quite an experience as well. That's where the caste system is even more evident. There are about forty to fifty brand-new cars with the newest, most expensive rims, tints, and stereo systems. These, of course, belong to the so-called bonus babies—the guys who were high-round draft choices who got a lot of money to sign.

For guys like me—and trust me, the vast majority of the guys here are like me—we just hop onto the shuttle bus if we have any place we need to go. But even if we did have someplace to go, we'd have no money to take with us.

In fact, let's chat about money. The sports pages are always full of the big bonus baby signings—that some first-round draft choice received a $5 million bonus or more for simply signing his name to a pro contract. Yes, that does happen. Or so I'm told, because nobody gave me a mil to sign with the White Sox. In fact, in terms of getting paid to play ball, minor leaguers don't even get paid in spring training. The ball club takes care of your motel room bill and provides meals, so I guess from their perspective a minor leaguer shouldn't have any other expenses. They do give us about $30 at the end of the week, I guess, for laundry money.

But the bottom line here is that from early March until you make an actual team and start playing real games in mid-April, there are no paychecks. That, by the way, seems to be the same policy with all the pro teams. Of course, if you do have that $5 million signing bonus in the bank, I guess you could spend some of the interest income that it generates. But for the rest of us, it's a long, long wait until that first paycheck comes in.

Speaking of which—according to the standard minor league player's contract, a player in Class A ball earns $1,250 a month … and that's before taxes. That doesn't cover too much, no matter where you're playing ball—especially if you want to splurge on such luxury items like food and shelter. But hey—no matter how you slice it, you are still getting paid to play baseball.

Today we had a late start on the field and it was freezing. The wind was whipping and it was quite an adventure. We tried to take some batting practice but every time we set the pitcher's L-screen up, the wind would immediately blow it right down. In fact, at one point, one of our pitchers was hit hard by a falling screen. He was dazed but okay. But the coaches decided it wasn't worth getting someone hurt, and practice was called off.

Because of the cold weather, all the Dominican kids had on about thirty layers of clothing. All we heard all day was "Mucho frio, mucho frio." Granted, it was pretty cold, but all things considered it was about fifty degrees or so. In fact, I thought to myself that this kind of baseball day in Cambridge would have been welcomed with short sleeves! Almost fifty degrees with a slight and gentle breeze!

• • •

John's observations about the "caste system" made me chuckle, because certainly there was a caste system in place when I was playing ball as well. I also recall walking through the parking lot in Tigertown and seeing all of the late model cars of all the guys who got big bonus dollars. (For the record, I signed for "a bottle of Yoo-hoo and a Schwinn bicycle," as the old line goes).

The odd thing about shelling out those big bucks for bonus babies is that so few of these kids ever really develop into major league stars. It's kind of a bizarre business. I recall once talking with Joe McIlvaine, a tall right-handed pitcher who played in the Tigers' organization with me and who went on to become a very successful major league general manager with the Mets and the Padres, about the millions and millions that were allocated for young prospects' signing bonuses. I recall Joe telling me that budgeting all that guarantee money was just a cost of doing business in baseball, and that of course it wasn't very cost-effective. But that's just how it is if your organization is going to sign high draft choices.

In any event, back when I was in the minors (and in those days, I think I made $650 a month), I recall watching some of the established Detroit Tigers come down to the minor league camp, and like John, I noticed right away that some of these guys just had "major leaguer" written all over them. I recall watching Al Kaline, Dick McAuliffe, Bill Freehan, and several others who would come and work out with us. You could just tell that they were a cut above. I also recall watching Mickey Lolich come over one day to play some wall ball to get in shape. Lolich, as you recall, always had that little extra belly that hung over his belt. But the day I saw him in spring training, I was stunned by how quick and nimble he was on his feet. He could really move for a big guy.

One last note about money. One morning in spring training in Tigertown I was summoned by one of the front office people and was told to hang around after practice finished for the day. Apparently, some TV producers were filming a commercial about joining the Army or Air Force, and they were featuring catcher Bill Freehan in the spot. They need an extra player (me) to stand in the batter's box while Big Bill got up from behind the plate and delivered his lines. Being opportunistic and, quite frankly, hungry, I boldly asked one of the commercial producers if *there was anything left over in the budget to pay me. He looked at me, probably took pity on me, and then fished around in his pocket. He gave me a $50 bill and made my day.*

March 23, 2006
Tucson, Arizona

I realized today that the legendary Japanese pitcher, Hideo Nomo, is in camp. He's on the AAA team and everywhere he goes in camp, he is followed by a massive entourage of Japanese media people. I haven't had a chance to see him pitch yet, but I'm secretly hoping that I can get a chance to hit against him. That would be great fun.

Also, here's another curious observation. You may not know it, but Nomo has an enormous head. His cap size must be the largest in camp. An average cap size is 7¼ or 7½—I'm guessing Hideo wears a size 9! I know some players get swollen heads when they get to the big leagues, but trust me, nobody has a swollen head bigger than Nomo's!

I was also surprised to learn that a lot of the young guys in camp are married. When my friend Matt Dugan said that he had to call "the wife," I thought he was being sarcastic and just referring to his girlfriend. As a result, when I made a passing remark about "the wife," Matt became a little upset and patiently explained to me that he has been married for about two years. I believe Dugan is twenty-two years old. Needless to say, this embarrassed me a bit. I mean, back in Cambridge, I don't think I went to class with anyone who was married. For most of my classmates, marriage is something they see for themselves far off in the future, if they see it at all.

• • •

When it comes to teammates being married, I too remember going through the same kind of culture shock. One of my best friends in the minors was Al Newsome, a power-hitting outfielder from the Atlanta area. Whereas I had a college girlfriend, I can still remember Al bringing his wife and two young kids to our games. As I recall, Al was maybe all of nineteen or twenty years old at the time.

Trust me, the concept of my being married and having children was an idea that I just couldn't even imagine when I was twenty-three years old—especially when playing minor league baseball.

March 24, 2006
Tucson, Arizona

Today is a rare rainy day here in Arizona, so we were dispatched to work out inside. If you were wondering, there are no off days here in spring training.

Let me tell you about walking into the White Sox spring training indoor facility. Not only is it enormous, but it has every possible baseball-related feature you could ever imagine, including huge indoor batting cages, pitching machines, weight rooms, unlimited equipment, and so much more.

This is not something I was used to back at school. True, Harvard had a decent baseball field, but of course our entire spring season really only lasted a month—the month of April. In addition, our indoor batting cages were located in the indoor tennis court area, so there was no guarantee that we would be able to hit if a tennis player had reserved the courts ahead of time. Also, there were only two batting cages; hence, it always turned out to be a challenge to fit a full college team into two cages in the middle of winter and to make sure every player to got enough swings.

Our other indoor facility was located in the basketball pavilion. The artificial turf would be rolled out over the hardwood floor and we could take groundballs and swings in there. Because the basketball team was in season during the winter we couldn't use the facility until late at night, so we would routinely have baseball practices that went well past midnight.

When we did finally venture outside in late March or early April, when the temperature rarely rose above forty-five degrees, our team rule was that if it was above thirty-two degrees we would go out. That, of course, didn't account for wind chills and forms of frozen precipitation. I can remember days when our outfield grass was white from frost and frozen absolutely solid. Fly balls that fell in the outfield would bounce like they were hitting concrete. I recall putting on four layers of clothes before every practice and then still freezing my ass off.

That was baseball at Harvard. That's why I'm so glad to be in the warm sun of Arizona playing baseball in nice weather. It's just so different, like a baseball nirvana. In addition to the state-of-the-art indoor facilities in Tucson, there are seven full-sized baseball diamonds surrounding the clubhouse, and each one is perfectly manicured and dragged every day for our practices and scrimmages.

The infield dirt is baked hard because of the hot sun, but you can't find a bad hop anywhere. Plus, of course, the weather is usually in the seventies under crystal clear blue skies. I'm probably going to regret saying all of this in a few weeks, because the weather in Arizona in March is pleasant. However, it does keep getting hotter and hotter. In leagues like the Gulf Coast League (GCL) or the Arizona League (AZL) the players play games at 10:00 A.M. or noon because it gets too hot later in the day during the summer months. That means players are on the field at 6:00 A.M. doing their drills and fundamentals. Early mornings, but at least it is cool before the sun comes up.

This is exactly the opposite of the way we played baseball at Harvard. Springtime in Boston is a cold, wet, and dreary time of year. I can vividly recall games against Northeastern University that were canceled in April because of gale force winds. We were snowed out two years in a row against Sacred Heart University when we tried to play them in late March. One time, a blizzard started in the seventh inning of our game against cross-town rival Boston College. Of course, we played through it. I can still picture our centerfielder from Southern California almost passing out from the cold when he was stubborn enough to wear short sleeves during our games. He was adamant that he couldn't play well with long sleeves, and soon learned that baseball was not created to be played in the freezing cold.

• • •

Sad to say, Harvard baseball has never been state-of-the-art. Not only were the facilities sparse when I played there back in the 1970s, I think it's safe to say that they haven't improved much over the last thirty years. Nor, despite the threat of global warming, has the springtime weather gotten any better. Let's face it—playing baseball in April in Cambridge is a really bad idea. Always has been, and always will be. And just when you get to May, when the temperatures begin to climb, the season comes to an end so you can take final exams.

By the way, this is not to suggest that there aren't some excellent baseball players who have attended Harvard. There certainly have been, and there have been a lot. Back in my day, in the early 1970s, Harvard was a frequent competitor in the College World Series in Omaha. From my era, star players at Harvard who became pros included Pete Varney, who was a first round draft choice, Dan DeMichele, Bill Kelly, Roz Brayton, Jim Stoeckel, Jamie Werle, and several more. Lots of Harvard kids have signed pro contracts over the years. But in my opinion, I often wonder how much better the program could have been if the facilities and the coaching instruction had been at a higher level.

March 25, 2006
Tucson, Arizona

Once a day during spring training, the position players are given a lecture on defensive positioning, leads and steals, bunting, and other important aspects of the game. It's actually quite a treat, because we get to sit on the well-manicured infield grass under the Arizona sun and listen to such famous former major leaguers as Bobby Tolan, Daryl "D-Bo" Boston, Nate "Pee-Wee" Oliver, Ozzie Guillen, Jerry Hairston, Rafael "Raffie" Santana, Manny Trillo, and many others talking about their beliefs on the proper way to play the game.

In many ways, this is a part of the minor league experience that

I always dreamed about—having a chance to just soak up years and years of inside baseball knowledge from some of the game's top players.

. . .

Harvard offers a lot of wonderful courses on all aspects of the classic liberal arts education, but believe me, there are no courses there on how to hit a ninety-mile-per-hour fastball, or on how to turn a pivot, or on how to hit a hanging curve ball to the opposite field. Yes, you can learn all about Shakespeare, or B.F. Skinner, or the latest on international and domestic politics, but the course catalog offers nothing at all on how to put a good sacrifice bunt down the third base line.

What a waste!

March 27, 2007
Tucson, Arizona

Sometimes, late in the day when things have calmed down, or when I'm just relaxing back in the motel, I'll reflect for a few moments about where I've been in baseball, and how lucky I am to have been given a chance to play pro ball. I know full well that there's no sense of permanence in this business—that the only thing that's constant in pro baseball is change. Rosters, players, lineups, etc. are always changing. That's just the nature of the game.

But all that aside, I'm keenly aware that a year ago, I was just hoping to somehow get a little more playing time on my college team. Sure, I worked hard, but a lot of kids who have similar dreams to mine also work hard. But perhaps it was because I didn't see much playing time in college that I was driven that much more and reached a little higher.

All I know is that over the course of several summers back in the New York City area, I did my best to find out about the various open tryouts that the local scouts ran. I went to a number of these, took my chances, and was always very gratified when the scouts seemed to like what they saw in me. I recall filling out follow-up cards for several teams, always a good sign that the scout thought you might have a chance. Or at least that's what I hoped.

Then, one day in the spring of my junior year, I was asked to attend what they call a closed tryout session for the White Sox, which was being held at Pace University in Pleasantville, New York. John Tumminia, a long-time and well-respected scout for the White Sox, watched me go through my paces, and I must say that I thought I put on a pretty good show. I was in a groove at the plate, lining balls all over the ballpark, plus I was making all the plays in the field cleanly and flawlessly. When the session was complete, Mr. Tumminia came up and chatted with me, and he said some very nice things about my performance.

Fast forward to June 9, 2005. I was waiting on the field for the start of the Stamford Robins' first game of the summer season when my dad came over to the dugout with my grandparents, Bob and Jane Wolff. Dad, a former head college coach and former coach in the Cleveland Indians organization, would rarely come over to me during a game. But on this night, he had a big smile on his face.

"John … Hey, John, come here for a second." My dad was standing in the bleachers behind the dugout with my grandparents. I could see they all had huge smiles, but I couldn't figure out what they wanted. Normally, all conversations would wait until after the game.

"What's up, Dad?"

"You didn't hear the good news?"

"Umm, no. What are you talking about?" And then it hit me: it was draft day. I hadn't been able to follow the draft closely because I was at the ballpark. Mr. Tumminia had told me a few weeks before at Pace that he might draft me, but I didn't want to get my hopes up. I simply tried to put it out of my mind.

"You were drafted! By the White Sox!" My dad and my grandparents all tried to hold back their excitement. My grandfather (Bob) and Dad gave me congratulatory handshakes, and Grandma gave me a big hug and a kiss as I tried to let the good news settle in.

I couldn't believe that it had actually happened. My childhood dream had come true! I had been drafted by a major league team! All the hard work and hours spent in the batting cage and in the weight room, running sprints, and training had paid off. I couldn't even put my excitement into words. All I could manage was, "How did you find out?"

Dad explained, "Your mother walked into the house late this afternoon and the Internet radio was on, and the first thing she heard was: 'The Chicago White Sox, with their forty-seventh pick, select second-baseman from Harvard University, John Wolff. Grandson of Hall of Fame broadcaster Bob Wolff.' Of course Mom started to scream with joy and she called me right away to give me the good news!"

As you might imagine, it was hard for me to focus during that night's game, although I did manage to cap off the night with a single to finish one for three. My mind raced all night long with wild thoughts of my new life as a professional baseball player! Plus, the word spread fast. My Stamford Robins' teammates were all very excited for me and my cell phone rang all night long as my college teammates and old friends heard the good news.

When I returned home that evening, I listened to that Internet radio recording of my being drafted over and over and over again.

· · ·

I remember the pure joy of finding out when I was drafted back in 1972. Like John, it was just after my junior year in college, and like John, I recall literally jumping for joy! It was a dream come true. That's the only way to describe it.

I also think that in our particular cases, because we both saw only limited time in college games, the thrill of being drafted was that much sweeter. It's one thing if you've been a star player at your respective school and you knew all along that you would be drafted. But when you've been relegated to a bench role, finally getting that chance to sign a contract is a tremendous personal validation of all the long hours you've put into your game for all those years.

I know firsthand how many terrifically talented amateur players never get this opportunity, and John knows as well. As I told him a few days later, getting a chance to play professional baseball is one of the great privileges in life. It's a rare, rare honor, and no matter what happens to your baseball career, for the rest of your life you can point with tremendous pride and self-satisfaction to the reality that you were good enough to have been drafted and signed as a professional baseball player.

TWO

EXTENDED SPRING? WHAT IS THAT?

April 1, 2006
End of Spring Training
Tucson, Arizona

Today was the last day of spring training. More cuts were made, but I survived. Of the guys who were released, two included my friends, first baseman Matt Dugan and infielder Joel Izquierdo. This was the first year of pro ball for them and their pro baseball dreams ended within one month. They didn't even receive a White Sox paycheck. They endured a brutal spring training only to be told that their services were no longer needed.

The good news was that I had made it through all the releases (and there were lots of them). The bad news is that I'm being kept in Tucson for what's known as extended spring training. That means I'll be here in sunny (and getting hotter by the day) Arizona until early June when the short season Class A teams start to play their schedules.

The players who were assigned to the higher classification teams (AAA or AA) left today for their summer seasons. Those of us stuck here in extended spring training just went back to the hotel and watched bad movies on television. Let me once again add that the off-hours in spring training tend to be pretty lame, especially if you don't have access to a car. You're either at the ballpark, or back in the motel, along with dozens of other bored ballplayers. And you do this every day, seven days a week.

In addition, all the extended spring players now have to find places to live. No more free room and board at the motel. We were given a few days to scour the area, find some new digs, and ideally, find some roomies. I decided to live with Matt Sharp, a catcher from Chicago who played ball at UCLA. Sharpie is a nice guy and seems like he could be a good roommate. Sharpie's father played for the White Sox in the major leagues for several years and was a star outfielder. Although Sharp grew up in Chicago, one might think that he born and raised in California judging by his clothing and accessories. I guess he learned his style at UCLA. Like Ryan McCarthy, Sharpie has a big smile and is always laid back. He wears huge movie star sunglasses, but Sharpie is somehow able to pull it off. He has a shaved head and wears long shorts with white socks pulled up to his calves. Vintage t-shirts and unusual shoes finish off his attire. He has a great sense of humor and is always up to grab a beer and shoot the breeze while hanging out by the pool.

Along with Sharpie, though, have come a few other roommates who I didn't realize were part of the deal. I'm sure they are all nice guys, but I can tell already that they are real characters. The other roommates are Brandon Johnson, Tim Murphey, and Matt Nachreiner. Brandon Johnson, or "Bayyyybay" as he known around camp, is certainly the life of the party. He is a good-sized third baseman from St. Louis who is always telling stories about wondrous pool parties at the University of Arizona where there are no shortage of ladies. More importantly, Brandon is outgoing, friendly, and also a fine ballplayer. Rumor has it that Brandon once put on an impressive showing outside a bar last year when he was playing for the White Sox in Great Falls, Montana. Apparently, three large fellows from Montana had a problem with Brandon and they forced him out of the bar. They were preparing to beat the stuffing out of him when Brandon knocked out all three guys with three quick punches. I'm sure this story is a bit exaggerated, but if you took one look at Brandon you would believe it, too.

Tim Murphey is a left-handed pitcher from Georgia and definitely a different kind of guy. I guess that's to be expected from left-handed pitchers. A high draft choice out of high school, Murphey is a tall, skinny kid who consistently fires a fastball clocked in the mid nineties. Murphey has one of the strongest Southern accents I have ever heard and sometimes, for a Northerner like myself, it's difficult to understand what he's saying. Murph is easily the most outgoing and fun kid I have ever been around, the kind of guy who will talk to anyone at any time. He's also the good-looking kid who can get a cute waitress to smile by saying something stupid like, "Excuse me, but I've lost my telephone number. Can I have yours?"

The other roomie, Matt Nachreiner, has been playing high-A ball and seems like a good kid. Curiously, he's been begging the Sox to give him his release so he can sign with another team. Matt just wants to get out of extended spring training, which, by all accounts, is a very tough experience. In any event, according to Matt, the White Sox refuse to release him. I don't know how to figure this one out. Matt was a high draft choice out of Texas and he doesn't feel he's making enough progress in the White Sox organization. That being said, it is always risky asking for your release. After all, there is no guarantee another team will pick you up.

This just in … the Tucson Banjo Convention was held today at the Riverpark Inn where we have been staying, and the banjo players appeared to be a huge hit with the locals. I'd say a good two hundred people toting banjos were seen walking into the courtyard at the Inn. For the rest of the afternoon all you could hear was the loudest banjo jam-fest in the history of the world. It was interesting for about twenty seconds. Then I had to leave. Or more accurately, I *wanted* to leave.

My girlfriend from college has been in town for a couple of weeks now and is planning on leaving to travel the world on Wednesday. We met at Harvard and have been together for about two years. She's originally from Washington, D.C., and now lives in New York City. She was very supportive of my baseball dreams when we were in college and thought it might be fun to come visit me during spring training. I also thought it would be nice to have her around.

But looking back, I don't think it was the best idea. The amount of time I spent on the field and away from her has put a huge strain on our relationship. I also would have the occasional bad day and not fully appreciate my time with her because I was angry with my performance on the field. Sometimes it was hard for me to separate my time on the field from my time off the field. She had been accepted into Columbia Medical School and was taking the year off before she enrolled, so most of her days have been spent relaxing by the pool, tanning, reading good books, and waiting for me to get off the field to enjoy our evenings together. We have had good times together, but we had never before seen firsthand what professional baseball is all about. Our relationship was a lot easier to manage in college. Baseball didn't occupy my life and we both lived in the same dorm (Dunster House) on campus.

In truth, I haven't always managed my time with her well, as sometimes I would come home to her so tired that I didn't want to do anything except sit on the couch, eat, and collapse. I'm sure that once she leaves Arizona to travel I'll miss her very much. However, I think we've both begun to realize that our lives are going in opposite directions. I am going to be playing baseball all the time and she is going to be even busier studying in med school.

In any event we have been seeing a lot of movies lately, but tonight we decided to try our hand at a little miniature golf. It seemed like a good idea until we got to the course and discovered that everyone else in Tucson also decided to play mini golf this evening. After playing just six holes in two hours, we called it quits. It wouldn't have been too bad if it weren't for the couple about five groups ahead of us on the course, who were playing like they wanted a green jacket or something. Both of them were sizing up shots, reading the break, discussing the best shot possible, and taking their sweet time. I had never seen people take mini golf so seriously, and I couldn't stand it. It reminded me of something out of *Curb Your Enthusiasm*, but at least the weather was warm and I had my girl with me.

As for actually playing baseball, we have an official "week off" from the usual grind of being up very early and at the ballpark. But when these days are over, extended spring training games begin again on Friday. We don't have any official or mandatory practices during the time off, but we do have optional weight lifting and batting cage time. The players are expected to show up at least for a little while; besides, what else are we going to do around here in the desert without a car?

In any event, my swing is feeling better each day and I am beginning to understand how to keep my approach consistent and hit the ball hard every time at bat. It is taking me a little while longer to make certain adjustments, but I have full certainty that in a few more days I'll be right on track.

· · ·

As noted, one of the little known realities about playing professional baseball is that once spring training ends, all the ballplayers are left to their own devices to go out and find a place to live. As you might imagine, this is not always easy, especially when you have very limited funds (e.g., your minor league paycheck). You have to find a teammate or two who you like, and then fan out throughout the area trying to find an apartment to rent on a weekly or monthly basis. If you don't have access to a car, well, you're just about sunk. Without a car, you might as well pitch a tent at the ballpark.

I recall my first year in minor league ball when I played in Anderson, South Carolina. I, along with three other teammates, found a nice quiet home on a shady residential street. The upstairs floor had a couple of bedrooms, living room, bath, and kitchenette. All things considered, it was quite nice. But it was tight, and I recall that one of my roommates liked to strum his guitar until the wee hours of the morning. Being a light sleeper, that was something I didn't fancy. But what really made it difficult was when the heat of summer piped in. The upstairs apartment didn't have any air conditioning, and before long, George Cappuzzello (a crafty left-handed pitcher on the team) and I found a trailer in a mobile trailer park on the outskirts of town. It was a miserable setting: no grass, no trees, red ruddy dirt, and lots of wacky neighbors. But the trailer had A/C, and trust me, when the temperatures started to hit ninety degrees with matching humidity, I was sure glad that it was frosty inside our mobile tin can.

April 2, 2006
Extended Spring Training
Tucson, Arizona

The last day of regular spring training offered something of a special treat for us players stranded in extended. Since all the other ballplayers who had to report to their assignments could carry only about three or four bats with them in their team bat bags, they left plenty of lumber in the minor league clubhouse. There were literally hundreds of bats left behind, and it was open season for anyone who wanted a bat or, for that matter, ten. I grabbed some fancy maple bats, some obscure models, and some other good stuff. It was like Christmas in April.

Also, after making all the final cuts as regular spring training ended, they posted the extended roster. The middle infielders who remain consist of the following: Acosta, Batista, Tavares, Rodriguez, and Wolff. Interesting. Only one speaks English. Can you guess which one?

· · ·

Baseball is truly an international sport, and has been for some time now. And to that end, English is not always the main language spoken on the field. If you're serious about a career in baseball, you had better brush up on your español. Fortunately, John was smart enough to take Spanish classes in high school and in college, so now in the minors he can at least communicate with his teammates, many of whom are from the Caribbean countries. I wish I had taken Spanish in school.

April 5, 2006
Extended Spring Training
Tucson, Arizona

Today we had another optional practice in the morning. I like to take swings with my buddy Josh Morgan because he's a talented hitter and he always helps me with my swing mechanics. Josh is also a truly genuine, nice guy, even if he is stereotypically Southern. Josh is from Alabama and attended the University of Southern Alabama, where he was one of the leading home run hitters in the country his junior year. Other famous players from the University of South Alabama include Juan Pierre and Luis Gonzalez. Josh is extremely polite and modest and only has kind things to say about everyone. He is well-liked by his teammates and coaches, and I respect him as a person and as a player. I haven't met too many people from Alabama, and Josh is a lot different from me. He sure acts differently and speaks differently than I do. But then again, now that I think about it, I'm sure that from Josh's perspective, I must seem just as strange.

We had to finally move out of the Riverpark Inn today. Unfortunately, our new lavish digs at the La Lomita apartment house won't be ready until late tomorrow. As a result, we needed a place to stay for the night. Fortunately, my girlfriend still had a couple of days open on her rented condo, even though she has already left to go travel the world. My three new roomies—Matt Sharp, Matt Nachreiner, and Tim Murphey—were thrilled to have a place to stay. Sure, it was more than a bit cramped with three ballplayers in a one-bedroom condo, but hey, it beat the alternative of camping out under the stars with the cactus.

After we got home from practice, Nach and Sharpie went to a bar to hang out and get some food while Murphey and I played Wiffle ball in the apartment house parking lot. We played for about thirty minutes until the plastic ball cracked and became unplayable.

"Damnit, Wolff … you got any more Wiffle balls?"

"Nah man. You want to keep playing?" I asked.

"Yeah. Let's just go to the store and buy some more."

"Murph, it's ninety degrees. And I'm not walking five miles to Walgreens just to buy Wiffle balls. And I sure as hell don't want to hitchhike."

"Great idea!" Murph immediately responded, and we started to walk down the barren street trying to flag down cars. At first we didn't have much luck; after all, let's face it—we looked more than a little sketchy. I mean, if you were driving along in the desert and saw two shirtless guys in their twenties walking down a heavily traveled road, would you be tempted to stop? In any event, a nice guy finally picked us up, drove us down to the local Walgreens and our mission was accomplished. On the way home we simply jumped into the back of a large man's pickup truck. Not a great idea, to be sure.

As we approached our apartment house, I yelled to the driver, "Hey man! You can let us out right here. This is our stop!"

No response. He just cruised right past our street. Murph and I locked eyes and decided that we should hop out at the next red light—which we did. We then ran through traffic across the highway and back towards our condo.

Once we were back home, the Wiffle ball game resumed immediately. As luck would have it, on the first pitch I drilled a home run onto the roof of the condo and we decided that was enough for one day. After all, neither one of us was in a mood to climb up on the roof and retrieve the ball.

We grabbed some dinner at the local grill and then my friends wanted to go across the street to Hooters and get some pitchers of beer. Personally, I find Hooters very depressing, especially when folks come in with their families and young kids. I find that kind of strange; however, my roommates seem to love it. After Nach and Sharpie got the phone number of our waitress we decided to meet up with the rest of the team at the local hot spot known as the Cactus Moon.

Tonight was my first night out at the Cactus Moon but it reminded me of the country-style dance club from the movie *Cool Runnings*. There was a large dance floor in the middle of the place where people were two-stepping and line dancing—real Arizona cowboy stuff. I was trying to lay low with my teammates Marquise Cody, Marcos Causey, Raleigh Evans, Matt Sharp, and the rest of the crew when a cute blonde-haired girl wearing a sexy cowgirl outfit started chatting with the guys. I was trying to avoid awkward conversation, but before I knew it she was standing next to me.

"Hey, why aren't you dancing?" she said with an inviting smile. I thought to myself, "Here we go."

I replied with a smirk, "Because I don't have anyone to dance with." She grabbed me and pulled me onto the dance floor. I didn't put up much of a fight and I could hear the rest of the guys laughing at me from back at the bar.

"So what are you doing in Tucson?" she asked while we were two-stepping.

I tried to think of something creative and funny but all I could come up with was, "I'm a construction worker and those guys over there are my coworkers."

You see, there are a few rules when talking to girls at bars or clubs. The number one rule is that you can't say that you play ball or who you play for. A common question is, "What are you doing here in town?" It is important to make up some ridiculous excuse such as, "I work for UPS and I'm just passing through" or some nonsense like that, or the other ballplayers might fine you in Kangaroo Court the next day.

There's a set of unspoken rules that the players follow and learn as they go. No one really enforces the rules adamantly, except in the team's "Kangaroo Court" in which players can be fined money for doing silly or stupid things. In most Kangaroo Courts, the oldest player on the team is the judge and the veterans serve as the panel to vote in close decisions. Everyone is fair game. Players usually are the main target because all the guys live together, but the coaches can also be fined. All the money collected is saved and used for a team party at the end of the year. Kangaroo Court is a good way to build team chemistry and also get a good laugh because every baseball team has a few characters.

I'll probably be in trouble or get fined for telling you this, but in Kangaroo Court you can get fined for wearing your team's hat, shirt, or gear at any time off the field. For example, if you play for the Great Falls White Sox and you wear a Great Falls Sox cap to a bar at night that is a maximum fine (usually $5). If you drink too much and make a fool of yourself, hook up with an unattractive girl, or go home with a "cougar," those are all also fineable offenses. If you are running the bases in a game and forget how many outs there are, that will definitely result in a fine. If your two girlfriends show up to the same game and you get caught, you can expect to be fined for that as well.

By the way, Nachreiner got released this afternoon, so this night at the Moon was his last night in town and he was quite eager to make something good happen. Unfortunately, he wasn't having too much luck with the ladies. But at least he had tried his best.

As you recall, Nachreiner had asked for his release in spring training because he felt he wasn't making fast enough progress through the White Sox minor league system, and he didn't want to go through extended spring training again. Sure enough, he got a call on his cell phone from Dave Wilder, Chicago's director of player development, in the middle of the afternoon and was told he had a plane ticket for home the next morning. It happened just like that. Sure enough, by the time I woke up the next morning, my roommate and friend was gone, and so were his bags and belongings.

• • •

John's getting a real taste of minor league life. Maybe for guys at the big league level, it's fun and exciting, but in the low minors, a big day is to play Wiffle ball, hitch a ride to the Walgreen's, and then make it home in one piece. Then, to top it off, hanging out at a local restaurant for some square dancing. Yee-haw!

Also, you have to understand that minor league baseball players, especially guys in low Class A ball, come and go on a routine basis. Yes, it's great, great fun to be a professional baseball player, but there is one certainty—and that is, nothing is certain.

Getting released or shipped out to another team is just a part of the business. You have to be ready to pack up your baseball gear and all of your clothes in a suitcase in a matter of minutes. I know that for the average fan, this all sounds terrible. And you know what? It really is.

April 7, 2006
Extended Spring Training
Tucson, Arizona

It is a beautiful day in Tucson, Arizona. I'm playing professional baseball and all my goofy college chums are back in cold and windy Cambridge studying for exams. Me? I just have to get up in the morning, put on my working togs, and play the game I love in the warm sunshine. It doesn't get much better than this. In spring training we have to wear full uniform everyday: baseball pants, spikes, and heavy mesh uniforms. In extended spring we get a bit of a break. We get to wear light mesh shorts, a t-shirt, and turf shoes, which are more comfortable than spikes. One of the main reasons for the wardrobe change is that it is just getting too hot for pants and heavy jerseys.

Thinking of my college buddies, it dawned on me that I hadn't written a term paper or studied for an exam in over four months. It's difficult to go more than a few days at Harvard without having to do some form of labor-intensive homework. I studied psychology in college and although I was far from one of the most driven students in school, I always prided myself on taking my academic work load seriously. And during these first few months of my minor league career I am experiencing sudden guilt that I should still be in school and catching up on my work. I have to constantly remind myself that I am now employed as a professional baseball player and that I don't have to worry about that art history exam coming up in two weeks. This is what Harvard University does to people.

"Hey Wolffy," shouted my manager, Nick Leyva, (also known as Cuz) with a devilish grin from the opposite end of the bench.

"What's up, Cuz?"

"Grab a bat," he replied with a chuckle. "You're on deck."

I paused for a second to let his words sink in. It is one hundred degrees out here in Arizona, it's the top of the ninth inning, and we're up by at least five runs. "He doesn't really want me to pinch hit," I thought to myself. I mean, I'm fried right now. I haven't moved off the bench in the last two hours, and we are winning the game easily. Not only that, I have the most at-bats on the team up to this point in the season. So what's going on here?

"Wait a minute, what'd you say Cuz?" I pretended to forget what he had said.

Cuz looked at me with a huge smile and said a little louder, "You'd better grab a bat, you're on deck!"

I scampered through my equipment in a frantic attempt to find my batting gloves, helmet, and any bat that resembled mine. I was so busy getting ready to hop into the batter's box that I didn't realize who was pitching until I was walking up to the plate. I finally took a glance at the pitcher and realized, to my dismay, that I had to face the Diamondbacks' fairly new six-foot-seven, fire-balling, right-handed pitcher they had picked up early in the draft last year. His name is Jason Neighborgall and he had been a third-round draft pick even though he didn't pitch much at Georgia Tech. He throws really hard and has tremendous talent; he just struggles with his control.

"Wolffy! Come here," Cuz motioned towards me to come chat with him down in the third base coaching box. I figured he would tell me to watch out for this guy's nasty twelve-six curveball, or something of that nature.

"Yeah Cuz?"

With that same mischievous smile, "You know this guy throws 103 miles per hour, right?" I nodded my head. I didn't even know how to respond to this. But I did realize that pinch-hitting me against this wild flamethrower was apparently a cruel but very funny joke to Cuz and the rest of the coaching staff. Geez, thanks guys! I looked back towards my bench only to see my hitting coach and some teammates waving goodbye to me. I even heard a few Dominican players yell, "Adios, Lobo," and start chuckling. I turned away from Cuz and started the baseball equivalent of what I thought would be my personal long green mile back to the batter's box.

I heard Cuz yell out one more reassuring line: "Hey Wolffy, I would rather chew on home plate than bat against this guy!"

I put one foot in the box and my life flashed in front of my eyes.

"Be careful. Don't dig in, buddy. I got no idea where this guy's ball is going," the catcher, Mike DeCarlo, muttered under his breath. I just smiled and very gingerly planted my feet. Thankfully, the first two pitches soared five feet over my head at about 101 miles per hour. I thought for sure the third pitch was going to drill me right in the hip but it somehow ended up coming in behind me. The fourth pitch was spiked into the grass in front of home plate and I happily took my base on balls. What a relief!

• • •

Too many fans think it's easy to hit professional pitching. They watch major league games on television from the safety and comfort of their sofas, and the camera angles—especially the ones from behind the centerfield fence—make it appear that there could be nothing easier than to hit a pitch that's clocked at ninety-six miles per hour. I mean, it looks so easy!

But trust me. Getting up to bat against a pitcher who throws the ball at ninety-plus miles per hour and who has lousy control is one of the scariest experiences on the planet. Look at it this way: a good high school pitcher probably throws seventy-five miles per hour. A top college pitcher is clocked around eighty-four or eighty-five. A good minor league pitcher throws in the low to mid nineties. In fact, ALL of the guys I faced in the minors threw in the low nineties. If they hadn't, they wouldn't have been signed in the first place.

Take that kind of velocity and couple with it the fact that a thrown baseball really hurts like hell when it hits you. Yeah, I know hitters get plunked all the time, and they easily brush it off as they make their way down to first base. But trust me—when you get hit by a ninety miles per hour fastball, it hurts like the dickens. And it hurts for several days.

So, when you have to face a young pitcher who throws hard but who is cursed with no sense of control, it's not one of the highlights of your day at the ballpark. You just hope to survive without getting bruised too badly.

April 7, 2006
Tucson, Arizona
Extended Spring Training

During extended spring training we have to be out on the field by 6:30 A.M., because it gets too hot in the afternoon to play ball. By the end of the day everyone is drained and cooked from the heat, and we can't wait to get off the field and head back to some shade and air conditioning. In fact, let me give you a rundown of a typical day at the field to show you how we spend our time:

> 5:15 A.M. – Morning routine (shower, brush teeth, shave, etc.) Yeah, that's right—5:15 A.M.!
>
> 6:00 A.M. – Breakfast (eat en route to the field in the car or in the clubhouse)
>
> 6:15 A.M. – Team lift (thirty minutes of intense weight lifting)
>
> 7:00 A.M. – Flips and batting tee work with coaches Bobby Tolan and Jerry Hairston
>
> 7:45 A.M. – Team meeting (short discussion with the coaches about yesterday's game: what we did well, what we need to work on)

8:15 A.M. – Team stretch

8:30 A.M. – Throwing program

9:00 A.M. – Team fundamentals drills (double plays, ground balls, bunt coverage, etc.)

9:30 A.M. – Catch the bus for an away game at either Diamondbacks or Rockies

9:45 A.M. – Stretch again; infield-outfield practice before game

10:30 A.M. – Game time (regular nine-inning game)

1:30 P.M. – Bus back to White Sox camp for more conditioning

2:00 P.M. – Shower up, and head back to the apartment

We do this same routine tomorrow, seven days a week.

One note about the weather. Curiously, by early April, the perfect time of day to walk out of the clubhouse and down to the fields is 6:45 A.M. The sun is shining at that time, but the air is still cool and crisp. It's a perfect temperature for baseball, especially when you consider how just a few hours later that dry heat is going to bake you and transform the soft, watered infields into cement.

That being said, I'm certainly not complaining about the weather in Arizona. You have to remember that the daily challenge at Harvard was trying to figure out new, secretive ways to stay warm on the bench without drawing attention from the coaching staff. My teammates and I tried portable space heaters, blankets, ski gloves, hand warmers, hot chocolate—pretty much anything we thought might be able to help us survive those long, frigid games.

I used to keep a hand warmer in my back pocket just to keep the feeling in my fingers.

One game I'll never forget was a match-up against Boston College on our field when it started to snow in the fifth inning. By the seventh inning it was really coming down. In fact, it was almost comical how hard it was snowing—it was practically a blizzard. Of course, the game continued even though we could barely see the ball through the white snow. The oddity was, if it had been a few degrees warmer and the snow had warmed up and turned to rain, the game would have likely been stopped and postponed. But because the temperature was in the low thirties and the snow was, well, just frozen precipitation, the umpires and the coaches saw no reason to stop the game.

This type of weather was more common than not. It was always hard to tell who had it worse: the players in the game freezing or the guys on the bench struggling to stay warm. It was a common sight in between each half-inning to see the bench players from both teams running up and down the foul lines in order to keep the blood flowing and to maintain some sense of body warmth. In my mind, I think these situations are toughest on the players who don't start the game but are inserted later on as pinch hitters or defensive replacements. Relief pitchers have it a bit easier because they get a little extra time to warm up and get loose. I'm definitely not saying that pitching in the cold is easy, but at least most guys can break a sweat when they're getting loose in the bullpen. On the other hand, the Harvard coaching staff would routinely tell someone on the bench who was ice cold to pinch hit when the batter was already on deck. That gave the pinch hitter no time to get loose, and many times he could barely get his fingers warm enough to grip the bat.

It is also very challenging to play defense when it is brutally cold. If your pitcher is throwing strikes and there is constant action, then you are able to keep moving in the infield or outfield and stay a little warm. However, in the worst case scenario your pitcher is not throwing consistent strikes because, well, he's cold, too. This leads to everyone getting tight in the field and before you know it some batter hits a laser beam at you using a metal bat. Needless to say, a lot of errors are made on days like these. In fact, one of our Harvard infielders broke the record for most errors in a game by one player, committing seven errors on a brutally cold day against Boston College. As you probably guessed, we didn't win that game. However, I can't blame my teammate. When it's that cold, sometimes your glove just doesn't work.

• • •

When I was playing in the minors, I never had to go through the grueling experience of extended spring training. But when I was coaching with the Indians, I recall spending some time each year with the players in extended spring. By all accounts, it's not a fun time. On one hand, as a player, you're getting paid a minor leaguer's salary, and each day you're working out with top coaches, and playing real games against kids from other extended spring programs.

But while the competition is top notch, none of the games has the same feel of playing in a real minor league game. For starters, the extended games are all played during the day; in contrast, the vast majority of minor league games are played at night under the lights. And of course, nobody comes to the extended games except for bored local retirees and perhaps a few lost tourists. Beyond that, there's just nobody there. There's no scoreboard, no music blaring, no roar of the crowd, no kids seeking autographs. Just a few whistles and occasional claps from the third base coach to keep you going. That's it.

Psychologically, it is very, very difficult to keep yourself pumped up during this kind of routine. Yes, the coaches are watching—always watching—to see who is doing well and who isn't. And yes, they definitely keep a scorebook to keep track of batting averages, RBIs, and the like, although these stats never appear on any official minor league website. Each week, the stats are posted on the clubhouse wall, so that all the players can see how they and their teammates are doing.

In addition to the psychological wear-and-tear, there is, of course, the heat to contend with. With each passing day, whether you're in extended in Arizona or Florida, the heat just builds and builds. There's no escaping it. Extended spring runs from early April until the middle of June, so you're talking about almost two-and-a-half months of scorching heat. I recall once going down to Winter Haven, Florida, to work with the kids in extended spring in early June, and it was so hot and humid there that I just talked to the kids about making sure that they were getting enough to drink everyday and to keep their weight up. Remember, those kids who make it through extended camp then ship out to play in a short-season minor league, such as in the New York Penn league or Pioneer League. Playing in those leagues is the real minor league experience.

But extended spring? Most minor league players will flat out tell you that once they've gone through that experience, they will never go through it again—that they'd rather quit playing pro ball. In short, life in extended spring training is flat-out brutal.

April 8, 2006
Extended Spring Training
Tucson, Arizona

Once we moved into our low-income apartment at La Lomita off of Broadway in Tucson, it became increasingly clear that we couldn't subsist solely on Wendy's, Subway, McDonald's, and Burger King for too much longer. One of us was going to have to cook, and it wasn't going to be me. Luckily, Matt Sharp had already lived on his own for a few years and had mastered the delicate art of cooking pasta.

But after a few days of being served pasta for breakfast, lunch, and dinner I began to realize how much I missed the Dunster House dining hall back at college. I would dream about my days of being able to walk up to Sue, the grill chef, and ask for anything I wanted. Grilled chicken, grilled cheese, huge omelettes, scrambled eggs, burgers, hot dogs, and pretty much anything else a growing college kid could possibly want to eat after a long day at the field. I always appreciated the dining hall when I was at college, but after suffering through Sharpie's non-stop pasta fests I began to have a whole new appreciation for the cuisine back at school.

. . .

Another part of minor league life that too many kids (and their parents) aren't aware of is that players have to find their own place to live and also learn how to feed themselves. Playing pro ball is a job. It's not like being in college. When you're in school, you go to class, have a meal plan, and have a place to sleep at night. You only have to worry about doing well in class and playing ball.

But when you're in the minors—even in extended spring training—not only do you have to find a place to live, but you have to cook and fend for yourself as well. Knowing how to cook pasta is a start, but as John found out, it behooves one to spend a little time and learn how to cook some decent meals. I recall when I was in my first year of pro ball, I somehow survived on lots of peanut butter sandwiches, breakfast cereal, and an occasional barbecued steak. But as you can tell, a four-star chef I was not. I was totally clueless in the kitchen.

And that continued right into my second year, when I played in the Midwest League in Clinton, Iowa. One night, I convinced my roommates that we should sneak out into the cornfields which, of course, are everywhere in Iowa, to help ourselves to a few ears of corn. I had learned how to cook corn in hot water and salt, and to this day I can still recall how much I was looking forward to a big meal of corn on the cob. But with my very first bite, I was aghast! The corn looked great and most inviting, but it tasted, well, like gravel. I tossed it out, along with all the other ears we had stolen.

I remember the next day telling this disappointing story on the bench to some of my teammates. They hooted and hollered at me, "You dope ... you were eating grain corn—the stuff they feed to the animals on the farm." And then, of course, a young pitcher who hailed from rural Missouri piped up, "And you say you went to Harvard? Don't you know nothing about living on a farm?" That really sent everybody into stitches.

But in truth and in my defense, I really didn't know nothing about living on a farm. And I don't think they offer agricultural studies as a major at Harvard.

April 9, 2006
Extended Spring Training
Tucson, Arizona

Although the days are strictly business, they are filled with occasional laughter and good humor. That's the fuel that keeps ballplayers going, and it helps to make the experience that much more fun. I'll probably never get used to waking up before 6:00 A.M. to play, but I'm still getting paid to play a game, and I do my best to never lose sight of that.

That being said, as soon as the long day is over my next move is to either head straight to the local pool or water park, or to flop on the sofa in the apartment to get some needed rest. Personally, I enjoy grabbing an ice cold beer before passing out on the couch. As for my roommates, Sharpie always falls asleep right away, while Murph prefers to play video games or watch television with me. Sharpie will walk through the front door and into his private room without a word. Eventually he'll wake and emerge from his room, but only because he's hungry and wants to make himself some pasta. Murph will grab a beer with me and challenge me to a baseball video game on Playstation 2. I'm not much of a gamer, though, so I usually get my ass kicked and get bored pretty quickly.

Because we only have one car among the three of us, we have to share it accordingly. There is a "hierarchy of uses" for the car. For example, top priority use of the car is reserved for the obtaining of food or groceries. Second priority is for going to the field. Third, meeting a girl or going to a bar for a beer. Fourth priority is for recreational excursions like going to a pool or the bowling alley. Finally, the last acceptable use is traveling to the local Riverpark Inn to use their wireless internet. Because the internet is at the bottom of the list, I take my computer to the Inn when Sharp is asleep and Murph is playing videogames. It's about a five minute drive, but it's annoying not to have internet in our apartment.

As for our setup, Murph and I share a small double across from the kitchen and common room. Our room is smaller than Sharp's and we each have a tiny single bed, off of which our heads, arms, and feet hang. I'm six-one and Murph is easily six-four. Two large guys sleeping on these tiny beds about three feet apart is an unusual sight. Sharp found the apartment and since he also pays more rent, he has the larger room with the king size bed. We all thought that was a fair arrangement.

Even on the mornings when we are at the clubhouse before dawn, we're greeted by our ol' buddy, Chet DiMedio, who has already finished exercising and is now ready to coach us. Chettie is a breath of fresh air. He's been a part of the White Sox organization for approximately twenty years and, before that, he was a legendary police officer on the Philadelphia force. He played ball at the AA level in the St. Louis Cardinals organization as a big, powerful catcher.

Chettie tells me that he arrives at the weight room every morning at 4:00 A.M. and does his routine long before the players get there. Chettie is the official cheerleader for the extended team. He's upbeat, happy, and always on the move. It's hard to feel sorry about your aches and pains when you're twenty-two and Chettie is running rings around you. Chettie is somewhat elusive about his age, but I would imagine he is somewhere in his early seventies.

However, I'm not sure about this because he is very focused on staying young, and if you ask him he might tell you that his age doesn't matter because he feels like he's twenty-five and that's all that counts. He told me that he stands on his head every morning after his workout for a few minutes to change the flow of blood in his body. He also only eats organic foods. In short, he's the picture of perfect health.

"Okay guys, how many sprints are we going to do today?" Chettie barks.

"One!" Manny Rodriguez yells in response, but we players all nod in unison.

"Just one more?" Chettie responds back, "Hey, that's what I heard Wolffie saying at the bar last night … just one more!"

"What can I say? I was thirsty!" I quickly fire back. Chettie and the rest of the guys crack a smile and we finish our daily sprints. If it weren't for Chettie and his good-natured humor and wit, well, it just wouldn't be as much fun.

April 10, 2006
Extended Spring Training
Tucson, Arizona
During early morning flips, in which a batter hits a ball tossed from a teammate into a fence, Nick Leyva, or Cuz as he's known, approached me with a serious face and asked me, "Hey, Wolffie, you went to Harvard right?"

"Yeah, Cuz, but I haven't graduated yet, so don't ask me anything too challenging."

"Okay ... but can you tell me how many seconds there are in a year?"

"Geez, Cuz. Hmm, well, I could probably figure that out if I had a calculator, but I don't want to make any promises. Besides, I majored in psych, not math."

Leyva couldn't wait to respond. "Well, by my count, there are twelve seconds in a year."

"How do you figure that, Cuz?"

"Well, there's January 2nd, February 2nd, March 2nd and so on." Cuz was roaring with laughter.

"Good one, Cuz," I shot back facetiously. "You think of that all by yourself?"

"Okay, Wolffie, here's an easy one for you. How many Ds are there in Rudolph the Red-Nosed Reindeer?"

I smiled with relief. "That one I can handle. There are four Ds in that phrase." I began to walk away when Cuz told me that I was wrong.

"Nope, sorry, Wolffie. There are 347 Ds in that song." And he began singing the song: "Dee ... dee ... dee ... dee ... dee ... dee ... dee ... " and so on, instead of the actual words. Leyva roared again. I stood there in the batting cage, absolutely dumbfounded.

Here I am, in Tucson, Arizona, at the crack of dawn and here's Nick Leyva, a former major league manager, getting a kick out of making a Harvard kid screw up riddles that he probably learned in the fourth grade.

But back to baseball. Today we played the Colorado Rockies in our first official game of extended spring training. We traveled to their training facility on the other side of Tucson, which used to be the spring training home of the Cleveland Indians. (For anyone who has ever seen the movie *Major League,* the training facility is exactly the same, except now it features Rockies' signage.) In any event, visiting the facility was also somewhat nostalgic for me because I happened to visit the training camp area almost ten years earlier when my father was working as the roving sports psychologist for the Indians. I couldn't remember a single thing about the ballpark from when I was younger, but as soon as I saw it today a whole rush of memories came back to me. I remembered watching Manny Ramirez take batting practice on one of the side fields when he was about twenty years old, hitting rope after rope. I remembered backing up a ground ball drill at third base and making a diving catch at age eleven when Buddy Bell fungoed a bullet past first baseman Jim Thome that I was able to snare. I even recalled playing Sega Genesis hockey with Alex Cole and Albert Belle back at the Indians' hotel. I think Alex Cole let me win, but I can assure you that Albert Belle took no prisoners.

These days, the Rockies' facility appears to be much older than the White Sox, or the Diamondbacks, training camps are. It consists of the major league field (which is also used by the Arizona Heat, a professional women's softball team) and four minor league fields that are all adjacent to each other. There is a large look-out tower situated in the middle of the four fields so the player development staff can watch all fields simultaneously. Water is tough to come by in Arizona, and the Rockies rarely water their fields. It is only mid-April and already the fields are turning into dust pits with few patches of green grass. Sometimes the dust gets kicked up so much by bursts of wind that it becomes hard to see and breathe in the infield.

We beat the Rockies' minor league affiliate 5-1 today. It was a clean, crisp game and a good way to start off the new season. I was pleased with myself and finished 1-for-2 on the day with two key RBIs that put us up 3-1 late in the game. They had a pretty good right-handed pitcher going and with two outs I laced an outside fastball to left field to drive in the runners from second and third. Even though there is no championship or playoffs at the end of extended spring, our won-loss record is kept as well as our statistics, so I was glad to start the season batting .500.

· · ·

Playing baseball is all about ... playing. That's the fun of the game. The drills and skills are enjoyable, but pretty much they are just work. The real enjoyment comes from competing in the game—and of course, whenever you do well, that just makes the experience that much more enjoyable. Even if it is only an extended spring game, there's nothing better than getting a key hit to drive in the winning run. That's what baseball is all about.

By the way, I'm amazed that John had recalled those early years of his life in spring training when I was with the Indians. But looking back, when you're eleven years old and have a chance to spend some time watching big leaguers go through their paces, that becomes the stuff of life-long dreams. People like Manny Ramirez, Jim Thome, Buddy Bell and his son, David—I had the opportunity to get to know these folks, and in addition to their being tremendous baseball players, I'm also happy to report that they were fine and classy people as well.

For years when I was growing up, my own dad would tell me that he always enjoyed being around ballplayers—that in general, baseball players were gracious, good, and gentle folks, and they were always fun to be around. I'm happy to report that I have also found that to be true over the years. And I'm sure that other baseball people will tell you the exact same thing.

There's just something so rare and unique about baseball players. It's the only fraternity I can think of where you can gleefully needle each other about your foibles, your strengths, your weaknesses, and so on. But it's never done in a harmful or mean-spirited way. It's always done with a smile. That openness, combined with ballplayers who have a real knack for quick retorts, makes for rip-roaring fun.

A guy who gets a couple of cheap bloop hits will find a rolled-up copy of The Sporting News *in his locker the next day—as a new bat to use. An infielder who has sure hands but unexpectedly boots a couple of grounders will find a can of Rustoleum in his locker—so he can get the rust off his mitt. A ballplayer who is prematurely bald will be nicknamed "Curly." A chubby pitcher will be nicknamed "Slim." A rookie will be told by a veteran to go back inside the clubhouse and find the key to the batter's box. Another rookie will be ordered by the manager to get a bat stretcher. And on and on it goes.*

Maybe on paper this doesn't sound all that funny or engaging. But in the company of ballplayers, this is the daily way of life. And trust me, it's a hoot. As noted, I don't know of any other part of conventional society where this kind of behavior is accepted or encouraged. It's just different with baseball, I guess. And that's fine with me.

April 11, 2006
Extended Spring Training
Tucson, Arizona

There was no official game today. Instead, we just had our usual morning workout, and then played an intrasquad scrimmage. We play the Diamondbacks tomorrow on our home field. Nothing new to report. Just another day at the ballpark.

But aside from baseball, we have a big problem back in our new apartment. Sharpie, Murph, and myself have been living here for only a few days and unfortunately, our air conditioning has broken down. Our small apartment has been transformed into a full-out sauna; It is just too hot to wear anything but shorts inside. I don't even know why I'm typing on my laptop right now. It is way too hot to even do that.

I tried to take a nap, but it's so hot that the sheets stick to you and it's flat-out impossible to get comfortable. Sharpie called the maintenance staff right away; alas, they explained that they have to order a special part in order to fix our air conditioner. Hopefully the part will be here by the end of the week, but until then, I honestly don't know how I'm going to be able to sleep and survive—right now, it's literally one hundred degrees in the apartment.

I'm going to the pool.

• • •

Today's ballplayer seems to take air conditioning for granted. Indeed, in many major league ballparks, the dugouts are even cooled by air conditioning just on the off-chance that the millionaire players break a sweat during the course of a game.

I can recall a Fourth of July, day-night double header my first year in pro ball between the neighboring Greenwood (South Carolina) Braves and the Anderson (South Carolina) Tigers. Greenwood was only a short drive away, so somebody decided it would be a neat idea to have us play a day game over in Greenwood, and then have the Braves come to our ballpark in the evening. I honestly don't recall the outcome of the games that day, or how I played. But I do vividly recall that by 1 P.M. that day, the sun was absolutely broiling and that everybody was drenched in perspiration before we even got off the bus in Greenwood. We tried to shower there after the first game, but the shower water was the temperature of warm bath water, so that was useless.

We all climbed back on the bus, returned to Anderson, and then laid around in our (un-air conditioned) clubhouse, waiting to suit up and play again that evening when the sun set and the temperature cooled off to eighty-nine degrees with matching humidity. Above everything else, I'll never forget what it was like to have to somehow put on the same, sweaty, dirt-stained uniform that I had worn that afternoon. That, my friends, was just gross. Absolutely gross.

April 12, 2006
Extended Spring Training
Tucson, Arizona

I was batting in the two-spot today and playing second base against the Diamondbacks on our home field.

The game was tied 8-8 after nine innings, but both managers decided to not play extra innings because many of the pitchers are still on specific pitch counts and the front office doesn't want them throwing too much this early in the season. It is a pretty strange feeling to leave a baseball game tied. To make things worse, the pitchers who did throw today were not throwing strikes. They just couldn't find the strike zone on a consistent basis. As a result, this game ran more than three and a half hours.

Games that last that long in the Arizona sun are a cruel form of torture because it just keeps getting hotter and hotter every inning. As the game progressed, the infield went from being a soft and nicely colored red clay (it was watered down before the game) to a barren moon-like surface. Hard hit ground balls that would have been routine in the first few innings started to take bad hops and sped through the infield for hits. That, of course, only made the game last longer.

Back at the apartment, the air conditioning still isn't fixed but the managers of La Lomita were kind enough to give us a key to a vacant apartment so we could get some sleep without sweating all night long. Hopefully our air conditioning problems will be solved soon. In the meantime, we have two apartments all to ourselves. We all agreed that once our AC is fixed we shouldn't give back the keys back until they threaten us with fines. A second apartment could always come in handy in case there are some girls in the area. Hey, you never know!

• • •

When you play minor league baseball and you're an infielder, you actually do pay a lot of attention to the texture and quality of the infield. Some are well-maintained, but most are rock quarries. Bad hops are part of the game and so are errors—but that doesn't mean you like them. In fact, if you want to survive in the minors, you learn very quickly how to cope with bad fields (e.g., playing a little deeper, taking the time to smooth the dirt right in front of you with your spikes, etc.). Ideally, for me, the best infield to play on is one on which it just rained and everything is still somewhat soft. That slows the ball down, and also ensures that the ball doesn't jump up and take a bite of your face.

I recall one night playing in Wisconsin Rapids, Wisconsin, against the Wisconsin Rapids Twins. I was playing second base, and the field was very, very sandy—almost like the beach. A young slugger named Gary Ward (father of Daryle Ward) smacked a low liner right at me. I instantly transformed my body into that of a hockey goalie's, hoping to block the ball, knock it down, pick it up and throw out Ward. Problem was, the infield dirt was so sandy that when the liner landed in front of me, instead of skipping into my gut or chest, it hopped up and banged off my chin.

I had no play. The ball bounced off into short right field, where I picked up while rubbing my chin, checking to see if I had lost any teeth. After making sure everything was okay, I happened to look around at the scoreboard where a big flashing "E" as in error was staring me in the face. Talk about adding insult to injury! Not only had I been punched in the face by a scorched one-hop line drive, I was being punished for my efforts by having an error tacked onto it as well!

Needless to say, I was not happy. The sandy infield had caused the bad hop, and clearly it should have been ruled as such. In any event, I was so ticked that after the game was over I did something I had never done before. I went up to find the official scorer in the hope of pleading my case. I know that is rarely done, but I really felt stiffed by the call. But as I asked around to try to find the door to the press box which would lead me to the official scorer, something funny happened: I ran into Gary Ward!

Turns out Gary was just as angry as I was. "I really smoked that ball,"
I recall Gary telling me, "How could that scorekeeper rob me of a hit?"

Once the scorer was confronted by both me (the fielder) and Gary
Ward (the hitter), he relented and changed the error on the play to a hit.
A happy ending for everyone—except for my chin, which still hurt.

April 13, 2006
Extended Spring Training
Tucson, Arizona

We ended up losing 9-6 to the Rockies in our game today. Our offense was hitting the ball very well, but we're developing some serious pitching problems. Our pitchers give up a lot of walks as well as two-strike hits. Nothing is worse than standing helpless in the infield while watching a pitcher walk the ballpark—and then watching hitters tee off on hanging curves and sliders. The innings just never seem to end.

Our hurlers are having some issues off the field as well. Everyday during batting practice, the pitchers who are scheduled to pitch or to be on-call in the bullpen are allowed to hang out in the locker room. They usually have a late breakfast, work out, watch television, or play cards. At the start of the game today against the Rockies our staring pitcher, a kid named Flores, was nowhere to be found. In fact, Flores wasn't alone—a large chunk of our pitching staff was missing. Finally, one of the back-up outfielders ran into the clubhouse and found them all, including Flores, still playing cards. Apparently, Flores had gotten so caught up in his card game that he missed his first start of the season.

Unbelievable. This is a good example of a maximum fine in any Kangaroo Court.

Not surprisingly, card games are now banned from the clubhouse.

• • •

The story about the kid being late for his first start is funny, but you can just imagine how embarrassed the kid was. You have to bear in mind that in the minors, it's totally your job and responsibility to be on time, and ready to go. Unlike college or high school where the coach or an assistant does a head count before the bus leaves for a road trip, in pro ball, you had better be there on time ... or the bus leaves without you. It's your responsibility to get the ballpark on the road, even if that means you have to rent a car to get there.

Same goes for being ready to play in a game. You have to be ready— that's your job. If you're not prepared or ready, there's always somebody else who'd be happy to take your job.

April 14, 2006
Extended Spring Training
Tucson, Arizona

We had a very light day today. We played a short intrasquad scrimmage and then had the remainder of the day off to relax and catch up on some sleep. It's clear that a lot of my teammates are getting worn down and that injuries are starting to become more and more common. I don't know how serious some of these injuries are, as guys usually come back and start playing again in a few days. But I have to admit that it does get very monotonous here in extended spring, mainly because every day is pretty much the same as any other. Plus, you play the same two teams over and over again. Maybe the front office is just trying to test us, or motivate us to play well and get moved up to a higher level. That, of course, would be great.

• • •

One of the aspects of minor league baseball that never seems to change is the total lack of communication between the front office and the player. By that, I don't mean that the coaches and players don't talk; of course, they talk all the time. What I'm referring is to the lack of communication between the director of player development and the players.

For some unexplained reason, it seems as though the director of player development (the man who oversees the minor leaguers) is always fearful to say anything meaningful to the players. As a result, the players worry incessantly about cuts, about who's doing well, who's not playing well, what team they will be assigned to, and so on. I have never understood why the front office can't simply sit down with each player and say, "Here are your strengths, and here are your weaknesses. Right now, you are slated to go to a high-level A team this spring, but only if you cut down on your strikeouts at the plate. If you don't, then you're a good candidate to be released."

It would be so much better if they would just be honest with the kids and let them know where they stand. Instead, every kid in spring training or extended spring is worried about how the front office really sees them and their ability. Not only is that bad for morale, but it's totally counterproductive for each player. Instead of focusing on their skill development, they spend most of their time being anxious about whether they're going to be cut.

It was done that way when I played in the 1970s, and apparently it's still done the same way thirty years later. It's a medieval way of running a business.

April 15, 2006
Extended Spring Training
Tucson, Arizona

Today was a brutally long day at the field. We took on the Diamondbacks, and our pitchers could neither throw strikes nor get anyone out. The D'Backs received countless walks and, when our pitchers did manage to throw a strike or two, they were launched as absolute missiles to all parts of the field. I was playing third base and it was almost frightening.

The first overall pick of the 2005 draft was Justin Upton, and today Upton was playing centerfield for Arizona. I had never seen Justin play in person before, and I have always been curious to see how good a first overall pick really is.

I was a bit skeptical, but after watching Upton hit home run after home run in today's game, I can now openly acknowledge that the Diamondbacks made a pretty good investment. Yep, he's that good. Plus he's only eighteen or so.

• • •

When it comes to scouting, superstars like Justin Upton are pretty easy to pick out. He has all five baseball tools (hitting for average, hitting with power, running speed, a great arm, and excellent hands). So, you can just imagine how much he dominated high school competition. It's with the vast majority of other players—the so-called "diamonds in the rough"—where scouts earn their stripes. Finding the kid who shows potential and then giving him the opportunity to develop that potential is what scouting is all about.

Of course, most minor leaguers never get out of Class A ball. But some do. Somehow, that magic of potential kicking in really does happen. Or the kid just physically and emotionally matures. Whatever the reason, the big leagues are full of superstars, to be sure—but there are always lots of players who weren't considered anything more than a long shot, yet they worked at their craft and got to the show. In fact, it happens so often that minor leaguers continue to cling to that dream.

When I was playing pro ball, I played against a number of talented players who eventually went onto to become big leaguers. Among the more notable names were Mike Hargrove, John Candelaria, Gary Ward, Alvis Woods, Jerry Garvin, Miguel Dilone, Joe Sambito, Tom Underwood, and many others. I played against these guys in A ball, and while they were all good, it wasn't obvious that they were going to become major leaguers. They were just hard-working and hungry players like me.

When I played in the Western Carolina League (now the South Atlantic, or "Sally" League), I was hitting about .280 over the first couple of months and was hoping to make the All-Star team. But then we played a three-game set against the Charleston (South Carolina) Pirates, and they had a number of excellent players, including a young second baseman named Willie Randolph. I remember calling home one night to my parents, telling them that it didn't look good for me to make the All-Star team that year because this Randolph kid fielded as well as I did, ran as well as I did, and hit better than I did. Plus Willie was four years younger than I was. Bottom line—this Randolph kid was good. And I guess he was, as Willie went onto play for eighteen years in the big leagues.

On the other hand, there was a kid playing second for the Gastonia (North Carolina) Rangers who was kind of small, choked up on the bat, and tried to punch the ball for base hits. I didn't think he was anything special. But, wow, was I wrong. That little second baseman—Brian Doyle—eventually made it to the big leagues and when he got his chance, he starred for the Yankees in the 1978 World Series.

Hey, you never know!

April 16, 2006
Extended Spring Training
Tucson, Arizona

Today is Easter Sunday. However, it is not exactly a typical Easter Sunday for me. I woke up around 9:00 A.M. to find that my roommates were still out partying somewhere in the Tucson area and were not answering their cell phones. Hence, I had no idea when they were going to return with our one and only car. There are no places to get breakfast within walking distance around here, so I was left to sit on the couch, eat a bowl of Cheerios, and watch television.

Around 11:00 A.M. my roommates returned full of laughs, but they were too tired to tell any stories regarding their late evening and early morning escapades. Both fell asleep on the couch within minutes. I took advantage of the empty car and drove to my favorite Waffle House where I was, in fact, the only person dining on this fine Easter morning. Sure, it was a little creepy, but at least I had an enjoyable, and quiet, breakfast.

I returned to the apartment to find Sharp and Murph still passed out. I watched a little baseball on television and then decided to go hang out at Josh Morgan's "pueblo" across town. Josh doesn't live with anyone from the team because he has a friend from Alabama who lives in Tucson; they live together off Broadway. In addition to his friend from Alabama, Josh lives with three guys from Mexico in a small clay hut, or pueblo, that looks like it is about to collapse at any moment. It's a classic Arizona pueblo with the banged-up screen door, the washing machines outside which make huge puddles in the backyard, weather-beaten cactus scattered all over the front yard, with some even growing through the windows, random dogs running around the house, and, of all things, a Boston Market restaurant as a neighbor right next door.

Josh, of course, says he loves it all and has become good friends with his roommates. However, he does admit that his roommates are very loud and that it's tough for him to get to sleep early enough.

I visited Josh because he wanted me to join his Bible study group, and I thought that might be a nice idea for Easter Sunday. In fact, they had made plans to study the Bible that day on Mount Lemmon, which is one of the better known hills in the Tucson area. When I arrived at Josh's place, however, the others were running late. By the time they finally arrived, I had to leave and go back to my place for Easter dinner with Sharp and Murph. Of course, the formal dinner never really took place. I ended up doing some laundry, munched on a few Clif Bars, a bowl of Cheerios, and gulped down a protein shake or two. I think Sharp and Murph went to Wendy's for dinner (Wendy's, the fast food restaurant—not a girl they had met).

By the way, here's a quick rundown of how our apartment has been transformed into our collective baseball home away from home. We have a cozy little two-bedroom apartment in the middle of the foothills. It came fully furnished but we certainly added some of our own personal flavor to it. In the television/dining/kitchen area you can find my laptop, one of my baseball gloves, a couple of wooden bats, a bunch of empty Gatorade and water bottles that I haven't thrown out yet, my Ritz crackers and peanut butter, my favorite hats, and a bag of chocolate mini-eggs for Easter.

Adding a little more life to my stuff is Murphey's dirty t-shirts, random pairs of jeans hanging over the chairs, empty Bennigan's take out boxes, empty water bottles filled with tobacco spit, dip cans, empty bottles and cans of various brands of extremely cheap beer, and dirty towels that he doesn't like to wash or hang up. Finally, Sharp, who is by far the cleanest of the group, still finds a way to leave his unique California-style sunglasses around the room along with some more beer bottles. Sharp is definitely the neat-freak of the group. He is pretty much the "housewife" of our apartment, as he can cook and has been living on his own for longer than Murph or myself.

By the way, you can always tell which beer bottles around the house are mine, because I prefer the dark beers (i.e., Newcastle,

Guinness, Killian's, etc.). I somewhat enjoy the taste, but I heard on ESPN that dark beers have bioflavonoids that help aid in muscle recovery. I don't know if it's true or not, but it gives me a good excuse to drink beer.

The car we all share is a 1980-something bright red Plymouth Neon. Of course, I should point out that only the left side of the car has paint on it; the other side is all scratched up and has gaps where the paint should be, or used to be. So far "Little Red" has worked okay—it gets us around, and the air conditioning usually works. But we're hardly driving in style. None of the hub caps match. The gas cap doesn't close properly so it just flaps back and forth in the breeze when we drive. And of course, the car constantly rattles and shakes. When we pull up to a red light and come to a stop, the car actually vibrates so much that everyone in the car gets a nice massage. It is also loud and sounds like it might explode at any moment. But hey—I just hope it'll last us until the end of extended spring training. Then it can fall apart all it wants.

I overheard Murph talking on the phone in the other room. He calls old girlfriends, current girlfriends, and pretty much any girl that will listen to him. When he talks to them he has a strange habit of throwing in random lines from rap songs. Today the line he used was, "On my ghetto report card I made the honor roll." On the speaker phone, I could hear the girl exclaiming in pure excitement, "Congratulations Tim! That is great news! You made the honor roll!" Tim is neither in school nor did he ever make the honor roll. The line is from a song by Young Buc, I believe.

"Hey Fox! Did you hear that?" Murph yelled to me after he got off the phone. "That dumb girl thinks I made the honor roll. Put that in your journal."

Duly noted.

. . .

Life with baseball roomies is different. Everybody knows that everything is transient. Nobody has any desire to make this apartment or rental home or trailer into a permanent part of their lives. You want to move on, ideally, to a step up the baseball ladder. And as far as your roomies are concerned, so long as they don't snore or steal, and they have some semblance of personal hygiene, well, that's all you can really hope for. And a car.

April 17, 2006
Extended Spring Training
Tucson, Arizona

The dog days of extended spring training are upon us, and we still have two months to go!

We have a player here named Jeury Espinal. We also have a pitching coach named "Espy." It turns out that Espy's full name is Roberto Espinoza and that he is the brother of Alvaro Espinoza, the former major league infielder. However, before I knew all of this information I wondered if Jeury was related to Espy in some way. So I was sitting on the bench today, next to Jeury, and innocently asked him, "Hey, Jeury, is Espy your dad?"

He paused for a moment, looked around, and then responded in a strange and unusual way using choppy English, "Hmmm ... I don't think so ... but, you would have to ask my mother to be sure."

Hmm. Maybe something was lost in the translation.

April 18, 2006
Extended Spring Training
Tucson, Arizona

John "J.O." Orton and Nick "Cappy" Capra arrived in town today. J.O. is the catching coordinator, and Cappy is the roving hitting coordinator. Both of these coaches are baseball lifers: J.O. played ball at Cal Poly and was a first round draft pick years ago; Nick played eighteen seasons of professional baseball but got only fifty-four major league at-bats. No matter. To play for eighteen years in pro ball, you have to be some kind of hitter. They are both full of information and always willing to discuss the game. J.O. is a very relaxed, friendly man and I always enjoy talking baseball with him even if it's about smallest details about how to be a successful catcher. Cappy, who I also like very much, is also very outgoing and friendly but can occasionally be stern when he is dealing with someone's swing mechanics. When he watches batting practice, or is doing flips, I can see some of the younger players start to tense up when he comes near their cage. I guess that is a part of the game but it is always interesting to see the different effects that certain coaches have on an individual player's performance.

That being said, I personally like when Cappy is here because I feel like we both buy into the same approach to hitting mechanics. Everyone in the White Sox organization is supposed to teach the same approach to hitting but each coach has a tendency to use different terms to explain the same mechanics. For some reason, the words that Cappy uses always register with my brain a lot more quickly than terms used by other coaches. He is not talkative about it, but he'll say something very simple and all of a sudden the adjustment will become clear in my mind.

Baseball, at least at the professional level, is all about making adjustments. Adjustments in your swing, adjustments when fielding, adjustments when pitching, and so on. The very best players are able to make adjustments practically from pitch to pitch. Other players need more time to make those changes in their mechanics. Problem is, if it takes you a few at-bats to correct a hitch in your swing, that's going to probably translate into a 0-for-4 day. The fellow who can adjust from pitch to pitch can turn a bad first at-bat in a game into a 2-for-4 as the game develops. Trust me, that's what it's all about.

Let's say you're facing a pitcher with a great change-up. If you make the adjustment to keep your weight back, then you have a good chance to hit that pitch two or three times in a game. And of course, the more times you hit the ball hard, the better your chances of getting a hit. Likewise, if you can't make the adjustment to keep your weight back on the change-up, you're doomed to a long day of whiffs and pop-ups at the plate.

• • •

Adjustments are indeed the essence of baseball. No at-bat, no pitch is exactly the same. You consciously make small, subtle, but important changes all the time. No, you really don't re-work your entire set of basic mechanics, but you do make small adjustments throughout the game.

I recall playing in Class A ball my first year against Mike Hargrove, who was one of the best hitters I ever saw. Mike learned early on in his career how to make adjustments at the plate, on a pitch-by-pitch basis. For those old enough to remember seeing Mike hit, you'll recall he was known as "the human rain delay" since he seemingly took forever between pitches. He would step up, play with his batting glove, fiddle with his helmet, tug on his shirt, and so on. What Mike was doing was not superstition—he was just thinking about the last pitch and how to make a proper adjustment for the next delivery. And he was superb at making those changes.

How good was Mike? As I recall, he jumped from low Class A ball to being the starting first baseman of the Texas Rangers the following season. Funny story about that: Len Okrie, who was a major league catcher for several seasons, was my manager for two years, both in Anderson, South Carolina, as well as the following season in Clinton, Iowa. It was that first year— when Len and I were in Anderson—that we saw Hargrove tear up the league offensively. We just couldn't get him out, but in truth, nobody else in the league could get him out either. He just hit line drives seemingly every at-bat.

In any event, the following spring, Okrie and I were in Clinton, and early in the season, Oke gets a phone call from Billy Martin, who at that time was the manager of the Detroit Tigers. Oke used to tell the story: "So Billy gets me on the phone, and it turns out that the Tigers are opening the season against the Texas Rangers, and he's calling me to find out about this kid Hargrove—y'know, how to pitch to him to get him out." Oke continued, "I told Billy ... if we knew how to pitch Hargrove and get him out, well, hell, Billy, he'd still be in Class A ball, not the big leagues."

April 19, 2006
Extended Spring Training
Tucson, Arizona

Today was the first day where I really felt the heat affect me. After I took infield and outfield practice at shortstop, I found myself struggling to catch my breath. I suddenly became very dizzy. I was clearly dehydrated and once I got some Gatorade in my system I was fine. However, those five minutes when I was gasping for air definitely worried me. I made sure no one saw me struggling, because I didn't want any of the trainers to worry or tell the manager to take me out of the game. You have to understand—the trainers around here are so attentive to the players that, one time, when I was sitting on the bench in the middle of game and just casually scratched my non-throwing shoulder, a trainer ran over to me and said, 'Hey, Wolffie, everything okay man? Is your shoulder bothering you?" Of course I explained that I just had an itch and not to worry, but he quickly responded with, "Oh okay, good, you scared me there for a second."

In any event, the Gatorade worked wonders. Within minutes, I was back and ready for more action. After all, I'm trying to make a ball club here, and the last impression you want to leave with the coaches is that you're either not in good shape or can't play well in the heat. There's always another ballplayer on the bench, just waiting to take your spot in the lineup.

• • •

Most kids today, including my son, probably have never heard the story of Wally Pipp, the famed first baseman for the Yankees who, one day, asked out of the lineup because he had a headache. His replacement at first was a kid out of Columbia University named Lou Gehrig, the original Iron Man of baseball, who didn't miss a game for, what, thirteen years straight?

In any event, players from my generation never asked for a night off, lest your replacement go out and have a giant game. I used to play, regardless of whether I had a fever, or a stomachache, or a hurting arm, or whatever. If I saw my name in the lineup, it was time to go to work. As a pro, that's what you do.

April 20, 2006
Extended Spring Training
Tucson, Arizona

The quote of the day came from roving coach John Orton, who dropped the following analogy on us: "Carbon is to steel … as perseverance is to the character of a human." Immediately after Orton said this to the entire group of minor leaguers, all of whom had blank faces, our manager Bobby Tolan blurted out with a big smile, "Hey, Harvard boy, if you would, please break that down for the rest of us."

I did the best I could, but in truth, I'm a long, long way from Harvard Square these days.

Today we had a nice thrill, playing in the big league stadium against the Rockies. Usually, most of our games are played on the practice fields behind the major league spring training stadiums. Hence, it was a nice change of scenery, although I have to admit that zero fans showed up. I guess the regular locals and the tourists couldn't find our game. Regardless, playing in a new venue made a big difference mentally; everyone was a little more pumped up and energetic about the game. That translated into a nice 2-for-3 day for me, including the game-winning RBI.

April 21, 2006
Extended Spring Training
Tucson, Arizona

Today was an in-camp day at the field, but it was a surprisingly long day. After a few days of lifting *before* our games and practices I have finally worked out a deal with the strength and conditioning staff to allow me to lift *after* we play ball. It just makes a lot more sense. Anyhow, the staff is cool about it but I'm not supposed to tell anyone about our agreement; otherwise, the weight room will get overcrowded after practice. I prefer doing my lifting and conditioning after I've had my baseball workout.

During the workout today, Chettie was telling me stories about the great entertainers of the minor leagues. Of course, some of the first names he mentioned were Bill Veeck and Max Patkin. But then he said a name that I had never heard of: Jackie Price. He enthusiastically explained that Jackie Price had far and away the craziest routines he had ever seen. In fact, Chettie had seen Price perform when he was a ballplayer many years ago in the Cardinals' minor league franchise. As Chettie detailed, Price would come out onto the field in a jeep with some sort of "baseball grenade launcher" in the seat next to him. Sure enough, Price would park the jeep in the middle of the diamond, shoot a baseball about a mile into the sky, and then maneuver the jeep in such a way that he could catch the baseball nonchalantly in his jeep while driving around. Chettie said he couldn't believe his eyes when he first saw this routine. Personally, I still have a hard time believing it. But it sure does sound cool!

Another act that Price would put on was an inverted hitting display. Apparently, he built a special contraption that enabled him to hang upside down from the batting cage next to home plate. Then, he would take regular batting practice upside down while someone threw to him. Chettie said Price would hit line drive after line drive while upside down. Now, that's impressive. I have enough of a hard time just hitting line drives standing the right way.

• • •

I'm not familiar with Jackie Price's routines, but I did see Max Patkin, the clown prince of baseball, perform a couple of times in the minors. Wearing a bedraggled and baggy old uniform with a question mark on his back instead of a number, Max was a long-limbed fellow with an amazing knack for striking goofy poses on the baseball diamond—all of them designed to elicit big laughs. He spent years and years traveling to all the minor league towns, entertaining fans (and ballplayers) wherever he went.

I don't know if there are any original baseball acts like Max Patkin anymore. He may have been the last of the breed, but he sure did liven things up. It was always great fun when Max was in town.

April 22, 2006
Extended Spring Training
Tucson, Arizona

Today we played the Diamondbacks again. I noticed that one of their players was Travis Tully. Tully was a former Cape Cod League teammate of my friend and former Harvard teammate, Zak Farkes, who now plays in the Red Sox organization. I chatted with Tully for a few minutes after the game, and he told me that he went to the same high school as Trey Hendricks and Josh Beckett in Texas. Trey Hendricks played baseball with me at Harvard and now plays in the Diamondbacks organization, and of course Beckett is a big league stud pitcher and was the MVP of the 2003 World Series. It sounds like they must have had a pretty darn good high school baseball team.

On Saturdays there are always huge pool parties thrown by the University of Arizona students. Usually 300 to 500 people show up, including all the local minor leaguers in the area. The best way to describe these parties is to think of MTV's *Spring Break* television show. They are quite impressive productions with live bands, lots of alcohol, and many good-looking half-naked people, especially girls. Unfortunately, I usually stand out at these parties because of the brutal farmer's tan that I get from being a white boy toiling on baseball fields all day. My tan has become somewhat of an inside joke with my teammates because my arms and neck are so red that it gives me a strange two-tone appearance that, I gather, not too many girls find attractive. I probably should start tanning just to even out.

There's a left-handed pitcher named Nick Walters who has become a frequent guest at our apartment. He is one of our good friends and hails from the Phoenix area. On occasion, he'll go out with his girl, or with Sharp and Murph, and Nick will leave his huge, almost-monster-like pickup truck at our place. He leaves the keys with me and I always seem to find something that I need to do because I love that truck. I've loved monster trucks since I was a little kid, and this is probably the closest I'll ever get to driving one around the streets of Tucson. It would be nice to own a huge pickup truck one day.

Maybe when I get to the big leagues.

April 23, 2006
Extended Spring Training
Tucson, Arizona

Remember when I wrote about Josh Morgan, and how much he was enjoying living in that pueblo? Well, Josh finally decided that he just couldn't stand his digs anymore and now wants to live for as long as he can in our extra apartment. We still haven't given the key back to the apartment managers, and they don't seem to care. So I felt that Morgan might as well take advantage of the extra apartment until somebody complains. Who knows—maybe he can even help defray the cost of our rent.

After we moved Morgan's stuff in, we went down to the Waffle House for a little Sunday brunch and bumped into our manager, Bobby Tolan. Bobby was all dressed up to go golfing and looked strangely similar to Chubbs Peterson, the golf pro from the movie *Happy Gilmore*. All he needed was a wooden hand and it would have been the perfect impersonation.

As you can plainly see, we live a very exciting and glamorous life as professional baseball players.

April 24, 2006
Extended Spring Training
Tucson, Arizona

We lost a tough game today to the Rockies. I don't mind losing too much as long as it's a hard-fought and clean-played game. After all, there is no championship or playoffs at the end of extended spring. That being said, we do have the best record of the three teams and it would be nice to keep it that way. I hate losing when pitchers can't throw strikes, or when too many errors are committed because of a lack of hustle or focus.

For example, we have one relief pitcher who came in today's game and took an absolute eternity between each pitch. We were already down about five runs at the time, and this was not what I wanted to deal with in the infield. This guy was like the "human rain delay" of the pitching world. If he had been effective and had gotten the hitters out I wouldn't have minded his slow pace, but that was certainly not the case. He would take about two to three minutes between each pitch.

Here's his thirteen-step routine:

1) Throw the ball.
2) Catch the ball.
3) Walk the complete circumference of the pitcher's mound.
4) Play with the rosin bag until his hand is completely covered in white dust.

5) Practice his follow-through a few times.

6) Pick up some dirt.

7) Throw the dirt back down.

8) Brush off the rubber with his hand.

9) Dig in the dirt a little with his shoe.

10) Look up at the sky for three seconds.

11) Take a deep breath and shrug his shoulders.

12) Get the sign.

13) Pause for a second or two—and then throw the ball towards the plate with an equally slow windup.

This is the absolute truth. And all these actions were done in an extremely slow and methodical fashion. It drives me crazy. Because after all these meticulous patterns of behavior were finally completed, the Rockies then proceeded to hit about six ropes off the pitcher in a row. My opinion is that if you're going to get hit, and hit hard, you might as well speed up your between-pitch routine—not slow it up. I mean, why torture all of us?

Tomorrow we have an in-camp day, but the best part will be that Manny Trillo, the former All-Star second baseman, is going to be in town. Manny's our roving infield instructor and he always has good advice on how to become a better infielder. The last time I worked with him he explained that fielding a ground ball "is like feeling a pair of boobs … you want your hands to be soft and away from your body." He of course demonstrated on an imaginary girl and then started laughing his head off. He told some of the guys that they might need some more practice on their Saturday nights. Manny is a funny guy and always finds a way to show off a little bit during the ground ball drills. During every infield drill he ends up hopping in with us and taking grounders. The best part is that he still has perfect mechanics and never misses or bobbles a ball. He's a lot of fun to watch and has great hands at second. He must have felt a lot of boobs over the years.

April 25, 2006
Extended Spring Training
Tucson, Arizona

In the middle of our workout this morning I heard a familiar voice shout, "Hey, Wolffie!" I turned around and it was Nate "PeeWee" Oliver, our base-running coach.

"I hear you dove head first on the base paths in a game the other day ... Is that true?" Nate asked in a loud and almost angry-sounding voice.

"Yeah, it was a high throw and I knew it was going to be a close play," I said.

"Were you safe?" he asked, seeming to calm down a little bit.

"Yeah, of course."

"Good ... because you owe me fifty dollars for sliding head first. I just wanted to make sure you got your money's worth," he said with a smirk.

"What? Are you serious?"

"Of course I'm serious. You know the rules! No sliding head first. Fifty dollar fine to me and you also have to buy breakfast tomorrow."

I looked for some sign in Nate's face or voice in the hope that he was joking and just messing with me. However, he neither laughed, smirked, nor cracked a smile. I began to get really nervous because I live paycheck to paycheck and I can't afford to just throw away fifty dollars to the Nate Oliver Fund. Finally, Nate walked away and I got back in line for more groundballs when Bobby Tolan walked up beside me.

"Hey, Harvard boy, relax. Nate is just messing with ya'. Don't worry about the fifty bucks, just buy me breakfast tomorrow and I'll take care of it."

Whew!

· · ·

Yep, that's right. In amateur ball, like high school or college, if the coach "fines" you for messing up a play, you might have to carry the water jug, or run extra laps, or some other menial chore. But in pro ball, the coaches don't have to be creative in terms of punishing players. They just take your money.

After all, you're getting paid.

Of course, for a kid in the low minors, there isn't much money to spare. So a fifty dollar fine may not seem much to an outsider, but fifty dollars for sliding headfirst can mean the difference between eating well for a few days or starving.

April 27, 2006
Extended Spring Training
Tucson, Arizona
News has spread that the shortstop at Kannapolis (South Atlantic League), Javier Castillo, injured his wrist and they are calling up

our shortstop: Leo Acosta. Kannapolis is having a really bad start to their season; based on their record, they are the literally the worst team in professional baseball today, with only two wins so far in over twenty games.

Who knows? Maybe management will look to shake things up a bit on that Kannapolis roster.

• • •

The sad reality of all pro baseball is that players get hurt. However, sometimes, one player's misfortune can spell good things for another.

That's why players secretly keep track not just of their own stats, but also they peek to see how their competition is doing as well. Hey, it's all about getting to the big leagues, and players can't wait to get out of extended spring.

April 29, 2006
Extended Spring Training
Tucson, Arizona

After about a month of extended spring training I am now batting .303 (10-33) with ten RBIs and a pair of doubles. I went 0-for-8 in my last few games, and I look forward to getting back on track come Monday and want to stay consistent through May. I have been somewhat reaching for off-speed pitches in my last eight at-bats. If I can relax and learn not to reach, I should be right back on track. I hit the ball very hard three times out of eight, but unfortunately my line drives went right at the defense.

Speaking of defense, I've made only one error so far. I'm making all the routine plays and turning some good double plays. I've played the majority of games at second base, but I have also played a few games at third and shortstop.

MAY

WAIT A MINUTE. I DIDN'T SIGN UP FOR THIS.

May 1, 2006
Extended Spring Training
Tucson, Arizona

As I was leaving the field today a familiar looking man was walking into the clubhouse with a Texas Rangers, bag. He asked, "Do you know where Scott is?"

"Sure," I replied. "I'll take you to his office."

As we walked down the corridor, I nonchalantly introduced myself to him. When he answered, I realized why he looked so familiar. It was the former New York Yankees, pitcher, Jeff Nelson, who also used to bring his family to live in Armonk, New York, for the summers. Armonk is my home town, and it's a one-stoplight kind of town. You can't miss Nelson—he's about six feet, six inches with a 1950s flat-top—and I recall seeing him around Broadway North Pizzeria and Manny's Barbershop back home.

I told Nelson I was from Armonk and we reminisced about the town. Nelson's a very friendly guy and has just been signed by the White Sox. He'll be here with us in extended spring training until he is healthy enough to be moved up to the big leagues. Hopefully I won't have to face him and his nasty slider.

Speaking of Armonk, after watching the Los Angeles Clippers on television in the NBA playoffs I was reminded of my childhood days at the local lake in town. Back in the day, the Clippers' Elton Brand was just a big friendly kid from Peekskill, who was trying to earn some extra money as a lifeguard. However, there was a slight problem with Elton trying to be a lifeguard. Elton was not an efficient swimmer. More to the point, he couldn't swim. One sunny afternoon Elton, who was in his mid-teens, took out a canoe by himself in order to clean up some of the sea grass on the outskirts of the lake. He was along the left side of the lake in a fairly deep area when his canoe capsized. I was only about ten years old at the time, but I remember seeing this happen from the beach and I yelled to the lifeguard on duty.

The lifeguard hustled out to reach Elton, but by the time he got there it was clear the big man had stopped trying to tread water. In fact, he was perfectly still. However, here's the funny part: Elton's head was still above the water. As it turns out, Elton was tall enough that when he finally got tired from treading water, he let his legs down— and he was fortunate enough to be hovering over an old submerged stone wall. He was tall enough to be able to stand on the wall, and had enough height left over to keep his head above the waves. After this incident, Elton wasn't assigned to any more chores involving the lake. He stayed on the basketball court at the local club and picked up little kids to dunk basketballs. I think his high school head coach, Lou Panzanaro, who was also the manager at the club, felt this would be a safer activity for his star ballplayer. Clearly he was right.

· · ·

Jeff Nelson? Elton Brand? That's the amazing thing about sports. No matter where you go, or how far you travel from home, you invariably see someone, or see something, that reminds you of just how small this world can be.

May 2, 2006
Extended Spring Training
Tucson, Arizona

We have an in-camp day today. My grandparents, Bob and Jane Wolff, arrive tonight to see me play for a few days. You should know that I have always addressed my grandfather as "Bob" for my entire life. Some people find that a little strange, but because I have done it since I was born it's now awkward for me to call him Grandpa. (However, I do call my grandmother "Grandma.")

Bob's a legendary sportscaster but has never liked to be called Mr. Wolff or Grandpa. He feels that "Mr." is too stiff and formal and that "Grandpa" makes him sound older than he is, so he prefers that everybody—including his grandchildren—call him by his first name. Sounds good to me. In any event, Bob broadcast the original Washington Senators for years and years and then eventually did the NBC "Game of the Week" with Joe Garagiola as well. He won the National Baseball Hall of Fame's Fred C. Frick Award in 1995, and is also in the Madison Square Garden Hall of Fame. He's the only sportscaster in history to have done the play-by-play coverage on all four major sport championships: the Stanley Cup finals, the Super Bowl, the NBA finals, and the World Series. Many baseball fans know Bob from his call of Don Larsen's perfect game in the 1956 World Series, or from his call of the Baltimore Colts-New York Giants famed overtime 1958 NFL Championship game. New Yorkers know my grandfather as the TV voice of the Knicks in the

1950s, '60s, and '70s, including their two championship seasons in the early 1970s. He also was the voice of the New York Rangers for decades as well. Bob's list of accomplishments is endless, and he's always been a great resource and inspiration for me when it comes to sports.

Unfortunately, because they are arriving late and because I go to bed so early during extended spring training, Grandma and Bob will arrive long after I have gone to sleep. I look forward to seeing them at the ballpark early tomorrow morning. It's nice to have them visit all the way from New York because it really helps break up the monotony of each day. Even more importantly, having them around for a few days might really help in getting some more good meals. Money and food are still hard to come by around here.

• • •

Anytime you get a visitor from home to come see you play, it just perks you up. Especially when it's your grandparents. Suddenly, the days are no longer boring or monotonous. In addition to wanting to do well for your visitors, you also know that the rest of the afternoons and evenings will be filled with family stories, food, and fun. Somehow, everything starts to become new, fresh, and enjoyable again. I can still vividly recall when my mom and dad came to watch me play in the minors. Today, as a parent of a pro ballplayer myself and having a chance to watch John perform, I now know first-hand how much pride and excitement my parents must have enjoyed when they came to see me play. It's really quite a thrill.

My favorite story about my parents watching me in the minors happened when I was playing in the Midwest League in Clinton, Iowa, in the mid-1970s. Once the general manager of the club heard that my dad was in attendance at the ballpark, he asked Dad to come up to the press box and do an inning or two on the public address system.

Dad was more than happy to oblige. I actually came to bat in the bottom of the first. I worked the count to 3-and-2, and then took a low, outside pitch for ball four. I tossed my bat off to the side and started to jog towards first when, out of nowhere, I heard the umpire bellow, "Strike ... three!"

I was stunned—so stunned that I immediately turned and got face-to-face with the ump. Back and forth we went, until I heard this voice from up above, making some comment about the ump's lack of visual acuity. Before I knew it, the ump was tossing me out of the game ... and then he turned, looked up at the press box, and exclaimed, "And the P.A. announcer is gone too!"

It has to be the only time in the history of professional baseball that a player and the P.A. announcer were tossed on the same play.

True story.

May 3, 2006
Extended Spring Training
Tucson, Arizona

Our ball club has been playing very well recently, and today we beat up on the Diamondbacks. I hit a shot off the right field fence for a double, and defensively I ranged way to my left at second base, grabbed a hard hit groundball and fired an off-balance throw to second base to turn a double play at a key point in the game. Even the opposing field manager complimented me on the play. I was glad to put on a show for Grandma and Bob after they had traveled so far and waited so long to watch me play.

May 4, 2006
Extended Spring Training
Tucson, Arizona

What a difference a day makes. Today I went a disappointing 0-for-3 at the plate. At my first at-bat I received the sacrifice bunt sign from Bobby Tolan and, sure enough, when I squared to bunt, the ball was high and tight on my hands. I tried to pull back the bat and get out of the way of the ball, but unfortunately, my attempt was fruitless. The ball deflected high in the air off my bat and was caught easily by the catcher. Very frustrating.

In my next at-bat the pitcher threw a very nice change-up which struck me out for the first time since the very beginning of extended spring training. Finally, I felt good on my last at-bat when I roped a line drive into left field, only to see it get caught easily by the left fielder. Tough day at the park.

May 5, 2006
Extended Spring Training
Tucson, Arizona

My girlfriend came back to visit me today after enjoying some time off traveling the world. Already graduated and accepted into medical school, she decided to defer her admission for a year in order to travel and relax before the stress of medical school takes over her life.

In truth, I don't think she's a huge baseball fan, especially because baseball keeps me away from her, but she has always been very supportive of me during my short pro career and all through college. These few days will probably be one of the last times I see her all summer, because I'll be playing ball and she'll continue her travels around the globe. Long distance relationships are always tough and many ballplayers try to avoid them. I'm curious to see how my relationship plays out over the course of the summer.

• • •

Yes, there's no question that it takes a very unusual kind of relationship to withstand the rigors and uncertainty of pro ball. This is not a typical nine-to-five job, with weekends, evenings, and holidays off. For better or for worse, your main preoccupation every day is getting to the field on time, being ready to play, and always trying to impress the coaching staff. This is seven days a week. And on the occasional off-day, you just want to sleep in and relax.

As noted, this makes for a very difficult kind of relationship, especially if the two people are thousands of miles apart and can only really communicate with cell phones and e-mail.

May 6, 2006
Extended Spring Training
Tucson, Arizona
Grandma, Bob, and my girlfriend all had a chance to watch my game today. It was a great thrill to have them all in the stands. I

wanted to make sure that I played my best and wanted desperately to show off a little for them.

But as you might imagine, as soon as you start thinking that way, you end up with an 0-for-3 and only one hard hit ball. I did happen to get walked with the bases loaded to drive in a run, but that was pretty much it offensively. However, the highlight of the day was making over ten plays in the field at second base. I put on quite a show with my glove and helped win the game. But in truth, I would have been just as happy to trade a few defensive plays for a couple of frozen rope line drives.

By the way, let me take a moment to give you a little more background on the rest of my family. This book is being co-authored by my dad and me, but I'd certainly be remiss if I didn't write about my mom and my sisters, Alyssa and Samantha. Mom, who's an English teacher in Chappaqua, New York, has always been my biggest supporter. She's seen all of the struggles and ups and downs of my athletic career up close and in person, and at the end of the day, she's always been there for me. Yeah, I know all moms are supposed to do that, but I really do think that my mom has been something special. She put her own teaching career on hold to stay home and raise me and my sisters, and she was rewarded by then having the opportunity to drive me to endless ice hockey practices, travel baseball and soccer games, and everything else in between. When I was accepted to Harvard and when I was drafted by the White Sox, Mom cried, because she was so happy for me. Mom, I can never thank you enough.

As for Alyssa and Samantha, well, you have to understand that the three of us are pretty tight. We get along great, and I'm just as proud of them as they are of me. Alyssa is two years behind me at Harvard, where she's an editor on the prestigious school newspaper, *The Crimson*. And Sam, who may be the best athlete in the family, is just finishing up high school in Armonk. Both of them are going to be stars.

. . .

I just want to echo John's sentiments. The absolute center of the Wolff family is my wife Trish. She's talented in countless ways, but most importantly, she's always been there to help our three kids find their way in their young lives, whether it be in sports, schools, theatre, or whatever. It all starts with Trish's amazing organizational skills, and her seemingly endless energy to help the kids to pursue their dreams. Every parent knows how tough the job is, but I lucked out. Trish is clearly the best thing that ever happened to me—and to our kids. She's flat-out amazing.

May 7, 2006
Extended Spring Training
Tucson, Arizona

Tonight was my girlfriend's last night in town, and Bob and Grandma took us out to one of the nicest restaurants in Tucson, McMahon's Prime Steakhouse. It was a wonderful dinner and the food was excellent. Later on in the evening I was scanning the cigar and beer menu and noticed a section listing the fine cigars they offered. I flipped through a few pages and found a cigar titled a 1953 No. 3 and listed at $5.45.

When I mentioned this, Bob told me some of his stories about selling Robert Burns cigars on television. He then offered to buy me a cigar. I thought about it for a minute and said that we should try the 1953 No. 3 and see what it's like. After all, it's only a few dollars. However, when Bob mentioned this to the waiter he quickly corrected us that there was a typo on the page—that cigar cost $545, not $5.45—a slight difference.

It was a pretty sobering moment when I realized that one cigar costs more money than I make in two weeks playing minor league baseball. Wow, that definitely puts things into perspective.

After dinner, my girlfriend and I went back to her hotel room and had a long chat. Our relationship has been very difficult to maintain while we've been apart these last few weeks. The phone calls and e-mails have almost come to a complete stop. It upset me very much and it's been tough to deal with since we've been together for so long. It feels like I'm losing my best friend, but there isn't much I or she could do about it. It's now clear that we're going in very separate directions, and she explained to me that one of the reasons for her trip to visit me now was to tell me in person that she wants to break up. I respect her for telling me in person rather than just calling me and breaking up over the phone. However, it's still tough to stomach. The girl I had dated for two years caught a cab to the airport and that was the end of our relationship. I'll probably never see her again, I thought to myself.

When I got back to my apartment Sharp and Murph were watching television. They had met my girlfriend earlier in the day. Circumstances were a bit unusual because our car overheated and broke down in the middle of Tucson, and we were all stuck. She wasn't too happy about our situation and it was hard for her to understand that we couldn't afford anything more than a crappy car that breaks down on occasion. Being stuck in this situation, she did not like Murph and Sharp and they didn't really like her either. So, as you could imagine, when I told Murph and Sharp that we had broken up they were excited to hear that I was single and that I could go out with them more often. In truth, I wasn't exactly happy to hear this from my buddies. I was hoping for a bit more sympathy and understanding, but at least they were honest.

May 8, 2006
Extended Spring Training
Tucson, Arizona

We won our seventh straight game today. I was 1-for-2 with a single. After experimenting with my batting stance I have found some success with a few minor adjustments. One, keeping my hands high helps me utilize my top hand and I drive the ball more efficiently to all areas of the field. Two, I have to be careful that when I keep my hands a little higher that I don't make the mistake of standing up too straight and losing rhythm. When I stand up too straight, it can be a challenge for me to get my front foot down in time. That makes me occasionally late on certain pitches and I tend to lunge at off-speed balls. Third, in order to correct this problem, I widen my stance only slightly and get better separation. I'm always eager to make adjustments like these so I can continue to improve my swing.

While baseball is going very well, my housing situation is

growing increasingly difficult. Sharing one car with three active people has become a struggle. In fact, living in such close and slovenly quarters has put me in a somewhat eager mood to get out of here. My roommates are great guys and I love them, but when living in such close proximity things can sometimes get heated. Whenever we start yelling at each other the only thing I can think of is a line from the movie *Dumb and Dumber* when the two poor guys have reached rock bottom of their finances: "We have no food … we have no money … our pets' heads are falling off." Yeah, that is what I feel like at times.

• • •

You have to understand that you spend so much time at the ballpark—from very early in the morning until late in the afternoon—that your time away from the ballpark becomes precious. You just want to come home, get out of the sun, collapse onto an easy chair or bed, and relax. You want your space to be peaceful.

The last thing you want is to come home to a cramped space, which is a mess, and which is populated by teammates who tend to be loud, angry, and sloppy. It just doesn't make for a good combination.

May 9, 2006
Extended Spring Training
Tucson, Arizona
In our game today we had a new pitcher on the mound, and I wanted to make sure that he was not nervous about his first

start here in extended spring training. As soon as he finished his warm-up pitches I jogged over to the mound and chatted with him briefly.

"Hey man, I know you are a little nervous right now ... but just try to relax and don't let the crowd get to you. They can get pretty loud at times so try and be cool." The new pitcher looked around the entire ballpark and saw maybe three pigeons, a sleepy spectator or two, and cracked a smile. He said, "This entire scene reminds me of Yankee Stadium in the playoffs."

Of course, the "new" pitcher was veteran major leaguer Jeff Nelson. It's not too often that I get to give some friendly advice to a veteran star pitcher, so I felt it was necessary to welcome Jeff to extended spring training with the White Sox. Believe it or not, I think he was glad that I came over and joked with him.

It wasn't too long ago that *Baseball America* voted Jeff Nelson as having the best slider in the bigs for the last ten to fifteen years. I had a chance to see it from the second base position, and I can assure you that every right-handed batter who faced him would literally dive out of the box, only to see the ball boomerang back into the strike zone. A few guys were able to get the bat on the ball but only managed to hit weak grounders to me at second base.

The highlight of the day came on a chopper that bounced over Nelson's glove and landed in between the pitcher's mound and first base. I raced in as fast as I could, called off my first baseman, and then fielded the ball and flipped it to Nelson on the run to get the third out of the inning. It sounds somewhat juvenile, but when Jeff Nelson came over after the play and patted me on the back it was pretty cool. It's not every day you get complimented by an established major leaguer. But then again, we Armonkians have to look for out for each other.

May 10, 2006
Extended Spring Training
Tucson, Arizona

"Gentleman, there are only thirty days of spring training left … Thank God we are almost out of here!"

Nick Leyva opened up today's team meeting with that uplifting sentiment. It appears that the managers and coaching staff don't want to be stuck in extended any more than we do. Thirty days still feels like an eternity here in Tucson, though. Every day it just gets hotter and hotter and more things turn from green to brown as the sun bears down and bakes every living thing in the area.

We couldn't get more than three hits against the Diamondbacks pitching staff today, despite some colorful advice from our hitting coach, Jerry Hairston. Among his helpful hints were, "Smack this pitcher around like he was your unwanted red-headed stepbrother," and "Beat this pitcher like he was a dead goat tied to a tree!"

Jerry Hairston is a pretty amazing guy. In addition to being a top-flight hitting coach, Jerry is a devout Jehovah's Witness and is probably one of the nicest guys you'll ever meet. He also happens to have one of the best baseball pedigrees in the history of the game. His father, Sam Hairston, was a famous Negro League star who also played for the White Sox. Jerry was a long-time major leaguer, and his two sons, Jerry Jr. and Scott, are both current major leaguers. And I think Jerry has a brother who also played in the show. Quite a baseball family. In any event, during a break in batting practice,

I asked Jerry, "Hey man, do you talk baseball all the time during family gatherings and dinners? I mean, your family must have some pretty good baseball stories." He laughed and said, "Awww man, you got to be crazy. We rarely talk about baseball. It is something we all share and enjoy but we don't talk about it as much as you might imagine." I guess I probably should have figured that.

Jerry Hairston has a very distinct way of saying the phrase, "Awww man." He draws out the "awwww" part and pronounces "man" more like "main." He uses this phrase on many different occasions. For example, he has been known to use it when somebody hits a rope, makes a great play, or does something stupid. Matt Sharp and I have picked up on this Hairston-ism and use it more and more frequently during the day. Sharpie told me that his dad (former major leaguer Bill Sharp) used that same phrase as well when he was a teammate of Hairston's on the Chicago White Sox years ago. I'm impressed that Hairston has stayed true to his trademark phrase for all these years.

It was a tied game in the bottom of the ninth when a routine fly ball was hit to our right fielder, Marquise Cody. I ran out a few steps from second base but was called off immediately by Cody. He was camped under the ball and waiting to catch the ball to make the final out when, inexplicably, the ball bounced off the heel of his glove and the winning run scored from second base. Cody was pretty upset about costing us the game.

• • •

I feel for Marquise Cody. There are very few experiences in life worse than making the key error that costs your team a victory. Yes, it does happen. And it happens a lot. But when it happens to you, there isn't much you can say, nor is there much that your teammates can do to ease the pain, except to give you a quiet pat on the back.

It makes for a long, long night and a lot of lost sleep—what did the manager think? Will the manager play me again tomorrow? Will I get cut? Should I go and apologize to the team? These are the kinds of endless questions that filter through your mind and soul for the rest of the evening. It's painful—very painful.

The reassuring thing about baseball is the knowledge that tomorrow brings a new day and a new game—and with it, the hope that you can somehow get that chance to redeem yourself. But it still is tough.

May 11, 2006
Extended Spring Training
Tucson, Arizona

We rebounded nicely from our bizarre loss yesterday to rally and beat the Rockies 5-3 today on their home field. I was 1-for-3 with a walk, a run scored, and an RBI. Unfortunately for our pitching staff, Jeff Nelson just got called up to AAA today; however, in retrospect, it wasn't really fair to have him throw against players in Rookie ball and A ball.

This evening, back at the apartment, I realized that I hadn't had a haircut in quite some time and that my hair is getting long. I thought it might look good at first with a little "flow" coming out from under my hat, but then I realized that it's just too hot out here to keep long hair. I decided I needed to get a haircut, and soon.

There are two obstacles, however: 1) I don't know of any barber shops here in the area, and 2) haircuts cost money.

Sharpie shaves his head every couple of weeks and he looks okay so I thought that might be a good way for me to go. I figured Sharpie could shave my head and my problem would be solved. However, the last time I shaved my head was my freshman year of high school and I seem to recall that it wasn't really a great look for me. If you ask my mom she would strongly agree, but I think most moms don't like shaved heads on their sons. Anyway, I decided to let Sharp shave my head, and I was quite pleased with the way it turned out. The one thing I didn't take into consideration, though, was that my longer hair had fully covered my pale white forehead while, in stark contrast, my face was extremely tan. Hence, with a shaved head it appears that I have a spectacular two-tone skull with a dark face and a very white forehead.

May 12, 2006
Extended Spring Training
Tucson, Arizona

The catching coordinator, John Orton, is back in town today and was the first coach to speak at the team meeting this morning. J.O. had a smirk on his face and as he addressed the troops, he boldly said, "Guys, let me tell you this … you can't always get want you want … " He paused for a few moments and then continued, "But sometimes … you might just find … you get what you need."

There was stone silence after J.O. finished his thought, but he still had that same smirk on his face. I looked around for a moment and then started to crack up with laughter. Everyone glared at me because they couldn't figure out what was so funny in John Orton's very serious message. J.O. immediately looked over at me and thanked me by saying, "Well, at least someone here gets my sense of humor!"

All the coaches then picked up on J.O.'s Rolling Stones reference; however, I think most of the players were still kind of curious as to what was going on—especially the players who don't speak English that well.

· · ·

Baseball is truly an amazing melting pot of different cultures and backgrounds, but everybody on your team is drawn together by the same dream—to get to the big leagues. And to do that, you have to rely on your teammates everyday. Example: John is primarily a second baseman who grew up in the upper-middle-class suburbs of New York City. He has to depend greatly on getting good feeds from his shortstop, who grew up in the poor sugarcane fields of the Dominican Republic. On those bang-bang turn pivots, it is essential that John gets a good solid throw from his infield mate. Likewise, the shortstop is fully reliant on John giving him a good feed on the double-play throws from second.

It makes no difference where they grew up, what kind of education they've had, or what kind of background they come from. All that matters is that in a key double play situation in a close game, if the opposing batter hits a chopper to short, John has to fully trust that his shortstop will get the ball to him in a quick and timely manner. If everything goes according to plan, the feed, pivot, and throw to first are made perfectly, and the team gets out of the jam—and the pitcher, who may be from Japan or Australia or backwoods Arkansas, is also extremely grateful that his trust in his teammates was rewarded. Indeed, when they come off the field as the inning ends, the pitcher will compliment and thank his shortstop and second baseman for making that key double play. To me, this is the international melting pot of baseball in action. It doesn't matter what language you speak or culture you come from—it only matters that you all trust each other to make the play.

May 13, 2006
Extended Spring Training
Tucson, Arizona

We got to an early lead this morning against the Diamondbacks but then fell behind on back-to-back home runs. We rallied in the bottom of the eighth inning with some clutch hitting, however, and went on to win again, our tenth consecutive victory.

I was pleased with my performance both in the field and at bat. I had to range way to my left at second base to make two plays in the hole and I was also 2-for-2 with two singles.

On our way home from the field we had to stop and get some gas. Getting gas usually involves some form of fight because no one ever wants to spend his money on gas. However, this afternoon we had a bigger problem to worry about. After filling up the car, we couldn't get the car to start. Apparently, the battery was fried. This was rather frustrating because only a few days ago our original car, the red Plymouth Neon, had overheated numerous times, forcing us to bring it back to the rental car place. In exchange, we received a 1987 red Monte Carlo with the aforementioned battery problem. We were able to get someone to jumpstart us and get back home, but we knew that once we turned the car off again it was not going to start without a new battery. We immediately called the rental car service and the manager told us to drive over right away and change cars. We didn't waste a single minute. As we drove over in our second crappy car we all hoped that we would get some nice new convertible or a sweet pickup truck.

What we got back was the same crappy Plymouth Neon that we had before! I couldn't believe it. All of us knew this Neon piece of scrap metal had overheated numerous times before we traded it in and, sure enough, we were only halfway to our apartment when it started heating up again. Unbelievable! We made it home, but it appears that the air conditioning in our sweet ride causes it to heat up way too much. Hence, we now have a car that has no air conditioning during the hottest period of extended spring. I think it was 110 degrees today. But they say it's a dry heat. Yeah, so is your oven but I wouldn't want to sit in that either.

May 14, 2006
Extended Spring Training
Tucson, Arizona

We had a much-needed and relaxing off-day today that was spent half at the local pool and half in our apartment parking lot playing Wiffle ball.

Now, understand that since I play ball all day for a living, the very last thing I wanted to do on my off-day was play Wiffle ball. But when Murphey told me that three girls from the University of Arizona were playing, I changed my mind rather quickly.

The girls challenged us to a three-on-three game of home run derby that, of course, we dominated. However, two of the three girls had nice swings and hit the ball well. One of the girls used to be a softball pitcher and she was throwing softball-style, which gave the Wiffle ball some nasty movement. At one point I was concerned that this U of A senior might actually strike me out. But I have to admit, having a few beers and playing Wiffle ball on a warm Sunday evening in Arizona with three attractive ladies makes for a pretty enjoyable and relaxing evening.

After the game, we went over the girls' neighboring apartment complex and they made us some dinner and we were able to relax and do our laundry for free. These are the things that matter the most.

We met these girls a few weeks ago at the Cactus Moon nightclub/bar and we had stayed in touch with them over the past few weeks. They had been very kind to us in terms of helping us out with our laundry and food situation. However, they were all seniors at the University of Arizona and their upcoming graduation was this weekend. With them leaving town we were going to have find some other local girls to take care of us.

I must confess that their graduation reminded me of Harvard, and I thought about what I'd be doing today if I had chosen to stay in school. Chances are I'd be in the middle of reading period preparing for exams and writing term papers. I called my old roommate, Tony Biagioli, and he did a good job of filling me in on the stories and gossip that I've missed the past few months. It was great to share a few laughs and he made me feel like I had never left campus.

"This is the best time of one's Harvard career," Tony explained. "For the first time you truly have no work to do and can just relax and party with your classmates." He said he was having an awesome time and that he was still adjusting to not having to worry about academic demands. That being said, Tony will have plenty of work to do once he arrives at Georgetown Law School in the fall. I'm glad to hear he is enjoying his light schedule. I forgot to ask whether he was playing any Wiffle ball.

. . .

I can sympathize with John about missing that last semester of college. That's the one chance that you really have time to sit back and relax after all the hard work you put into high school and college, and have some good times with your buddies.

I don't recall what I was doing exactly on what should have been my graduation day from college, but I do know I was playing a game somewhere in South Carolina. And yes, I much preferred to be wearing a double knit baseball uniform that a cap and gown. But there is something to be said about honoring the day one graduates from college, especially from a school like Harvard.

That's why the following spring, when I was playing in Clinton, Iowa, I decided that I had to make plans to somehow get back to Cambridge for that year's graduation (I was originally in the Class of 1973, but since I didn't finish my studies until January 1974, the next official graduation I could attend was June 1974). These days, I read in the papers that major leaguers routinely ask for and get days off for any number of personal reasons. But a generation ago, these kinds of requests just weren't made, especially at the minor league level. Regardless, once I had been assigned to the Midwest League for 1974, I did make a personal request to my manager, Len Okrie, for a day off to attend my college graduation.

I recall Len looking at me. I'm sure he was thinking, "Nobody gets a day off in the minors ... especially not for a college graduation." But somehow, Len relented and said, "Okay, I'll give you one game to miss ... but you had better be back for the next night's game."

I assured him I would. I planned it all out. I drove a rented car to O'Hare from Clinton (as a I recall, it was a couple of hours), boarded a flight from Chicago to Boston, and arrived the night before the graduation ceremony to greet my parents. So far, so good. The next day's ceremony in Harvard Yard was indeed something spectacular, and yes, I am very glad that I made the effort to attend and be part of it. Mom and Dad were there to see me get my diploma, and it was a glorious day in all regards.

But now came the tricky part. The ceremonies ended around one or so. I was booked on a mid-afternoon flight back to Chicago, where I would pick up the rental car again and hustle back to Clinton, Iowa, for that night's game. Everything was working on schedule until we started to circle O'Hare. The pilot announced that there was a lot of air traffic and we'd been placed in a holding pattern. Of course, this is long before phones were installed in airplanes, so there was no way for me to communicate with my manager or the team. I was beginning to panic.

The plane finally landed and I sprinted to the car rental place, jumped in my rental, and zoomed due west to Iowa. But I had lost a lot of time, and as the minutes ticked off, it was clear I was going to be late for the 7:30 game start. I fiddled with the car radio, and was able to pick up the pre-game show. I was still thirty minutes out of Clinton, and the announcer was about to give the starting lineups. And then, I got a break.

The broadcaster came back on and said, "Well, friends, we're sitting through this sudden cloudburst ... but the tarp is on the field, and I imagine we'll be starting in about twenty or thirty minutes."

A rain delay! I was elated. I finally got to the ballpark, parked the car, raced to the clubhouse, and jumped into uniform. I immediately let Len Okrie know I was there, and he nodded his head and added, "Have a seat on the bench."

But the story doesn't end there. Late in the game, the score was tied and Okrie beckoned to me go up and pinch-hit. My sense of drama was with me. I mean, how cool would it be to get up there, smash a base hit, and help us win the game on the day I graduated from college some eight hundred miles away!

Well, I wish I could say I hit the first pitch for a home run, or even a base hit. But in truth, I whiffed on three sliders and sat back down on the bench. Oh well.

Lesson learned? Even newly minted Harvard grads can't always get a hit.

May 15, 2006
Extended Spring Training
Tucson, Arizona

Everyone who has played professional baseball knows that you very rarely feel one hundred percent, but despite your ailments and aches and pains, you still have to go out there and get the job done. It makes the game that much more of a challenge. I would like to think that I learned this lesson early in spring training, but trust me, it's not that easy.

Let me explain. I had a terrible game today. I was 0-for-3 with two broken bat ground balls and a line out to centerfield. I've broken only two bats since the first day of spring training, so my cracking not one but two bats in the same game was rather frustrating, not to mention expensive. I also made my first error at second base, which I couldn't believe. A Rockies, batter hit a hard one-hopper at me and it skipped up off the baked ground, smashed off the heel of my glove and then ricocheted off my shoulder into shallow centerfield. I knew I should have just tried to knock it down and keep it in front of me, but instead I tried to get a little fancy and make the "great" play. I ended up with an error. Brutal. At least one of my broken bats helped move a runner over from second to third, but that's the only positive thing to come out of today's game for me.

Sometimes, this game sucks.

•   •   •

Yes, it's a tough, tough game. It takes a long time to come to grips with how to even out the peaks and valleys. The truth is, you try as hard as you can every day. But some games bring you hits and great plays while others bring you strikeouts and errors. You try just as hard in both kinds of games, and you hope and pray that you'll have many more good games than bad ones.

May 16, 2006
Extended Spring Training
Tucson, Arizona

We had a short in-camp game today and I was able to play second base behind Nate Cornejo, who pitched four years in the bigs for the Detroit Tigers and who also happens to look a lot like the movie character Shrek. Nate's an off-speed, control type of pitcher who throws a very good change-up. He induces batters to hit a ton of ground balls and, as expected, I fielded a bunch of them today.

After the game today I went home, turned on Murphey's Playstation 2, and played a game against the New York Yankees. I chose to be the Detroit Tigers and my starting pitcher was, as you might imagine, Nate Cornejo. How cool is that?

May 17, 2006
Extended Spring Training
Tucson, Arizona

Josh Morgan had been living in our "free" apartment for the last few weeks, but the manager finally made us give back the key yesterday. Josh bought a huge, king-sized blow-up air mattress and is now sleeping where our kitchen table used to be. In addition, Chris Brennan was sent down to extended spring training from our Class A affiliate Kannapolis Intimidators and he has nowhere to stay. Even though we had no room to offer Chris, we told him he could stay on the couch and help us defray the cost of rent. Instead, Brennan showed up at our apartment with another king-sized air mattress and took up the remaining space in our television room. Brennan is from Alabama and attended Birmingham-Southern College. He is a crafty, left-handed pitcher who played last season in Great Falls, Montana. He pitched well in spring training and made the Class A Kannapolis roster. However, for some reason he was bumped off the roster and came back to extended spring. He was not happy about being sent back to extended and told me he contemplated retiring and applying to medical school. Brennan is one of the most outgoing players I have ever met and will talk your ear off if you give him the chance. He's the kind of guy who wakes up at 6:00 a.m. with a huge smile on his face. He starts laughing and talking loudly long before he even drinks his morning coffee. I hate morning people. They drive me crazy. In the morning I want quiet and more sleep. That being said, Brennan has one very entertaining gift. He can break any bat over his knee in one swift and powerful action. He's a strong and muscular guy, but he's no Bo Jackson. So, watching him destroy bats over his knees like they are twigs is a pretty amazing sight.

With the two enormous air beds it is now impossible to walk around the apartment without stepping on one of the beds. I don't mind that much, though I wonder why the air mattress manufacturers can't make a regular size inflatable bed. That would solve a lot of problems for us.

May 19, 2006
Extended Spring Training
Tucson, Arizona
We got paid a few days ago, fortunately, as our rent and car payments were due today. Every time I have to go to the ATM

and hand over large wads of cash to my landlord and car rental guy I feel like someone is ripping my stomach out of my body. Money is so hard to come by around here that spending it on things you can't really hold or eat seems like the devil. Every month we try to push off our rent and car payments for as long as we can, as if they will magically disappear if we wait long enough. However, they never do. It's terrible.

. . .

Welcome to the real world, my boy. Even minor leaguers have to pay rent and buy groceries. Yes, they cost money. And no, they won't magically disappear.

May 20, 2006
Extended Spring Training
Tucson, Arizona

We've got a home game today against the Diamondbacks. My father will be in town, which should be nice because he doesn't get a chance to take time off from work very often to travel so far to watch me play. The boredom out here is becoming unbearable. When I'm at the ballpark I'm fine and the baseball is great. It's the time off the field that can really get quite monotonous. A person can only watch so much network television and play so much Playstation before his mind goes numb. I finally decided to go out and buy a bunch of books in order to keep myself occupied during the evenings. I figure it's a cheap way to keep myself from losing my mind. The irony is that I spent the last three years in college trying all sorts of ways to avoid reading books and doing homework. But for the first time in quite awhile, I was actually somewhat excited about reading again. I'm clearly going nuts.

• • •

Can you imagine? My son has become so bored that he actually went out and bought some books to read! This is clearly one of the great positive side benefits of his playing pro ball.

That being said, I can certainly relate to the relentless tedium. When I was in Anderson, South Carolina, I recall being so bored that I would actually go to the local library in town. Not only was it nicely frigid due to the air conditioning (it gets really hot in South Carolina), but it was quiet and I could read any number of magazines and books in a peaceful setting. Trust me, like John, I wasn't any bookworm in college. But somehow, it was quite enjoyable spending time in the library on those mornings and early afternoons before night games.

May 21, 2006
Extended Spring Training
Tucson, Arizona

It sure is a great treat to have my dad here. Most players don't get a chance to see their parents or families at all, so I'm grateful to have the chance to relax with Dad for a weekend.

Dad and I drove over to Chandler, Arizona, today with Josh Morgan and Chris Brennan to visit our close family friends,

Inset As a member of the Harvard baseball team that captured the 2005 Ivy League championship. That's me, on the far right, in the black sweatshirt, kneeling down. *Courtesy of the Wolff Family*

I was absolutely thrilled when White Sox scout John Tumminia came to my home to sign me. *Courtesy of the Wolff Family*

Spring training March 2006 … I couldn't wait to get to Tucson, but I didn't
know my spring training experience would last into June.
Courtesy of the Wolff Family

A couple of shots of me batting during extended spring training in Arizona. Everyday was hot and dusty. But remember, it's a "dry heat"...
Courtesy of the Wolff Family

Above   In my first game in Bristol. Curiously, I started at first base, not second. *Courtesy of the Morgan Family*

Opposite   Josh Morgan and I as Bristol White Sox teammates. *Courtesy of the Morgan Family*

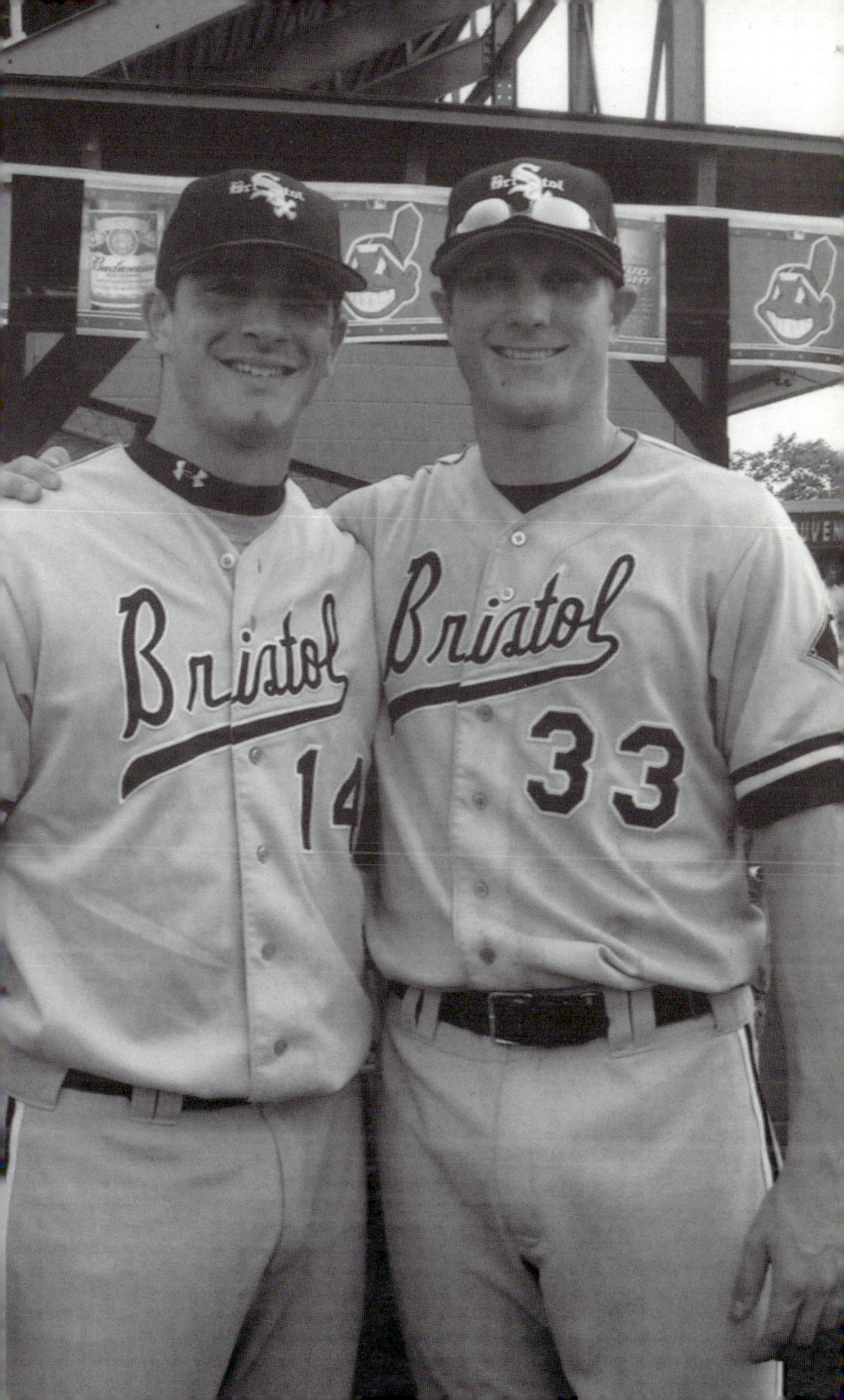
Bristol
14
Bristol
33

My mom visiting me after a game in Kalamazoo. She helped me drive all the way out there. *Courtesy of the Wolff Family*

My grandparents … Bob and me … Grandma and me.
Courtesy of the Wolff Family

Above Turning a double play against the Traverse City Beach Bums in the Frontier League. *Courtesy of Ron White Photography*

Opposite Banging out a base hit for the Kings. I was hitting around .270 before I injured my shoulder late in the season.
Courtesy of Ron White Photography

RLWhite

Above   My host parents in Kalamazoo, Ted and Louise Greene. They took good care of me on their farm. *Courtesy of Ted and Louise Greene*

Opposite   Ready to make the throw to first.
Courtesy of Ron White Photography

Signing for a young fan ... a baseball tradition that I always enjoy.
Courtesy of the Wolff Family

My dad and I in Tuscon, Arizona. He was lucky he never had to experience extended spring as a player. *Courtesy of the Wolff Family*

In the offseason, I stayed in shape by playing for the Harvard junior varsity hockey team. I hold my high school's all-time scoring records, and many thought I would choose to play hockey in college instead of baseball.
Courtesy of the Wolff Family

Here's me with my younger sisters, Samantha and Alyssa, at home in Armonk, NY. *Courtesy of the Wolff Family*

Dad was ready for action back in the day in spring training in Tigertown in 1973. *Courtesy of the Wolff Family*

Jack, Joanie, and James Rapoport. It was a rare Sunday off, filled with great food, company, and tons of baseball stories from all of our college days. That's one of the very best parts about playing ball—having the chance to trade stories with your teammates and friends.

. . .

As a father, there are few moments as gratifying or meaningful as watching your son play ball, especially at the pro level.

When I arrived at the White Sox facility today, I came over a gentle hill from the parking lot, and beyond the fence I could see John playing second base. The game was already in progress, and he was clearly engaged, doing his job.

I have been blessed with all sorts of wonderful moments and events in my life, but getting a chance to see my son play professional baseball is a thrill that will truly last me a lifetime. It's a wonderful memory that I will keep playing and replaying in my mind forever.

May 22, 2006
Extended Spring Training
Tucson, Arizona

We had a game today across town at the Colorado Rockies' facility. The short trip was quite an enjoyable experience for my dad because the Rockies' facility used to be the former Cleveland Indians' complex. As I mentioned earlier, my dad worked for the Cleveland Indians' organization for five years in the early 1990s as their roving sports psychology coach. As he walked around the complex, he was surprised to see how little the facility had changed in more than ten years. It brought back a lot of nice memories for him.

Before batting practice, Dad came up to me and jokingly reminded me of what Vince Lombardi once said, "Son, play well because if you don't … you are no longer part of this family!"

Oh wait, maybe Homer Simpson said that. Anyway, I was able to muster a 3-for-7 day with two singles and a double in our 24-6 trouncing of the Rockies. I was very glad Dad had a chance to see it.

. . .

It's true. If you had asked me back in the 1990s whether I would expect to see my young son grow up and play pro ball in Arizona , well … I guess I could have dreamed about it. But I also know from being in pro sports that it's a very, very difficult path to pro ball, and once you get there, it only gets harder. But for today, for this special moment, I looked around at the fields, the green grass, the blue sky, and looked on at my son in a White Sox uniform with the kind of pride that only a parent can feel.

May 23, 2006
Extended Spring Training
Tucson, Arizona
Today was an in-camp day and, unfortunately, the last day my father would be in town. The last few days went by too quickly. I

was able to put on a good show for him, however, and went 3-for-5 with two doubles, a triple, and a walk. I come from a baseball family, and nobody loves baseball more than I do, but I will say it is getting harder and harder to stay mentally focused for these games because there are no fans and no playoff incentive to do well.

I'm excited to get the season started in either Great Falls, Montana (Pioneer League) or Bristol, Virginia (Appalachian League). On that note, when I handed my laundry in after practice today I bumped into the clubhouse manager, Dan Flood. We have become very good friends over the past few months and we help each other in any way possible.

"Hey, Hahvahd boy, I saw the flight arrangements for the upcoming weeks."

"Oh yeah?"

"Yeah, man, I saw your name on the flight to Great Falls, Montana. Is that where you want to go?" Floody asked.

"Well, I don't know too much about Montana, but I hear they get great crowds and that would be a nice change of pace from the desert."

"Remember, this isn't official but I just wanted to give you the heads up," Floody said as he walked away into the laundry room and I thanked him. He put up his right hand in acknowledgement and I waited in the clubhouse for my roommates to head on home. I was excited to be heading to Great Falls in the Pioneer League.

• • •

Watching extended spring training games is a surreal kind of experience. Yes, the players are all top notch. They can all hit, run, and field. And yes, the pitchers all throw in the low nineties, with curves and sliders. And yet, it's somewhat bizarre because even though the talent level here is outstanding, there's no sense of drama or excitement since there's no scoreboard, no fans, no music, no nothing. It's almost as though a group of eighteen baseball players decided to get together for a spontaneous game on one of the nicely-manicured baseball fields in a local Tucson park.

The players go through all the motions of hustling on and off the field, the infielders make chatter and whistle between pitches, and when a kid hits a rope, his teammates on the bench applaud. But beyond that, there's nothing added in. I have always thought that extended spring was the roughest way of playing professional baseball—all of the romance has been totally bleached out of it—and clearly, the players are just hoping and praying to get moved up as soon as possible. Or that extended spring comes to an end as soon as possible.

John's as mentally tough as they come. But with every day melting into the next one, without any change of scenery or sense of accomplishment, it's a brutal way of playing a game you love.

May 24, 2006
Extended Spring Training
Tucson, Arizona

We lost to the Diamondbacks today, but I was able to break up a no-hitter in the fourth inning with a smoked line drive up the middle. I finished the day 1-for-3 with that line drive into center, a line out to the centerfielder, and a strike out, and I've noticed that I hit much better when I maintain my rhythm.

I received a painful phone call after the game today from my now ex-girlfriend. We had been dating for a long time and I think we are both going through a difficult transition phase. We are still important to each other and we are trying to figure out over the phone what our relationship is going to be like now. The clichéd idea of staying "friends" is certainly an option, but that didn't really sit well with either of us. So we decided to let some time go by and revisit the topic once things cooled down. I thought that was a good idea and we left it at that.

After that, there was really only one more order of business between my ex-girlfriend and me: giving back her stuff. As anyone who has been in a tough breakup knows this can actually be one of the most awkward and painful parts of the breakup. In an unusual arrangement, I was using her laptop computer to keep track of my diary in Arizona. Naturally, she wanted it back right away. I can't blame her. I would've wanted my computer back, too. I thought about asking for all of my t-shirts and clothes back in return, but the absurdity of that idea made me laugh. I agreed to mail her computer right away and let her keep the shirts.

May 25, 2006
Extended Spring Training
Tucson, Arizona

The countdown has finally begun. When extended spring training is finally over I have five whole days off to relax before I have to report to Montana. I haven't decided what I want to do just yet, but one good idea would be to do something to correct my brutal farmer's tan.

May 26, 2006
Extended Spring Training
Tucson, Arizona

Let me go back to my situation with my college girlfriend. One thing that isn't discussed too often is the strain that minor league baseball puts on relationships. My girlfriend (as well as many other teammates' girlfriends) was not ready to handle the distance and the time apart. There are no vacations during the minor league season, and many people don't understand why you can't simply take a weekend off work and go to the beach or go travel somewhere. By the nature of minor league baseball, you often find yourself playing in small towns in remote areas all across the United States. If your significant other is not prepared for this type of lifestyle then chances are the relationship will not last more than a few months.

Over the past few days, I've experienced a bunch of different emotions stemming from the breakup. At first, I was a little angry. Then I was disappointed and hurt. And now I've resolved to get my mind off the ordeal. I guess that's what you need to do in order to stay focused for the games. The one thing about playing ball every day is that it doesn't let you get down on yourself because you have to go out and perform constantly. There is no time to feel sorry for yourself when you go to the ball field because, in truth, your teammates and coaches don't care about your problems—much in the same way that you don't really want to hear about theirs.

May 28, 2006
Extended Spring Training
Tucson, Arizona

Josh Morgan, Enrique Escolano, and I wanted to take a break and do something a little different on our day off today. A couple of days ago, we found a brochure for a water park in Tucson and we decided to go check it out and cool off. We thought it would be a great idea to break up the deadly dull monotony.

Much to our chagrin, however, when we got to the water park it became clear to us that it was not designed for people over the age of eleven. There was a nice wave pool about the size of a basketball court and three water slides, but that was pretty much it. Three water slides. No more. I guess we were expecting to find a good chunk of the Pacific Ocean or maybe something like Jones Beach to be there. But we finally had to come to grips with the fact that we were in the middle of the desert and even though the slides were for elementary school children, we had to do the best we could.

So we pressed on, even though the three of us must've looked like something out of the movie *Billy Madison*, when Adam Sandler goes back to kindergarten. Josh is about six-three and 225 pounds, Enrique is six-eight, and I'm six-one. We were strolling around the water park sandwiched between hundreds of kids ten years old or younger on line for the three water slides.

Now, admittedly, most normal people our age probably would have seen the troubling situation we were in and left the park and try to find a better one in the area. But we decided that would be fruitless. So we just waited in line for the three water slides over and over again. To our surprise, we had a great day despite all the strange looks from concerned parents who clearly thought we were a danger to their children.

May 29, 2006
Extended Spring Training
Tucson, Arizona
Supposedly we find out officially where we will be assigned sometime this week. Everyone is starting to get anxious, as the countdown to end of spring training on June 8 continues.

• • •

Once the last cuts have finally been made in spring training each year, everybody's attention starts to focus on where they're going to be sent. It's a little bit odd, because there is so much nervous energy during spring training expended on who stays and who gets a plane ticket home. But when the cuts are finished, all of that negative energy transforms into positive enthusiasm. It's always exciting to think about the new and exotic spot where you're going to be shipped.

May 31, 2006
Extended Spring Training
Tucson, Arizona

We took on the Diamondbacks at their place today. It was the best 0-for-3 game I have ever had in my career. I hit the ball on the nose three times, got walked once, and made some standout plays in the field at second base. Our team got beat pretty badly, however, since our pitchers couldn't throw strikes consistently.

As the days pass by here in extended spring training my notes get shorter and shorter. This is mainly because people here in extended spring training are not too happy to be here. In fact, everyone is secretly depressed and frustrated that it's almost June and they are still stuck in Tucson. Yes, the games are still intense and important; however, it's clear that the players and staff are not in the same "relaxed" mood that they were a couple of months ago.

As recently as a few weeks ago the coaches were making jokes, laughing, and kidding around quite a bit. Now, since everyone can feel themselves itching to get out of here, the joking and fooling around has slowed down, and therefore there have not been many good stories to report. Even the players who enjoy partying and going out routinely have slowed down in their ways and as a result the stories of beer, women, and partying have stopped. The one good thing about this dip in morale is that it'll all be over in about a week's time. I noticed the itinerary for the Great Falls team was posted in the clubhouse today, and it looks like after we arrive in Great Falls we have some light workouts and then some activities that could be quite fun. I think I saw a media day, a "Meet the White Sox" day, an exhibition game versus a local high school all-star team, and other promotions. That all sounds nice, but I'm most excited about playing in front of fans again.

FOUR

JUNE

FINALLY, A CHANGE OF SCENERY!

June 1, 2006
Extended Spring Training
Tucson, Arizona

Before the game today, Nick Leyva stunned me by telling me I'll be playing in Bristol with him this summer.

I must confess that I was both surprised and somewhat disappointed. Even though Bristol and Great Falls are both considered to be the same level of pro ball, I was looking forward to being in Montana. I know it doesn't really matter which team I'm on so long as I get the chance to play a lot, but I was hoping to be in Great Falls because I heard the league is very well run and that they get lots of fans. On the other hand, I don't mind being assigned to Bristol because I happen to like Nick Leyva and Jerry Hairston quite a bit and I enjoy playing for them. Of course, I can't be sure, but I think that Leyva and Hairston are big supporters of mine, and maybe they wanted me in Bristol with them. Either way it is not worth over-thinking. I'll be in Bristol, Virginia, in a week or so.

By the way, today's game lasted twelve innings in 110 degree heat. We were down by one run going into the last inning and I was having a tough 0-for-5 game. There were runners on second and third with two outs when I got my sixth at-bat. I tried to put the thought of going 0-for-6 out of my head and focus on hitting the ball hard somewhere. Sure enough, the pitcher threw me a low and inside slider and I hammered it to right field. Both runners scored, and we won the game.

• • •

I will say this. Both John and I have do seem to have a flair for the dramatic. There is, of course, nothing better than winning a game with a clutch hit.

My best baseball experience actually occurred not when I was playing for the Tigers, but rather, some fifteen years later, when I was thirty-eight and came back and played a three-game series for the South Bend White Sox in 1989.

This is going to take a little explanation. In short, the success of films like Field of Dreams *and* Bull Durham *helped to revive interest in minor league baseball in the late 1980s. One afternoon, I was chatting with a friend of mine, Vic (short for Victoria) Boughton, an editor at* Sports Illustrated, *about how minor league baseball had become glamorous in recent years, and I assured her that the minor league life was still very tough and demanding.*

She told me that if I could somehow get signed to a player's contract, she'd give me an assignment to write a magazine piece for S.I. *Problem was, if you think it's tough to get signed when you're twenty-one, you can just imagine how tough it would be for a guy who hadn't played pro ball in years and who was now thirty-eight, going on thirty-nine.*

I made a flurry of phone calls, but in the small world of baseball, it was my former coach, Al Goldis, who made it all happen. At that time, Al was a scout for the White Sox, and after signing a bunch of waivers that I wouldn't sue the organization if I got injured, I was dispatched to South Bend, Indiana, to join my new teammates.

Remember, the original theme of the piece was to write about how challenging and difficult it is to be a minor league ballplayer. That is, I was supposed to write about the painful 0-for-4s and seeing one's batting average hover around the Mendoza line (.200).

But something inexplicable happened—something I still can't explain. As a lifetime .240 hitter in pro ball, I stunned everyone— myself especially—by going 4-for-7 with three RBIs in my short stay with South Bend in the Midwest League. I doubled off the center field wall in my last at-bat!

Mind you, I was playing second base next to a nineteen-year-old shortstop. At one point, I looked at my fielder's glove, then at the kid over at short, and realized that my mitt was older than he was. No matter, I ended up, unofficially, as the team's leading hitter with a solid .571 average, and when the White Sox went on to win the league championship, they even voted me a championship ring which I have and still cherish to this day.

How was I able to hit ninety-mile-per-hour fastballs at age thirty-eight? I haven't got a clue. My only regret is that I didn't do it when I was in my early twenties. Who knows? Maybe I would have given Lou Whitaker a real challenge at second base.

June 2, 2006
Extended Spring Training
Tucson, Arizona

I woke this morning and realized that graduation for Harvard's class of 2006 is only a few days away. Because of my choice to leave school to play baseball, however, I won't be graduating with my fellow classmates.

I'm happy with my decision to play ball, but when I get drunken phone calls late at night from my roommates and school friends back in Cambridge, I do get a bit nostalgic and wish I were there with them partying it up.

Yes, even kids at Harvard like to drink beer and party.

June 3, 2006
Extended Spring Training
Tucson, Arizona

Every day after the game or practice I enjoy taking a few extra swings in the cage to finish the day's workout and make any adjustment that I wasn't making in the game. I do this regardless of whether I played well or poorly. In fact, it's become a bit of a superstitious routine that I must go through each day if I want to keep my peace of mind. Then again, maybe it's the early stages of obsessive-compulsive disorder. After all, I know from my baseball history that as the season continues, my superstitions will only get worse.

• • •

Superstitions are indeed part of every ballplayer's daily regimen. From my experience, even the guys who say that they aren't superstitious are, in fact, usually quite fastidious about how they prepare for games and at-bats. Superstitions, of course, have no real scientific explanation, except that all performers usually find themselves trying to imitate their daily (and successful) routines on a regular basis. The thinking is that whatever worked for you yesterday should work for you again today.

Everybody knows about Wade Boggs and his obsessive superstitions about eating chicken every day, running sprints at exactly the same time before the game, making marks in the infield sand, and so on. At least Boggs was open about his routines. The vast majority of ballplayers never reveal their superstitious activities; after all, they fear that if they told people, their superstitions would immediately lose their magical powers.

June 4, 2006
Extended Spring Training
Tucson, Arizona

The clubhouse manager, Dan Flood, always busts my chops and tells me to go home and lay out in the sun. He knows about my terrible farmer's tan and yells, "Hey, Wolffie, I don't know about New York ... but the sun is free down here in Tucson!"

"Hey, Floody, my farmer's tan is now so terrible that I have just given up. Plus, I don't want to go tanning too long—I might end up looking like you!"

Floody grew up in the Chicago area and has been a die-hard White Sox fan since he was born. He got the job as the clubhouse manager and moved out to Tucson with his family to make the travel a little easier. He's tall, skinny, and dark-haired but put together pretty well. People usually tend to congregate by his clubhouse door after workouts because he has a huge refrigerator full of Corona. He also happens to hold the key to all of the equipment distribution. He has bats, gloves, shirts, bags, catcher's gear, and everything you could think of at his disposal. Hence, it is in everyone's best interest to be on Floody's good side. One good way to get on his good side is to tip him in addition to the clubhouse dues. Every couple of weeks all the players that Floody takes care of have to pay clubhouse dues. Some people try to avoid it, some players don't tip, and others go out of their way to get Floody some extra cash because you never know when you might need him to help you out. He keeps careful track of who pays and what amount, and I always make sure to tip Floody well.

Back at the apartment, we saw our first change of weather in months. We have been so accustomed to looking out the window and seeing cloudless skies and the hot sun that when dark thunderstorm clouds rolled in we were all glued to the window. The wind started to pick up and the sky became really dark. At first, I thought it might be a tornado. I have never seen a tornado in real life. It looked like it was at least going to be a serious thunderstorm, but then the only thing that happened was that a ton of desert dust blew outside and then within five minutes everything was back to sunny skies and 110 degree heat.

•   •   •

Rule number one in pro ball: You have got to make sure the clubhouse trainer is taken care of. You take care of him, he'll take care of you. It's as simple as that.

June 5, 2006
Extended Spring Training
Tucson, Arizona

We had our last away game at the Rockies' complex today. It was another twelve-inning game and it was absolute torture. We all got back to the apartment and passed out only to wake up at 7 P.M. eager to enjoy our Monday night. Of course, there didn't seem to be much going on in Tucson on this Monday night, until we found an old dilapidated bowling alley off Main Street. We all agreed we could use a few beers and a friendly bowling competition.

For the past few months, we have all wondered where the Tucson locals go on weeknights to have fun. Well, it looks like we found the place! It was nine o'clock on a Monday night and this old bowling alley was packed. In the back of the lounge area they had a dog-racing book similar to an OTB, and that was packed too. We wanted to go watch a few races but we couldn't even get a seat. It was quite a scene: as soon as we walked in, we saw older people yelling at the greyhounds running in circles on television, and then these senior citizens threw their beer cans at the TV screen when their dog lost.

My buddies and I quickly retreated back to the bowling alley, where we mingled with the local folks—older people, younger people, high school kids, college kids, and even some cute girls. Everyone was there, and it was great. We must have bowled for three hours. Funny thing, I hadn't bowled in a very long time and I surprised myself with how bad I was. However, by the end of the night I learned how to put spins on the ball and was busting out strikes left and right.

I learned from the best, and the best was certainly my roommate, Chris Brennan. I mean if baseball doesn't work out for Brennan he could definitely make a run for the professional bowling tour. He was like a young Roy Munson or Ernie McCracken from the movie *Kingpin*. He was doing trick shots and crazy spins all night long and was still bowling in the mid-200s. It was all rather impressive. On our score sheet we used some nicknames that I felt were quite funny and very appropriate/honest:

> Chris Brennan = Tourette's
> Josh Morgan = Steroids
> John Wolff = Get Sun Boy
> Tim Murphey = Cracker Barrel
> Matt Sharp = Slump

These nicknames are somewhat self-explanatory. Brennan is extremely hyperactive and is always screaming, yelling, singing, and blurting out random stuff. Half the time I don't think he even knows what he's saying. Hence, he is fondly called Tourette's, as in Tourette's syndrome. Josh Morgan is a good old corn-fed southern boy who does not take steroids but has a body that resembles most "juice-heads." He's very muscular and put together like a small car. My nickname? Well, we've covered that matter. Tim Murphey is a good ol' boy from Georgia, so the "Atlanta Cracker Barrel" name was a natural. Matt Sharp has been in a terrible slump since the beginning of extended spring training. Sharpie hit close to .400 in regular spring training, but during extended he just couldn't break through his hitting problems. Obviously, we had a good time together.

June 7, 2006
Tucson, Arizona
Extended Spring Training

Today was our last game against the Diamondbacks in extended spring training. As a result of playing the same two teams over and over again, I have become pretty good friends with a lot of the players from the Diamondbacks and Rockies. We said our goodbyes (mostly in Spanish) after the game and wished each other the best of luck during our seasons. In particular, I became very good friends with the D'Backs' middle infielders Jojo Batten and Lester Contreras. Every time one of us would wind up on second base we would have a good chat in the infield.

I played well today and it was a nice day to end on. I hit the ball hard my first at-bat and then I laid down a great bunt single along the third base line. After that, I was walked three times in a row. The highlight of my day, however, came on the first play of the game. Travis Tully, the speedy leadoff batter for the D'Backs, hit a ground ball to my right. I backhanded the ball, jumped up Derek Jeter-style, and threw the ball to get him out by half a step at first base. What a way to get the game started!

Later today I learned on the Internet that my old teammate and good friend, speedy outfielder Andy Mead, was drafted by the White Sox. There is a good chance that we might be reunited as teammates in Bristol, Virginia, this summer. That would be a nice surprise. Andy and I played together in the Atlantic Collegiate Baseball League before our senior year in college. Andy played ball at Cortland State, which is located in upstate New York and, despite the cold weather there in the spring, it has a top flight college baseball program.

For our last night in Tucson, my four roommates and I went out to a family dinner at the local Olive Garden restaurant. Whenever we had a night to eat out we always chose the O-Garden because of their never-ending soup, salad, and pasta combinations. You can't beat it when you're on a tight budget.

We had a great time at dinner and it finally hit us that our long, hot, and dusty extended spring training was over and we had somehow survived. I can't wait to start playing for a "real" minor league team in a "real" minor league town.

June 8, 2006
En route to Las Vegas, Nevada
Today, finally, is the last day of extended spring training. I was packed up and ready to go early this morning. I have a plane to catch at 5:00 P.M. headed to Las Vegas. We have three days to get to Bristol, and as it turns out, my Dad is giving a sports parenting speech in Vegas this week. My Mom is joining him for the trip, and they've invited me to come along as well—just to get a break from baseball for a few days.

I'm really looking forward to seeing Mom and Dad in Vegas, playing some blackjack, exploring the city, and just having some fun for a few days before I report to Bristol.

June 9, 2006
Las Vegas, NV
Josh Morgan came with me on the Vegas trip and we stayed in the Luxor Hotel, which is next to the Mandalay Bay where my parents

were staying. On our first night, I made a quick $200 playing blackjack and roulette. Good start.

After spending some serious time on the Strip, Josh and I snuck into the Mandalay Bay pool area and got a chance to look at some of the marvels of modern day cosmetic surgery around the pool. Incredible.

Beyond that, one of the many highlights of the day was checking out the roller coaster at the New York, New York Hotel & Casino. It certainly was not anything off the charts, but for two guys who'd been stuck in Tucson for the last three months, this roller coaster was a most enjoyable change of pace.

June 11, 2006
En Route to Armonk, New York

Josh, my parents, and I flew to New York today. From there, Josh and I will get my car and we'll make our way to Bristol, Virginia. I tried my hand at a little more gambling before leaving Vegas, but I lost early in blackjack and decided to walk away before I threw away all of my hard-earned cash. Something tells me that I'll need every dollar I have once we arrive in Bristol.

June 12, 2006
En Route to Bristol, Virginia

It's a ten hour drive to Bristol, Virginia, from my home in Armonk. Josh and I can't wait to get started. My car is all packed with bats, gloves, spikes, you name it. We're ready to get going.

• • •

There are few better feelings in life than packing up your car and shoving off for the start of a brand new season. In John's case, this is actually the third "season" for him—regular spring training, then extended spring training, and now the start of the 2006 Appalachian League season.

Just imagine—these kids are playing baseball—and getting paid for it! Life just doesn't get any better than this.

June 13, 2006
Bristol, Virginia

We finally arrived in beautiful downtown Bristol, Virginia, today. From Tucson to Vegas to New York to Bristol, it's clear we're hitting all the hot spots in this country!

We actually stopped last night in Purceyville, Virginia. It's about the halfway point between New York and Bristol. Josh Morgan's old friends, the Casemans, opened their house to us and we spent the night there. In fact, we arrived around 5:00 P.M. and had time to play some golf on the local course with Dave Caseman. I shot a seventy-four, which I felt was pretty good. We only played nine holes, though, so I guess that score isn't all that impressive. It was my first time golfing other than the occasional trip to the driving range, and I enjoyed every minute of it. It's definitely a game that I want to learn more about and improve my skills in. I seemed to have a good feel for the irons, but the woods gave me a lot of trouble. I would hit a terrible three-wood, and then follow it up with a beautiful iron shot. This happened over and over again. I'm sure some golf expert can tell me exactly what I'm doing incorrectly.

The town of Purceyville is beautiful. It is very hilly and covered in green foliage. Everyone appears to have huge yards and beautiful homes. In fact, the Casemans have stables and plenty of horses on their farm, and Mrs. Caseman and her daughter both ride horses and compete frequently in equestrian events. Their home reminded me of something out of an old-fashioned movie set in the countryside.

I also got my first taste of "real Southern cooking" at the highly popular Cracker Barrel off Interstate-81 in Virginia. I have to admit, I was a little nervous at first to eat all the country fried steak and stuff, but it was surprisingly good, as was the sweet tea.

Once we reached Bristol, we first stopped by the field to drop off our bags and then we checked into the hotel. The hotel is a run-down Howard Johnson located right in the middle of town. The town seems like a nice, quaint, and quiet town with beautiful homes and friendly people. There are a few colleges here as well and the campuses are filled with old brick and green surroundings. Overall, I'm impressed.

As for my impression of the ballpark: well, it's not as bad as I expected. I had heard some mixed reports about the field itself and, in truth, those reports are fairly accurate. Not to be picky, but the infield is way too soft and sandy, the outfield has dangerous divots and hills, the warning track is nothing but a bunch of large rocks in the dirt, the grandstand is dilapidated, and the field is used by a high school team for most of the year so it is not exactly well-maintained.

The clubhouse is right out of any minor league movie and is certainly not stylish. It's made of old cinderblocks and cement. No paint and no decorations. The showers are painfully small and the shower heads are so low you have to bend down awkwardly to wash your hair. The weight room is the size of a king bed. The lockers aren't too bad, but they have chicken-wire fencing separating them. It isn't all that bad, though, and I have to admit that I'm excited to be here.

• • •

When I first arrived in Anderson, South Carolina, in the spring of 1973, my first stop was also the ballpark. I recall that the infield was filled with pebbles and small rocks, and that there were only sprouts of grass in the outfield. Unlike those romantic, lush green infields you see in the major leagues, the infield in Anderson looked like the surface of the moon. It was not a pretty sight.

Then I visited the home clubhouse, which was a cinderblock bunker. No windows and no air conditioning meant that it would make for a steamy environment once summer hit. And it did. But the absolute worst part of the clubhouse was that it had been constructed down the right field line, and it was located right next to the town garbage dump!

Talk about a lack of urban planning. Not only was the smell overwhelming on those hot, humid days and evenings, but the cockroaches that strolled over from the dump into our clubhouse were unbelievable. I'm not talking about your garden variety or home roaches, either. These things were as long as your finger—the kind of roach you see in sci-fi horror movies. They would crawl in your fielding glove, hang out in your baseball spikes, clog up the drain in the shower, and find their way into the urinal where they drowned.

Let me stop there, because even thirty years after the fact, I still get the shivers about this.

June 14, 2006
Bristol, Virginia

We had a team breakfast this morning at the local Shoney's, which is a Southern family-style buffet place where the food was pretty good. I even tried some grits for the first time. I'll admit that I don't know what grits are, but it seemed to be the big attraction for all of the locals so I felt compelled to put some on my plate and taste them.

We have to be at the field by 2:00 P.M. today in order to work out, but in the meantime it is Apartment Hunt 2006. After staying in a tiny apartment in Tucson, I'm eager to find a place with a little more space. We drove around Bristol for about two hours checking out houses, condos, and apartments for rent. Along the way, I think we met the strangest man in all of Bristol.

His name was Sam and he approached me while we were looking at his neighbor's house. Sam had been sitting on his porch drinking a beer in his boxers and wife-beater until he walked up next to me with his tattoos and mangled teeth and said, "Hey, yankee, you from New Yawk?" I replied that I was, quickly realizing that Sam had spied the New York license plates on my car. He laughed and told me that he was also from New York—Albany to be exact. However, some years ago he was forced to leave New York State because he was being too crazy and rowdy, so he said. So he moved to Florida with his mom at first, but then she was scared of the hurricanes. Hence, Sam is now living in Bristol. That's his story. But maybe he isn't all that crazy. After all, Bristol doesn't get many hurricanes.

Back to our house searching. I met a girl at the mall last night and she called me today to recommend that I look at a house off Main Street. We had to go to the ball field, but we'll check out that house after practice. We can stay in the Howard Johnson for three days before we have to officially move out on our own. There's a certain amount of pressure here, because we certainly can't afford to stay in the motel, and I guess the alternatives are either sleeping in my car or seeing if I can room with goofy Sam from Albany.

• • •

Finding a suitable place to live for a few months on a ballplayer's salary is a daunting task. Just imagine—you move into a town where you literally don't know anyone, nor is the ballclub particularly helpful in finding you a spot to live. In some towns, the ballplayers get lucky and they end up living with a host family. A typical host family doesn't charge the player any rent, but invariably there are other complications to that kind of set-up.

But while it's challenging and exciting to find a place to live for the next few months, you also have to learn how to budget your dough. You need money for rent, for food, and of course for gas and the occasional bottle of beer. Ballplayers get paid twice a month, and you have to make every dollar count.

June 15, 2006
Bristol, Virginia

I'm feeling a little nostalgic again, realizing that I'm missing my graduation from Harvard. All of my friends and their families are celebrating and I'm hundreds of miles away. I would never trade baseball, but at times I do feel a little bit left out. Because I'm on such a different schedule these days, it's hard to keep in touch with many of my good friends from college.

Even with cell phones and e-mail, I still have to stave off the occasional bout of loneliness, especially when all of my buddies from college are enjoying their last semester before entering the real world as investment bankers, law students, medical students, and the like. While they're back in Cambridge toasting each other at private parties in swank clubs and talking about whether they should take a year off and travel around Europe before they head off to some prestigious graduate school, I find myself sleeping in a dusty and dirty old house wondering if I'll have enough money in my wallet to afford lunch at the local Denny's.

Even more stark, whereas in college my day revolved around going to stimulating classes in the morning, hanging out at lunch with my buddies in the afternoon, going to baseball practice for two or three hours and then going to an evening event at one of Harvard's clubs (I belonged to the Owl), here in pro ball, my everyday existence is defined by whether I get a hit or go 0-for-4. It's pretty simple—get a hit and I'm happy. Get two hits and I'm ecstatic. Go hitless and I'm miserable.

· · ·

John does a pretty good job of breaking down the ballplayer's lifestyle. It's all very transient, and everything revolves around your stats. Would I rather hit two squibs for two hits and go 2-for-4? Or hit four line drive outs, and have an 0-for-4?

Trust me, people forget the line drive outs. But those two cheap hits magically transform into solid hits in the next day's box score.

I know in college that you get grades at the end of the year, and that getting a B- instead of a B+ can really flatten your spirits for a day or two. But you get over it, and you move on. In baseball, every day is the end of the marking period. Every day is a final exam. And nobody wants to hear any excuses or alibis. Just be ready, get the job done, and get your hits if you want to be in the lineup the next day.

June 15, 2006
Bristol, Virginia

The top story of the day concerns our young catcher, Balthazar Valdez, and why he's not here in Bristol. He was supposed to board the plane in Tucson with the rest of the team, and he did. However, before they closed the doors, he freaked out, had some sort of a panic attack, and wasn't able to stay onboard. Valdez missed the flight.

The White Sox immediately bought him another ticket for a later flight that day, but the same thing happened again. So, unfortunately for Valdez, he might be end up being released because of his fear of flying. I can't imagine the Sox would pay for him to travel via bus or car to Bristol all the way from Arizona.

Valdez is from Sonora, Mexico, and he drove to Tucson for spring training. I believe that his flight to Bristol was going to be his first experience on an airplane. (As it turned out, he kept trying to get on flights and finally made it after quite a few attempts. All I know is that some two weeks later after we were all settled in, Valdez finally arrived in Bristol.)

We put down the money today on our new crib. It's an enormous house with three floors, albeit quite run-down and dilapidated. In truth, it's sort of like a beat-up fraternity house. Hey, what do you expect on a minor league salary? That said, I'm excited to get out of the routine of living in small, cramped apartments and hotel rooms and to be moving into an actual house. Imagine this: we have ten guys living here and we all get our own rooms! The guys are: me, Josh Morgan, Matt Enuco, Andrew Mead, Jacob Jean, Marquise Cody, Marcos Causey, Stefan Gartrell, Scott Madsen, Alex Woodson, and possibly Jeury Espinal. The house has plenty of space, but after only a few hours of being totally exuberant about this place I can already tell it's somewhat of a creepy house. I'm sure that's why we were able to get it so cheap. Our rent is $2,000 a month, so divided by ten or so players, we each pay about $200 a month. Not too bad.

Okay, I'll be honest. There are a few problems with the house: 1) We don't have any hot water. This isn't too much of a problem because we can shave and shower in the clubhouse at the ballpark. I can overlook that. 2) We don't have any furniture except for air mattresses. I would like to have a nice comfortable couch or something of that nature, preferably a real couch and not an air-couch. But furniture costs money. Did I mention that we have no money? 3) We have very limited electricity. Some outlets work, but most of them don't and the house, which was built in the 1930s and hasn't seen much in terms of upgrades over the years, is very dark and shadowy.

I ventured down into the basement, which resembles an enormous catacomb, and I found all types of strange stuff from old, beat-up wheelchairs to life-sized clown dolls that look like something out of a horror movie. There was a washing machine and a dryer down there as well, but when I opened them up and peaked inside, it looked as though something was living inside them. I didn't care to explore any further.

On the upstairs floor there are a bunch of locked doors that we can't open and we have no idea what's on the other side of them. At night we hear noises coming from behind the closed doors but we can't figure out a way to check what they are. Hopefully we'll just get used to the weird sounds after a while, because it's unlikely that we'll ever figure out what they are.

On the baseball front, Major League Baseball had its annual free agent draft the other day, and some of the new White Sox signees are finding their way to Bristol. One of the new pitchers is from Iowa and his name is Colt Smith. I could tell Colt was still pretty nervous because today was his first day with the ball club. Now, I'm by no means a veteran of pro ball, but after being in extended spring training for so long I feel like I've been in uniform forever. So I took it upon myself to welcome the new guy.

I called Colt over to my locker and introduced myself. I even made some mindless small talk for about five minutes. While I was untying my spikes I nonchalantly asked Colt if he could do me a favor. "Hey, Colt, do me a quick favor and run into Cuz's office and ask him if he knows where he put the key to the batter's box." Smith eagerly nodded and ran into the office all excited. He came back two minutes later, more than a bit embarrassed. "Cuz told me the key was right next to the box of curve balls." We both laughed and Colt admitted, "I guess I should probably learn to relax a bit." I just grinned, as did half of the team.

During practice today, my grandmother's brother (my great

uncle), Jim Hoy, stopped by the field to say hello. I had never met him before but Uncle Jim is a wonderfully nice guy, as is his wife, Jean. Cuz called me over to speak with them while the team was stretching, and then when Jim left the field Cuz asked me who he was. I jokingly responded that he was one of my old long lost relatives who I had never met before. Cuz laughed and said, "Just wait until you get to the big leagues. Once you get there everyone thinks they're related to you."

By the way, I spoke with a few of my friends back at school via e-mail, and they told me that graduation was great but that it poured all day long. They said that Ty Moore, our Class of 2006 president, included a nice mention about me in his Class Day speech, and that made my day. I guess all my friends have not forgotten about me even though it seems I'm a million miles away here in Bristol.

•   •   •

No matter where you go in pro ball, you get homesick. I don't care how nice your surroundings are, invariably at some point during the course of the day or evening, your mind begins to wander its way home. You think about what your friends are doing, what your family is doing. Do they miss you as much as you miss them?

As noted earlier, at least kids today have instant access via cell phones and the Internet. Even more amazing, depending on the team you play for, your friends and relatives can often hear the play-by-play of your games online. When John was broadcasting mens' and womens' ice hockey in school over the last few years on the college radio station, I was able to pick up his broadcasts not only on my home computer, but at my

*office in New York City, and for that matter, pretty much anywhere. I
recall one time I was in Florida and I was able to hook up to a computer
and listen to John do a hockey game from Minnesota. For an old-school
technophobe like me, that was exciting!*

*But my original point is that despite all these electronic breakthroughs,
loneliness is a major companion for ballplayers. Yes, you hang around
with your teammates, you play hard, and you work hard at your craft.
But there's nothing better than to look up in the stands and see a friendly,
familiar face at the game.*

June 16, 2006
Bristol, Virginia

After practice today—we took batting practice and lots of ground
balls in the infield—we spent most of the day taking care of errands
and acquiring essential items we needed for around the house. We
bought bedding, fans, chairs, and other necessities from Wal-Mart,
Lowe's, and a few local tag sales. While at Wal-Mart, I noticed that
all the air conditioners that they sold were designed for placement
inside a standard window. However, the windows in my bedroom are
much too big and old-fashioned to custom fit an air conditioner.

I know that the summers in Virginia get pretty hot and having
an air conditioner in the bedroom would be a great plus. I wanted
to buy a cheap, portable air conditioner but it looked like I might
be out of luck as they all ran into the hundreds of dollars. Just when
I was about to give up hope I noticed a beat-up, mangled box that
contained a portable air conditioner that would be perfect for my
room. When I checked the price of the machine I noticed that it,

too, was more than $300. Immediately, I realized that buying this machine would consume an entire two-week paycheck. Besides, who knows whether it would even work? After all, the box was all crumpled. I debated for a good fifteen minutes about what I should do. I phoned my father and he convinced me that it was a good investment to take a chance, buy it, and stay cool for a long, hot summer. And that's just what I decided to do.

But when I got to the cashier, the box was so beat up that she couldn't find the barcode to check the price. She called the manager and some other department members over, but none of them knew the price of the item. After ten minutes of waiting and holding up the entire checkout line, the cashier finally said to Matt Enuco and me, "Do you know what the price of this item is?" I laughed at first, and then tried to keep a straight face and say, "Uhh, about fifty dollars maybe?" I knew I was lying, but I couldn't afford anything else more expensive. To my amazement, she said, "Okay, sounds good to me," and rang up the sale.

Matt and I were off and out of the store before anyone could tell us that a mistake had been made. And here's the kicker: the air conditioner works so well that everyone (all five guys) who lived on the second floor moved their air mattresses into my bedroom in order to sleep in the air conditioned room. The room is packed from wall to wall with all of our beds now.

Later that evening our landlord, Chris Ketron, stopped by the house to give us all our house keys. When he walked into my room I was reading a book on my air mattress and he started laughing. I asked what was so funny and he said, "Hey, good choice of rooms. The guy who lived here before you was a gay crack head. When you're sleeping at night you can think about all the good loving that took place here." I grunted in disgust, but Chris just started laughing his head off. My room suddenly gives me the creeps. I just hope that the previous resident doesn't return in the middle of the night in search of pleasant times.

Right before I went to bed, Matt Enuco came by to chat. A new signee, I could tell he was still a little nervous and curious about being a pro ballplayer and what was expected of him. We grabbed a few beers and sat out on the front porch and chatted for a while. It was kind of an ironic situation for me because, after all, I'm still a rookie myself, but I remember all of the nerves and emotions that I went through during extended spring training. Matt is a fellow infielder from New Jersey who went to Rowan College, which is a Division III powerhouse in the Northeast. He's a pretty talented kid. Matt is not only a terrific baseball player but was also a standout swimmer and football player in high school. He's also a good guitar player and enjoys reading a lot. In any event, I hope I was able to make him feel more at home in our broken down palace.

Chris, our landlord, happens to be a big fan of the bestselling book, *Rich Dad, Poor Dad*. He told me that any time I wanted to get some lunch with him and discuss how to become a real estate investor, just give him a call. I might just do that. I figure if I can learn to make my money work for me while I'm still playing ball, I could conceivably extend my playing career through financial independence.

Then again, if I get moved up to the big leagues, I'll at least be able to buy an air conditioner that costs $300 or more.

• • •

There are certain essentials for ballplayers. First and most importantly, you have to take care of your body. That means that you have to find an apartment or house that is quiet and safe. Remember, ballplayers usually sleep from late at night to late in the morning. You don't want to find yourself in a place where people have regular jobs; that means getting up early in the morning, making noise, and going off to a nine-to-five.

In addition, you've got to have air conditioning. You need your sleep, and since you play ball in the summer, you need a cool place at night. And of course, when it comes to food and drink, your top priority is eating well and keeping your body hydrated.

Again, these are essentials. And this is where you should spend your hard-earned cash.

June 17, 2006
Bristol, Virginia

We had a short intrasquad game today and I led off against my roommate, Jake Jean. Jean is a left-handed pitcher who played at the University of Kansas and was signed as a free agent. He played last season in Bristol and is back here again because he is rehabbing his shoulder. In any event, on the second pitch I saw, he drilled me squarely in the hip. Thanks, roomie.

Jean yelled, "Hey, Wolffie, I'm sorry, man. You okay?" I replied with a smirk, "Yeah, it's all good. Besides, you don't throw hard enough to hurt me anyway." He smiled, because we both know that Jake throws pretty darn hard.

My next at-bat came against one of our younger pitchers. On the third pitch of the at-bat, I took an inside fastball over the right field fence. In fact, it just missed clearing the second fence that protects traffic on the local street beyond right field. In other words, I really crushed that one.

I'm not going to lie; it was a pretty nice feeling. Between you and me, just a few more feet and that one would have been clear *over* the street.

When we got home from the field all nine of my roommates grabbed some lunch and, to a man, all passed out. It was pretty amazing to see nine guys asleep at the same time in the middle of the day. On the other hand, it does make sense—because there isn't much else to do here except play Playstation 2, read, drink beer, or sleep. And, oh yeah, play baseball.

$$\bullet \quad \bullet \quad \bullet$$

Hitting a homer in batting practice always feels good, but it feels especially good when you do it in a relatively new setting. Pro ballplayers don't like to show much emotion about their hitting prowess, but trust me, there's no better feeling than hitting one right on the sweet spot of the bat and seeing it take off over the fence. Especially when everyone on the field takes notice.

John's blast reminded me of my first few weeks of playing ball in Anderson. As the story goes, the guys in the bullpen had apparently started a pool for which of the position players on that 1973 Anderson Tigers team would hit the first round-tripper in a game.

Now, understand that I used to choke up a good two inches on my Louisville Slugger and that I had one of the more condensed swings on the team. I used to hit home runs in high school against kids throwing seventy-eight miles per hour, but in pro ball, it was clear that if I wanted to have any kind of batting average I had to shorten my stroke considerably and try to consistently hit line drives into the gaps. Occasionally, I would get hold of one and the ball would go over the fence, but trust me, that was relatively rare, and indeed, more of an accident than something I planned.

Anyway, we were playing a Sunday afternoon game, as I recall, in Anderson in mid-April. Sure enough, the opposing pitcher threw me a change-up (note to pitchers: never throw a bad hitter a change-up). In any event, I pounced on the pitch, and lo and behold, drilled a clean line drive homer over the fence in left-center. I practically sprinted around the bases (in retrospect, I should have taken my sweet time) and tried to act nonchalantly as though this happened to me all the time. But I couldn't. A huge grin was all over my face.

Back to the dugout. Lots of high fives, claps, etc.

"Hey, I wonder who had my name out in the bullpen?" I asked out loud, "Y'know, the first on the team to hit one out!"

Embarrassed silence greeted me. Turns out that, alas, nobody on the Tigers' pitching staff had chosen me to be the first to hit a home run that season.

That brought me back to earth in a hurry. Plus, that home run turned out to be my only one for the entire season.

Like I said, enjoy those homers when they come.

June 18, 2006
Bristol, Virginia

Seven of my roommates and I went out last night to see what kind of nightlife they have here in Bristol. We stopped at two bars and two clubs and to our dismay, they were all empty. We couldn't believe it! I mean, they were all open for business, but no one was inside. This was the one night of the season in which we could have gone out and had a pretty good time without worrying about the game tomorrow, and instead we ended up back on our front porch drinking beer and reminiscing about all the fun college parties we used to attend. For added entertainment, Matt Enuco serenaded us with his guitar playing and sang a few songs.

In short, it was a real hot time in Bristol!

We still have no furniture in our house and we desperately need a couch to relax on. Josh Morgan called a local family that he became good friends with last season here in Bristol and they offered to lend us their old couch, recliner, and television. They didn't have to offer twice: we immediately took off for their house and picked up the goods.

The family is a fairly young couple with a six-year-old son who is very talented at baseball and also very energetic. While we were moving the furniture out of their house the little guy was messing with me and Josh. Of course, I was just trying to play along and be a nice guy and show the kid some attention. He would punch my leg and I would pull his shirt over his head like in a hockey fight. At one point I grabbed him softly and said to Josh, "Hey free punches!" Obviously, just a joke. I wasn't holding the kid very firmly and he wriggled his way free but in doing so he landed on his head on the hard, cement floor. His teeth clacked together and it sounded pretty bad. I felt terrible! Here I was, in these very friendly people's home, borrowing their furniture and I dropped their kid on his head.

Thank goodness the youngster seemed to be fine. Plus, his

parents weren't too upset because they knew it was an accident. Regardless, I still felt guilty about the incident. I guess I better be more careful about how I conduct myself.

June 19, 2006
Bristol, Virginia

We have our first evening practice today in over four months. Practice tonight starts at 5:00 P.M.

It sounds silly but I haven't worked out in the early evening or nighttime since I was back at school in Boston, training in the batting cages of Watertown, Massachusetts. I'm so accustomed to practicing in the morning that I really don't know what to do with myself all day today. I did my laundry, played some video games, watched a DVD, read some articles and then, in effect, did nothing. I was so bored I even cleaned up some of the garbage in our kitchen.

It's like my entire baseball schedule has been turned upside-down. I used to have free time in the evenings, and now I'll have free time in the mornings. Remember, in spring training, we were up early and out on the field. By late afternoon, we were done. We didn't play any night games in spring training. Same in extended. Up early and out to the field. Home by evening and early to bed. Again, no night games. But now, of course, a traditional minor league baseball schedule has pretty much all night games, with the exception of a rare Sunday afternoon game. As a result, I have to rearrange my lifestyle.

There are still a few necessary items that we need in our new home in order to live a bit more comfortably. Our landlord said he will take care of these requests, but who knows if he will or won't. We need hot water, shower curtains, blinds for our windows, and more keys to the house. I have given up showering and shaving at the house because the water is too darn cold.

As bad as our new house is, it's all relative. I drove a few of the Dominican players home after practice yesterday and learned that they all live together near the field in someone's garage. Yes, a garage. Not a converted garage or anything like that. They live in someone's garage and they seem pretty happy with that. They have cots and air mattresses on the concrete floor and that's about it. No windows and only one door. It doesn't look all too glamorous. I wonder about what will happen to them as the temperature begins to heat up over the next couple of months. I also assume that they have access to a bathroom as well, but who knows?

After our late practice, Enuco and I wanted some burgers and a few beers. We drove down to the local bar—the State Line—and watched some television and ate dinner. It was a nice relaxing evening, though Matt and I were secretly hoping there would be more than a just a handful of people at the bar; especially some good-looking girls. However, when we arrived we quickly discovered that we accounted for two of the five total people in the bar.

I thought the evening would be depressing, but it turned out to be surprisingly fun. We quickly made friends with the few locals there and they told us to hang around until midnight, because that's when the bar fills up. So we hung out for a couple of hours, the locals bought us some beers, and we were having a good time. However, at midnight, only about ten more people showed up. Hardly crowded at all, but we were content just to be out and talking to new people.

A couple of the older ladies kept trying to hit on us saying to themselves but loud enough for us to hear, "Why are all baseball players always so damn cute! I've never seen an ugly baseball player." At one point, the older ladies started to try and hook us up with some of their friends' daughters. They started showing us pictures and bragging about how wonderful these girls were.

All in all, it was a terrific evening. We hung out until about 1:00 A.M. having some laughs and then decided it was time to go home. However, the nice thing about starting the real season is that you can stay up late and still get all your sleep because you don't have to be awake before noon. It's the exact opposite of extended spring training. "Early to bed, early to rise" has now become "Late to bed and late to rise."

· · ·

It is true. Minor league ballplayers become local celebrities in minor league towns. That's probably been true forever.

Even when I played in Anderson, South Carolina, and in Clinton, Iowa, whenever my teammates and I walked into a bar or restaurant, once it was known that we played for the local team, it was very rare that we ever had to pay for a meal or a bottle of beer. Everything was on the house.

It's a wonderful feeling to be treated with such kindness. Not only

did we save money, but it was just great to be so embraced by the fans.
No matter where I played, it was just a glorious feeling. I'm glad that
John and his teammates had the same kind of experience in Bristol.

June 20, 2006
Bristol, Virginia

Tonight the front office held their annual "Meet the Sox" event.
A large portion of the town turned out, which made for quite an
interesting evening. For the first time since last summer, I had a
chance to play in front of a large crowd. Before we took batting
practice, all the fans were allowed onto the field and we mingled
with them, shaking hands and signing autographs and talking
with the friendly people. It really made me feel like a professional
ballplayer. After all those days in extended spring training in which
it seemed like no one cared about us at all, today it all changed.
The local fans loved to come down and hang out with us and to be
around the ball club. It was a real treat for us, just as it was for the
fans.

The other aspect of minor league baseball that became apparent
after Meet the Sox and practice were over was the appearance of
the "Bristol Birds." The Bristol Birds are a bunch of girls who love
to be around the ball players. I guess "baseball Annies" would be
another name for them. They seem nice enough, and some of them
are even kind of cute, but in the world of pro ball, home team players
learn early on to keep their distance from the local talent.

The best looking girl at practice this evening was actually the
photographer. I was hoping to get a personal interview with her,

but she didn't talk with anyone except the coaching staff. After practice, as all the players left the clubhouse the Bristol Birds just hung out in the parking lot waiting for the players to walk to their cars. Maybe they're just trying to see what kind of car each guy drives, or maybe they're just trying to get a glimpse of the new batch of players. I don't know, but honestly I wasn't too interested either way. Well, maybe I was a little bit interested.

Tonight is the night before Opening Night. Having a large crowd in the stands tonight during practice gave me quite an adrenaline rush. I'll have to remind myself when I'm playing tomorrow night to relax and do what I did all through extended spring training. Just go out there with a lot of confidence and get the job done in the field and at bat. The only thing that I'm thinking about tonight is seeing my name in the starting lineup tomorrow for the home opener.

June 21, 2006
Bristol, Virginia

It's Opening Night here in Bristol and we are taking on a farm team of St. Louis, the Johnson City Cardinals. The game tonight starts at 7:00 P.M. but we have to be at the field by 2:00 P.M. in order to get our early work done. Before every game we have lifting, batting practice, fielding practice, throwing, stretching, and then some time to rest, change clothes, and maybe get quick bite of a protein bar or something. It seems like a lot of our time is spent at the ballpark, but I'd rather be there than bored at home watching *Chappelle's Show* over and over again.

Now that all of my friends have graduated college and have finished up their partying for the spring semester, I'm now starting to get more consistent phone calls and e-mails from them. They've all either returned home for the summer or moved to new cities to work for large consulting or investment firms. Obviously, when they're all partying together there's no need to call me and tell me about all the fun I'm missing. But, now that they're finished with school and are working, they've been checking up on me and are curious to hear how professional baseball is treating me. It's always fun to hear from them, even though sometimes it's tough to think about all the fun times I missed back at school during senior spring.

After all the excitement and build-up to my first "real" minor league game, when I got to the field I discovered that I wasn't even in the lineup. So, in my first professional game, I received a DNP for "did not play." After the game was over I called my dad and he laughed. He told me that he was just as excited to play on opening night in his first professional game, but he also didn't play. Apparently, the parallels between our careers persist.

I must confess, though, that not starting tonight came as a bit of a shock to me, because I feel that I played well throughout extended spring training. In something like fifty games, I hit .296 with lots of RBIs and made only two errors in the field. I really felt that I had proven myself and had earned the start at second base. But for whatever reason, that's not what went down. I can't lie—it was disappointing.

My dad reminded me that it's a long, long season, and to look forward to tomorrow's game. Every game, whether it's opening night or the next night, counts in the final stat sheet. I guess he's right, but I sure was psyched to play tonight.

My roommate and good friend Josh Morgan went 4-for-5 on the night and I was excited for him because his parents were in town for the game. After the game, I went up to Mr. Morgan and told him that during extended spring training I taught Josh how to hit. We both laughed because we all know that Josh could hit with his eyes closed.

By the way, before the game I went up to Cuz and laughingly said, "This is the worst lineup I have ever seen!" He smiled and said, "Because you are not in it, right?" I replied that he was correct and then he said, "Well, in that case, it can only get better. I'm getting some pressure from the player development people to play the new guys and see what they've got. Don't worry, Wolffie, they just want me to get an assessment of the newly drafted players."

Not playing in tonight's game obviously stung my ego a little bit, but like Dad said, it's a long season and the best way to get back in the lineup is to stay positive and help the team win, even if I'm on the bench. During the game I tried to make myself visible but not obnoxious by cheering on my buddies, sitting near Jerry Hairston, and coaching first base if needed.

• • •

Here's the problem with pro ball: only nine guys can play at one time. And on most low Class A teams, the roster is overflowing with players—maybe twenty-five or thirty-five or even more. In addition, as Leyva pointed out to John, in early June the free agent draft takes place and as new signees come on board, all of them are eager to show what they can do. And especially in those cases, the signees often receive big bonus checks just for signing their name to a contract, and the front offices want to get a quick look at what exactly all that bonus money has purchased.

All in all, it's an exciting but also very nerve-racking time. Remember, in pro ball, the only constant is change. Everything is changing all the time. Lineups, rosters, players, you name it. And while you're trying your best to have a good day in the field and at bat, you also know that with every new kid who shows up ready and eager to play, that means somebody else will probably be let go. After going 0-for-5 in a game, it makes for some restless nights. Trust me, I know, because I went through the same experience some thirty years ago.

When I was drafted in June, 1972, I recall being advised by the late Emil Gall, who was a long-time, highly regarded scout for the Tigers. "Rick, I know you're eager to get going on your pro career," Emil told me, "but if I were you, I would forego signing right now. Play another summer in the Atlantic Collegiate Baseball League, and then sign in the fall."

I found this advice curious and asked why. "Because," Emil explained, "you're a relatively low draft choice. If you sign now, you'll be assigned to the Tigers' Rookie ball team in Bristol, Virginia, in the Appalachian League (yes, the same Bristol where John is now). Trust me, they'll have thirty-five guys there, all waiting for their chance to play. Maybe you'll get forty or fifty at-bats for the entire summer. You're a lot better off playing everyday in the ACBL, getting more experience, and then signing in September. Then you can go to spring training next year in Tigertown, where you'll get a good long look."

Looking back, it was absolutely the smartest advice I ever received in my pro career. A year later, when I did go to spring training, I learned that most of the kids who had been drafted in the same draft as I had found themselves sitting on the bench in Bristol, rarely playing. I was glad I had a full spring training to show what I could do. I would have gone nuts sitting on the bench in Bristol, waiting for a rare chance to play.

But for John, now he's in Bristol and, after paying his dues in spring training and in extended spring, he's ready to get his official minor league career started. The problem is, how many new second basemen did the White Sox draft and sign to contracts? Will those kids be reporting to Bristol? Regardless of how John performs, there are forces at work beyond his control. That's the dark side of pro baseball that most fans don't know about.

June 22, 2006
Bristol, Virginia

We had another home game tonight against the Johnson City Cardinals. Curiously, I started tonight's game—not at second base, but at first base. Let the record show that I was drafted as a second baseman, but I made my first professional start as a first baseman. When I make it to the major leagues that could be a good trivia question.

Unfortunately, we lost the game miserably and I finished 0-for-2 with a fly out to left and a hard hit ground ball to first base. It was hit so hard that I actually hit into a double play, which doesn't happen too often—the first baseman fielded my shot cleanly, fired to second for one out, and then the shortstop rifled the ball back to first to nail me. But again, at least the ball was well struck.

The unusual story of the evening, however, was my first defensive play of the game. In the first inning, the pitcher overthrew the bag and I took off running after the ball into right field. I got to the ball but as I tried to put on the brakes, I totally wiped out on my backside, kicking the ball accidentally past our right fielder. I didn't get an error on the play, but it was certainly the strangest defensive blunder that I have ever made in my career, and of all things, it happened on my first professional play. I bounced back after that incident, kind of chuckling to myself at the absurdity of the play, and I made a bunch of nice plays at first base during the rest of the game. I even saved our second baseman an error by making a stretching dive off the bag to get an out.

. . .

And so it begins. Even though spring training and extended spring training are all part of professional baseball, it's not the same as playing in a real game in a minor league ballpark with fans in the grandstand, music being played, scoreboards lighting up, and all the other sights and sounds that go with playing minor league baseball.

There aren't too many other experiences as much fun in life— especially after you've toiled so diligently to make this dream come true. I do hope John took a few moments just to soak it all in. He's worked extremely hard on a daily basis to make this happen. He's overcome all sorts of heartbreaks and setbacks, and nobody is more deserving than he is of this magical moment.

Just for the record, in my first professional game and in my first at-bat, I lined a triple to right center. I recall getting to third base, calling time, dusting myself off, and thinking, "Wow, what a great way to start a pro career—with a triple!" Unfortunately, as with my solitary home run my first year, my career was punctuated with a lot more grounders, pop-ups, and strikeouts than homers and triples.

But in the end, it's not so much what your final batting average is, it's really all about the experience. For many years after my playing days were over, I served as the editor of The Baseball Encyclopedia, *the classic thick-as-a-Manhattan-phonebook reference work of all the records of all the players who ever got to the big leagues. I recall noting that, ever since records have been officially kept since 1876, only a little more than 15,000 men have ever gotten to play in the majors—many of them just for the proverbial cup of coffee (think Archibald "Moonlight" Graham of* Field of Dreams *fame).*

When you think about how only 15,000 of the millions and millions of baseball players who have dreamed of making it to the bigs ever actually got there, you begin to realize that playing pro ball in the minors is truly a rare and wonderful experience. My wife Trish and I are so very grateful to all the people, coaches, and scouts who helped John see his lifelong dream come true.

June 23, 2006
Bristol, Virginia

We had the last home game in our three-game series against the Johnson City Cardinals tonight. I did not play again. It's pretty clear that there are so many players here that the coaches are going to have to use some sort of rotational system until they figure out who can play where and get the job done.

We won the game this evening and took two out of three from the Cardinals. We leave for Burlington, North Carolina, early tomorrow morning, so I'd better start packing tonight.

Hope I get in the lineup again tomorrow.

June 24, 2006
Burlington, North Carolina

We left for Burlington at 8:00 A.M. We had to pack the bus by seven, though, which means I had to be awake by six. We didn't even get back from the game and dinner last night until around 1:00 A.M. So much for that theory about staying up and sleeping in late. Oh well.

However, I got lucky and got the very best seat on the bus: the very last row. I sprawled out back there and passed out for the entire bus ride. We had about three hours to kill when we arrived in Burlington, so one might ask, "Why didn't we just leave later in the day?" My answer is that I don't know. I guess they want us to just relax and hang out before the ball game.

The only exciting part of this bus trip was when we hit a little traffic and the driver slammed on the brakes and everyone went flying forward. I was dead asleep at the time and before I knew it I woke up on the floor with all my stuff on the floor around me. It was quite a wakeup call.

Before tonight's game they staged an Old Timers' game and Jerry Hairston and pitching coach Roberto Espinoza both played. Actually, Roberto was bringing some pretty good cheese, and Jerry, who must be in his fifties or older, almost knocked one out of the ballpark. It was amazing to see how well Jerry could still swing the bat. What's the old saying? You can hit until you go blind? Apparently so. Looks like Hairston will be able to hit forever.

I started at second base tonight and batted in the eight hole. It was definitely the largest crowd that I have ever played in front of, and in truth I was a little nervous at first. Fortunately, I quickly made a few plays at second base and calmed down right away. On the other hand, my night with the stick started off rocky. I struck out in my first at-bat on a good outside slider and also struck out on my second at-bat against an old friend, Kyle Collina, when he made some very good pitches. I had faced Kyle numerous times over the summer when he pitched for Quakertown, Pennsylvania, in the ACBL while I was playing for Stamford, Connecticut.

In any event, I put those first two at-bats out of my head and then recovered from my tough start with a walk on four consecutive pitches. I then rang up my first professional in-season hit. It came in the ninth off the Indians' closer and though I eventually came around to score, our rally came too little too late and we ultimately lost the game.

I remember stepping up to bat and trying to clear my mind and not to put too much pressure on myself to try and salvage the day. The pitcher had a lot of movement on his ball; it looked like everything tailed away from left handed batters. I took a first pitch fastball strike, since we were down a few runs, and then I realized that it was time for me to let it rip. He threw me an outside two-seamer. I waited, let the ball come to me, and then lined a shot into left field.

As soon as I got the barrel on the ball I knew it was going to be a hit and it all felt like something out of an old-time sports movie. I was running hard down the line and around first base, but it felt like I was in slow motion. I was just enjoying the moment.

I know it must sound a little silly since I had plenty of hits during extended spring training—but to line a shot to left field in front of 5,000 fans is a pretty nice thrill compared to the barren and empty stands back in Tucson.

I have discovered that when you're on a road trip, the best way to survive is to find a player with parents in town and stick by them. Food is so hard to come by that you really need a car to find any kind of decent restaurant, and of course, the only people with cars on the road are parents. Luckily for me, Josh Morgan's parents have been in town and they have been taking me out to lunch, dinner, and breakfast just about every day. Minor league ballplayers have very few luxuries, so when someone is offering to buy you food, you gratefully accept every time.

• • •

I don't know if John even remembers this, but several years ago when I was working for the Cleveland Indians, one of my yearly stops during the season was to Burlington, North Carolina, when the Tribe had a rookie league team there.

One summer, I recall bringing John down to a game—he couldn't have been more than nine or ten years old—and the field manager for

*the Indians, Dave Keller, was nice enough to let John serve as the bat boy
that evening. John absolutely loved the experience. The problem was, the
game went deep into extra innings. By the time the game was over and
we headed back to the motel, all of the fast food restaurants in Burlington
were long closed.*

*John and I were starving. Unfortunately, the only place we
could get some food (if that's what you want to call it) was from
the vending machines in the Holiday Inn. John was seemingly more
than happy to munch on cheese and crackers and diet soda. He didn't
seem to mind at all; he was still very happy and very tired from his
night's labors.*

*Pretty ironic that a decade later that he would gather his first
"professional" hit at the same field where he once served as a bat boy.
I just hope he had a better meal after this game than he had twelve
years earlier.*

June 25, 2006
Burlington, North Carolina

We have another away game at Burlington tonight and we need
a win to get back over the .500 mark. But when we got to the
field today it started to pour and the game was cancelled by late
afternoon.

As you might imagine, there isn't all that much to do on the
road during a rain-out, except to have dinner with the Morgan
family once again—which was very nice of them. Tomorrow we'll
play a double header. There's more rain in the forecast, though, so
we shall see how that goes.

June 26, 2006
Burlington, North Carolina

It continued to rain all morning, but fortunately for us the tarp was on the field and we were able to get both games in tonight. We got absolutely smoked in the first game, the highlight being Ramon Olivardo, the Indians' right fielder, who hit three absolute moon-shot home runs. It was amazing to watch, as each one was hit farther then the one before it. I guess when you're hot, you're hot, because in the second game Ramon struck out three times. After the game I told our young pitcher, Justin Edwards, who worked in the first game, that he'll probably be receiving a Christmas card this year from Olivardo for serving up those three meatballs. He laughed and agreed, saying that his neck was sore from the whiplash of watching all those balls travel so far in such a hurry.

In the second game, I played second base and batted second in the lineup. We won 3-1 and I finished 0-for-2 with a walk. I played solid defense and made the plays when they were most important. Despite the 0-for-2, I felt good at the plate, because I hit the ball well. In fact, I hit a rope into the hole between third and short and thought for sure I had a hit before the third baseman made an unbelievable diving catch to rob me.

During the game, some odd-duck woman perched herself on top of our dugout and sang a brutal rendition of "Green Acres," complete with hand motions and everything. At first I ran in and yelled for someone to just throw a ball at the woman and put her out of her misery. Even Jerry Hairston started to chuckle. Then I quietly went over to my teammate, Kent Gerst, when he was in front of a bunch of guys and said, "Hey Kent, I didn't know your mom was such a good performer. You must be really proud."

Everyone started to laugh, even the quiet Gerst. Kent is the youngest player on the team, drafted straight out of high school in the eighth round from somewhere outside St. Louis. This minor league life must seem completely bizarre to him.

After the double header we all boarded the bus and took off back to Bristol. The four-hour drive home didn't seem too bad. We arrived home around 2:00 A.M., knowing full well we have to be back at the field tomorrow by 1:30 P.M. for a game against the Kingsport Mets.

Looks like we're back to going to bed late and sleeping late. I just hope I have enough time tomorrow to get some breakfast or lunch before heading back to work.

• • •

Travel in the minor leagues is not glamorous. I think most fans just assume that the trips from one town to the next are quick and easy, but that's hardly the truth. By most accounts, a four-hour bus ride in the middle of the night is relatively short. I recall trips in the Midwest League that lasted ten hours. That is, you'd leave the stadium at 11:00 P.M., ride all night on the bus to your next stop, arrive at the motel right before noon, straggle up to your room, take a quick nap and shower, find some food, and then head back out to the ballpark.

Now, that's what minor league baseball is really like.

June 28, 2006
Bristol, Virginia

We lost our game against Kingsport today due to a bunch of throwing and fielding errors. My roommate Josh Morgan, who has a torn labrum in his throwing shoulder, unfortunately made two costly errors at first on pickoff plays, twice overthrowing our shortstop covering second. At least Morgan is still hitting the stuffing out of the ball.

The second baseman for the Kingsport Mets was Anthony Manuel, the son of Jerry Manuel. Jerry Manuel was the first round pick of the Detroit Tigers the same year my dad was the thirty-third round pick. More parallels.

We lost again tonight and the team needed to blow off some steam after two tough losses, so fourteen of us went to the local Irish pub down on Main Street. We danced for a few hours, some guys had some drinks, and others left early with some local girls. Enuco and I were dancing, or trying to dance, with a few girls when two gorgeous twins walked in the door. They looked like something straight out of *Maxim* magazine.

Being two studs, Matt and I immediately left the dance floor and went over to talk with the twins. We spoke for a while, used some terrible pick-up lines, and found out that they were Bristol born and raised. We haven't been out much around here but I can't imagine that girls like these are too common in Bristol. But hey, maybe I'm wrong. Enuco and I ended up taking a trip back to their apartment later that evening. Nothing wild occurred, but it was just nice to be in an apartment with furniture!

June 29, 2006
Bristol, Virginia

Our game against Kingsport got rained out tonight. The field was already damp, but it rained extremely hard for about ten minutes during batting practice and the game had to be called off. It didn't look too bad but the grounds crew said that it was unplayable. So, it looks like the next time we travel to Kingsport we will have to play a double header. We had to wait at the field until 8:00 P.M. until the final decision was made. Those hours were spent listening to Espy's stories of how he was hired by Don Mattingly to throw batting practice for the New York Yankees and what it was like to be with those famous Yankees of a few years ago. The other half of the time was spent playing pepper in the wet grass. One of our best pepper players is John Orton, the catching coordinator and former big leaguer for the Angels. He's one of my favorites.

Since we had a quiet night, we decided to see what the State Line karaoke night was all about. We went for about an hour, and it looked like we didn't miss too much. Although by the time we finally got up enough courage to go sing a song, the management had decided to shut down the karaoke machine for the evening. Don't worry—we'll do it next time.

June 30, 2006
Bristol, Virginia

Tonight we have a home game against the Bluefield Orioles. The word on the street is that Bluefield is our rival. I don't know. I mean,

I don't know a soul on their team, so why should I view them as a hated rival? In any event, it sounds strange to me.

One other note. My parents are coming to town this weekend and should arrive in Bristol at some point this evening. It's a ten-hour drive for them from our home in New York, and it will be nice to see them. Plus I'm sure I'll be able to eat well while they're in town.

June 30, 206
Bristol, Virginia

I was in a pretty good mood when I left for the ballpark around 1:00 P.M., but I had no idea what was in store for me when I got to the field.

Surprisingly, one of my roommates, outfielder Marquise Cody, had gone to the field early today to get his paycheck. As I was just getting ready to leave the house, Marquise had returned home and, without saying much, started packing his belongings. Apparently, when he went to get his paycheck, he was also given his unconditional release. Even worse, it was done in the same horrible way it was done in spring training: Marquise innocently walked into the clubhouse and went to his locker, only to find that his uniform was missing—the sure telltale sign that his services were no longer needed by the Chicago White Sox.

This sent shock waves down my spine. My gosh, would they really release a good ballplayer just two weeks into the season? I mean, Marquise had gone through all of spring training, all of extended spring, and had survived. Now, he had seemingly earned a spot on the short season Bristol team, only to be let go before the season really got going. How unfair I thought that was. How cruel.

But if I was feeling sorry and outraged for Marquise Cody, you can just imagine the shock I felt when I walked into the clubhouse to find my own uniform missing from my locker.

I couldn't believe it. There had to be a mistake. I just stood there and stared at the empty locker. My teammates and buddies were going about their business, getting ready to go out and practice. But I was frozen. Frozen with all of the emotions were racing through my mind, body, and soul.

I was very upset. Even before I got the official news from Cuz, I had to walk outside for a few minutes to try and calm myself down. I couldn't believe that this was happening to me. It just didn't seem right. I kept replaying the last few months in my head and the honest, absolute, objective truth was that I had been playing well. I had the third highest batting average in extended spring, lots of RBIs, played solid defense, and so on. Plus I'm a well-liked and respected player. I also knew that I was a personal favorite of Leyva's and Hairston's.

How could this be happening? Getting released just as my career is beginning to take off! Heck, don't release me, I'll catch bullpens. I'll do anything to stay.

After venting to myself outside the clubhouse for a few minutes, I finally walked inside. My best friend in pro ball, Josh Morgan, looked at me and didn't know what to say. I stepped into Leyva's office where Jerry Hairston and Cuz spoke to me for about forty-five minutes. I didn't say a word. I just sat there on the couch as they tried to explain to me what happened. They didn't do a great job explaining the situation and the truth is, I'll probably never know exactly why I was released because they kept telling me that I didn't do anything poorly or wrong. In fact, both openly encouraged me to keep playing somewhere else and that if I ever needed a recommendation to call them and they'd put in a good word for me. That was a great compliment, but I wanted to say, "Why can't I just stay here?"

Leyva did finally say to me, "John, you're a smart kid. You know that this game is a business. And we're in the business of developing kids who will go on to become major league players. Honestly, I see you as a very solid Class A player—you have great hands on defense and a quick bat—but I also see you topping out in baseball at either high Class A or maybe even Double AA. But no higher."

In short, that was his professional evaluation. For better or worse, after watching me play all through spring training and extended, Leyva felt that the time had come to let me go. The oddity, of course, is that compared to several of the other players on the Bristol team, I was doing great. But in pro ball, as I was learning the hard way, it's not so much about stats—it's about your long-range potential.

On my way out as I cleaned out my locker, I got hugs and handshakes from all the players as well as the staff. Dale Torborg, John Orton, Espy, and Nate Oliver all told me to keep my head up and that things would work out. They told me that another team would pick me up because I'm too good of a ballplayer to be out of the game long.

Their sentiments meant a great deal to me, because they weren't saying these kind words to the other guys who had been released along the way.

I tried my best to hide my tears as I left the clubhouse, but I'm sure everyone could see my eyes beginning to water as I packed up my glove and spikes and left.

Now what?

$\bullet \quad \bullet \quad \bullet$

My wife and I were driving down the interstate in the middle of Virginia when John called on his cell phone. I answered, and could tell right away that something wasn't right.

As a parent, I did the best I could to comfort John. Yes, I know full well that professional baseball is a business. I know that it's the high round draft choices and kids who get a lot of bonus money who get treated better than the other kids, and yes, I know that the player development guys are looking for those players who have the five tools you need to get to the big leagues.

But as a former pro player, pro coach, and of course as a parent, John's release just didn't sit right with me. In all my years in baseball, I had never heard of a drafted kid being let go in his first year of pro ball. Okay, maybe if the player had broken the law, or been a serious pain to a management, they'd let him go. But here was a youngster who had been an ideal member of the White Sox organization, who busted his butt, and who hit .300 in spring training and in extended spring.

No one has ever told us their rationale for letting John go, but my pro baseball instincts tell me that the White Sox had just drafted and

signed another 25 players from the June draft, and they already had
too many players on their Bristol and Great Falls rosters. So, the front
office simply ordered Leyva to cut those kids who were low draft choices
or free agents—regardless of their ability. And that, I assume, is what
happened. In effect, it was a simple accounting move to keep the roster
numbers fairly tight.

Here's the irony. I had just spoken with John Tumminia, the scout
who had drafted and signed John for the White Sox. Every day, there's
a full report that goes on out on the minor league players, and just a day
before he got released, Tumminia had told me that the reports on John
had been excellent. Indeed, when my son called John Tumminia to tell
him he had been released, poor John Tumminia was just as stunned and
shocked as my son was.

Also, when a player gets released, it's like he's immediately transformed
into a person with a serious contagious infection. That is, your friends all
feel sorry for you, but they suddenly don't want to be around you too
much. They don't know what to say, nor do they want that "contagion"
to spread to them.

It makes no difference how well you were doing. There's nothing to
say. You just shake hands quietly and leave.

And so you do. Problem is, if you still want to play professional
baseball, you have to figure out a way to sell yourself to one of the other
organizations. And you can just imagine their very first question: "If you
were doing so well, why did the White Sox let you go?"

It's a tough question, and even tougher to answer. Especially when
you look at John's total stats in his Bristol, Virginia, career: 1-for-7.

FIVE

JULY

IS THIS REALLY HAPPENING?

July 1, 2006
Bristol, Virginia

As much as I felt sorry for myself for getting released, I felt even worse for my parents for driving ten hours to watch me play, only to be greeted by the news of my release. Fortunately, my mom and dad were very supportive despite their and my disappointment. Dad, in particular, understands the dark side of this business. He knows that once you get your release from an organization—regardless of the reason why—you have to move on. And quickly.

As a bit of sad irony to cap it all, I understand there was going to be a big feature article in the local Bristol paper tomorrow about me, my background, how I was doing, etc. There was even a small preview about the upcoming piece in tonight's paper. I assume that, by now, somebody from the Bristol front office has quietly told the paper that I have been released.

So my parents and I stayed overnight in a Bristol motel, and early the next day, we glumly packed up the car and started the long drive back to home in New York. I said my goodbyes to my roomies the night before in the rented house, and even left them the fifty-dollar air conditioner to remember me by. It was all very sad and confusing. The guys didn't understand why the White Sox had pulled the plug on my budding career, and of course I had no idea either. But there was now no reason for me to linger in Bristol any more. It was time to move on.

To that end, the very first question my dad asked me after he heard the news about my release was, "Do you want to keep playing pro ball?" I replied immediately, "Yes, of course!" "Well," he counseled, "after you get home and have a chance to get your bearings straight, you might want to get on the phone and start making some calls, either to affiliated teams or to independent clubs."

I took Dad's advice to heart, but I didn't have any reason to wait until I got back to New York to start working the phones. I figured that since I had a ten-hour drive ahead of me I'd grab my trusty cell phone and go to work, rather than just sitting there looking out the car window feeling sorry for myself. The night before, I had looked up dozens of phone numbers on the internet for pro teams and general managers in independent ball as well as in affiliated ball. During the drive home I was on my cell for at least five of the ten hours calling scouts, coaches, player procurement directors and other contacts—anybody who might help me find a place to play right away.

To my luck, one team in the Can-Am League, one of the stronger independent leagues, called me back right away: the North Shore Spirit. Turns out they were in need of a middle infielder, and they wanted to work me out at their ballpark in Lynn, Massachusetts, on Monday, July 3.

Now, I know some people might be thinking to themselves, "Why doesn't this stupid Ivy League kid just let it go and go make some money in a real job? He could certainly make a good living for himself with his education." But even in this dark time I'm not willing to give up on dream I have held for my entire life. Sometimes I think about life after my playing days are over, and my sense is that I would love to work in the front office of a baseball organization. But I don't want the future of the "real world" to be in my face right now. I'm just not ready to terminate my playing days yet. I played well in spring training and even better in extended spring. I have no idea why the White Sox let me go, but from my perspective I've had too much success in this short period of time to hang up the spikes. I've got to give it another shot. If I didn't, then I would always hate myself for giving up on my dream prematurely.

• • •

As you might imagine, Trish and I were reeling from John's release. We felt so sorry for him. Here's a young man who had worked his tail off to improve his game—dating all the way back to high school and then college and now into pro ball. I still can't get over the White Sox's decision to let him go so quickly into the season.

But no matter. This isn't about me, it's about John. And as I led our small caravan home from the backwoods of Virginia (I was driving the lead car and Trish and John following behind me), it looked in my rear view mirror like John was just sitting in the passenger seat, simply staring straight ahead.

What I didn't know until we eventually stopped to refill the gas tanks was that John wasn't just sitting there staring into space forlornly, but rather he was working his way back into pro baseball. When I heard that this team in Lynn, Massachusetts, had invited him for a private tryout, I couldn't have been prouder of my son.

After all, he had somehow taken the sting of being released and had channeled his anger and frustration into finding a pro team that was eager to see what he could do. Amazing.

I must confess that I don't know much about this North Shore team, but I sure do like their enthusiasm.

July 2, 2006
Armonk, New York

Today was just a nice, quiet, relaxing day at home in Armonk, New York, after that long drive yesterday. It presented me with a welcome opportunity to sleep in my own bed, get some good food in me (my mom is a terrific chef!), and get my wash done.

Tomorrow begins another adventure for me, as I'll be back out on the road headed to the tryout in Lynn, Massachusetts, a suburb on Boston's north coast. All in all, it's about a four hour drive. But I'm ready.

July 3, 2006
Lynn, Massachusetts

The tryout for the North Shore Spirit was held this afternoon at Fraser Field, a beautiful and well-manicured stadium. It was hot and sunny, and my workout was slated for 1:00 P.M. All in all, the tryout was just what I expected—a coach throwing me batting practice, a sixty-yard dash, a bunch of ground balls at shortstop and some throws over to first. Even better, it was nice to have this closed tryout and be the only player working out.

The North Shore Spirit is managed by John Kennedy, who's been around professional baseball forever. He came out and watched me go through my paces. He didn't say much, but I had a sense he liked what he saw.

And I will say this: I put on a solid showing, both defensively and offensively. I don't think I muffed one ball from all the grounders they hit me, and I stroked dozens of line drives all over the ballpark. My instincts proved correct, too, as my showing was well-received by the coaches and front office personnel. In fact, as soon as the workout was over, Kennedy offered me a contract on the spot. Kennedy and his coaches Tom Donahue, Jim Tgettis, and Frank Carey were watching me work out, and they all seemed pleased with what I had to offer their ballclub.

Here's an interesting note. During the workout they let me catch my breath for a few seconds, and in that time they discovered that I had played ball at Harvard. They told me that one of my college teammates, Josh Klimkiewicz, had worked out for North Shore a few weeks ago, and they said that they were interested in signing him as well. He happened to play the same position as the Spirit's veteran team captain and resident slugger, Vic Davilla, however, so as a result they ended up not signing Klimkiewicz. Last I heard he was playing in the American Association, for a team in El Paso.

After I signed the standard players' contract they told me that they wanted me to dress out for that evening's game, which was in only a few hours. They showed me my locker and got me fitted for pants, caps and everything else. As I was receiving the different home and away uniforms, it dawned on me that only a few days before I had been playing for the Bristol White Sox. In what seemed like an instant I was now playing for a different team 1,000 miles away. Yes, it's still baseball, but that's about the only thing that's the same.

One thing about the North Shore Spirit is that they have an unbelievable array of uniforms. They have whites, blues, reds, blacks, cut-offs in all colors, and combinations of all these colors, not to mention batting practice jerseys as well. With the White Sox, all we had was white jerseys for home games and grey jerseys for away games. But now, in Lynn, I was like a kid in a candy store. I loved having a ton of jerseys with my name on the back. The Spirit plays on a brand new field that is half turf and half grass. The infield is turf and it is outstanding, while the outfield is all grass. The ballpark itself is fantastic, with a huge grandstand and big league scoreboard in centerfield. Even the clubhouse, which was more or less a converted trailer, was nice and full of good food before and after the games.

At game time that evening I realized my role on this team will be to back up the Spirit'sstar shortstop, Chris Rowan, who happens to be from the same general area of New York as I am. Chris, who's twenty-six, is a well-built, power-hitting infielder who played a number of seasons in the Milwaukee Brewers' organization. He's also an outgoing guy with a happy demeanor about him.

Speaking of Chris's age, I was quickly discovering that the Can-Am league is an organization comprised primarily of veteran pro players who have spent considerable time in organized ball. Yes, there are a few kids in the league who never played pro ball and signed out of college, but the vast majority of these guys are in their mid-twenties and have logged two to four years of pro ball. At age twenty-two, I'm clearly one of the youngest, if not the youngest, member of the Spirit's team.

No matter to me. I'm back playing pro ball, albeit in an independent league. That's okay with me for the time being. I'm in uniform, waiting for my chance to show what I can do.

• • •

Lynn, Massachusetts, is sort of a tired suburb of Boston. As a result, the Spirits' refurbished ballpark, which sits behind a couple of strip malls and some fast food restaurants, is like a gem that gleams in the dust. It's been around forever, but recent renovations have transformed it into a real beauty.

Plus they're one of the top teams in the league, they average several thousand fans for every game, and they have all the attractions and charms of any top minor league organization. Lots of noise, lots of music, and so on. It makes it an exciting atmosphere for the players.

My sense is that the caliber of play is probably at the AA or High Class A level. This is clearly not Rookie ball (like the Appalachian League) nor even Low Class A ball. In the Can-Am league, the pitchers throw strikes and know how to change speeds, the fielders make the plays, and the batters hit with authority. In short, this is a good league.

July 4, 2006
Lynn, Massachusetts

The city of Lynn, Massachusetts, used to be infamously referred to as "Lynn, Lynn, the City of Sin." The North Shore Spirit decided to try and change this image by consciously promoting the change of the word "Sin" to "Win" and even putting a patch on their jersey sleeves with the slogan. I don't know if this campaign has changed many local attitudes yet. Only time will tell.

In any event, we got rained out tonight and we'll play a double header tomorrow against the New Jersey Jackals. It's a strange sensation when you join a team halfway through the season. Because North Shore signed me, they had to release someone else to make room for me on the roster.

In this case, I believe the player who was released was infielder Andy Howdeshell. I have never met the kid but I can tell from the clubhouse atmosphere that Andy was well-liked, and of course, everyone on the team sees me as the sole person to blame for their friend getting released. As I expected, most of the players were not all that eager at first to come over, shake my hand, and introduce themselves. A few guys said cursory hellos, but I think it might take a few games for them to warm up to me.

Also, as a general rule, players are always a little nervous when new guys come into the clubhouse. I remember it was the same way in spring training with the White Sox. Whenever a new guy walked in with his gear, it was a nervous time. On the one hand you want to be a nice guy and a good teammate, but on the other you know that this new fellow might steal your job or your friend's job. That's just the reality. It is a very cutthroat world in minor league baseball.

On the plus side of the ledger, the living arrangements in Lynn are like night and day compared to Bristol. I went from living in a dilapidated flophouse to staying at the Marriott Extended Stay Hotel—real big league digs! Apparently, the Lynn Marriott sponsors the North Shore Spirit and every player gets his own spacious room with full kitchen efficiency, king size bed, pull-out couch, and cable television. It is a beautiful setup for any minor leaguer and I can't believe my good fortune. No more sleeping on crappy air mattresses with bad air conditioning. I feel like I'm staying at the Ritz and playing in the big leagues. When I walk in the front door, the hotel manager knows my name. The staff treats us all like important baseball prospects, and they are always happy to help with anything we need. It is a great change of scenery and a great feeling to be at a place like this after my garbage apartment in Tucson and the worn-down dump in Bristol.

•   •   •

John's right. Whenever a new player shows up in the clubhouse, the rest of the team gets nervous. Who is this guy? And most importantly, what position does he play? Is he here to take over my spot? Those are the immediate and alarming questions that go through your head and heart.

On the plus side, John's also right about his new digs. After that rundown house in Bristol, the Marriott in Lynn is a welcome relief. Clean, cool, private, and the total charge is nominal. John is going to get spoiled in a hurry!

July 5, 2006
Lynn, Massachusetts
We split the double header tonight against the New Jersey Jackals. I played a few innings as shortstop at the end of the second game and made a few nice plays including a smooth double play turn. I got my first at-bat, too. I saw the ball well but unfortunately grounded out to shortstop.

My father drove to Lynn with me on Monday to help share the drive and let me rest before my workout. He's been staying here in Lynn since then and we have an off-day tomorrow. I wanted to give him a break, so we drove home back to New York late tonight after the game in order to get him back home. But as it turned out, he still ended up doing most of the driving because I was tired from the game. I promised him I wouldn't fall asleep in the car, but I did anyway. He didn't complain. He never does.

· · ·

Poor kid. He's really been on an emotional roller coaster these last few days, and even though he's excited to be playing in front of big crowds on a talented team, it still must be rough for John to have gone through all of these ups and downs of pro ball.

As a father and former college and pro coach, I try to be very, very careful not to put any kind of pressure on my son. He's a smart kid. He knows that the odds of any talented high school or college kid getting a chance to play pro ball at any level is extremely rare. Indeed, he's the first graduate of Byram Hills High School in Armonk to ever sign a pro baseball contract, even though the high school has had some very talented athletes over the years. Getting to play college ball is quite a leap from high school varsity ball, but going from a college program to the pro level is even tougher.

No one works harder at his craft than John does. Quite literally, I don't think a day has passed over the last several years that he hasn't worked long and hard hours to become the best ballplayer he can be. That means weight training, constantly working on his sprinting and foot speed, strengthening his throwing arm, breaking down videotape of his batting stroke, and of course, taking tons and tons of batting practice. He has gotten to the point now that if you throw him ten strikes in batting practice, he will hit nine ropes. That's what pro players do—they become more consistent than amateurs.

But hard work and endless desire don't guarantee you're going to be good enough to become a pro. You need the talent. Clearly John has that. He's got excellent hands and a great stroke, he's a smart base runner, a superb bunter, and so on. All he needs is the chance to prove himself. Don't get me wrong. Pro ball is tough, and everybody struggles. But before you can get a real assessment of what a kid can do, he needs to play a full-length season where he plays every day and gets between 400 and 500 at-bats. That's when you can do a real evaluation.

July 6, 2006
Armonk, New York

Today was my first sanctioned off-day in quite a while. Since I was home in Armonk, I went over to the ProSwing batting cage where I used to train at in nearby Mount Kisco. Dan Gray, the owner of the facility, caught in the Dodgers' organization for a number of years and coached me when I played ACBL ball. I wanted to stop in and get a few hacks in as well as to give Dan, who's become a close friend, an update as to what's been going on with my season thus far.

Sure enough, big Dan was surprised to see me walk in, because he thought I was still in Virginia. But Dan also knows the reality of the baseball world all too well and was happy to hear that I had signed on with another pro team.

I was going to drive back to Lynn tonight after seeing Dan Gray but instead I made a pit stop in Providence, Rhode Island, to visit my old friend Nicole Mayhew, who I hadn't seen since high school. Nicole is a very talented artist who went to the Rhode Island School of Design. She now lives in Providence, and I spent the night at her apartment with a few of her friends from college. After I met her friends we all went out for karaoke at the local American Legion Post 10. Because I'd never been to an American Legion Post on karaoke night I didn't know what to expect, but the karaoke singers performing that night were fantastic. I couldn't compete, even though I once won a karaoke championship in Harvard Square. By the way, just for the record: my go-to karaoke song is always Annie Lennox's "Walking on Broken Glass."

•   •   •

John has played for all different types of baseball coaches during his high school, college, and pro career. Clearly he was quite fortunate to have played for Dan Gray for two years in the ACBL. Dan brings an eternal joy to the game and knows that you can't perform at a top competitive level unless you are relaxed and loose. Unfortunately, very few college and high school baseball coaches seem to understand this fairly simple concept. I don't know why.

July 7, 2006
Lynn, Massachusetts

I took off early this morning from Providence and drove back to Lynn. It was an easy, one-hour drive right up I-95 into Massachusetts. We have an away game tonight against the Brockton Rox. Like the Spirit, the Rox have a beautiful ballpark and draw huge crowds. In addition, we happen to be in a first-place race against these guys so this is an important series for both teams. The first half of the season is coming to a close, and the team that finishes in first place at the end of the first half receives an automatic bid to the playoffs.

July 8, 2006
Lynn, Massachusetts

After losing the series opener, we beat Brockton tonight in solid fashion. Unfortunately, I didn't see action in either of the games, as my role is to continue to back up Chris Rowan at shortstop.

I understand my role on the team and the manager, John Kennedy, has made it clear to me that I could be playing any position in the infield at anytime. I'm fine with that and I accept that. The problem is, like all ballplayers, I just want to play.

. . .

Independent ball is different in its philosophy than organized, or affiliated, baseball. That is, in affiliated ball, you're there to develop as a prospect. Yes, the minor league manager wants to win, but he also knows that his job is to develop kids into prospects who will someday (ideally) make it to the big leagues. As such, they stress "development" over their win-loss record.

This is not the case in indy ball. Here, most of the players have their careers in affiliated ball behind them. As such, the indy owners want one thing—to win, and to win all the time. They are not concerned or interested in developing prospects; they want to win, because the more the team wins, the larger home crowds they'll draw. Or at least that seems to be the prevailing attitude as these indy teams shed players and make roster moves like most people change their clothes. It's just extraordinary how many players come and go on these indy teams.

July 9, 2006
Lynn, Massachusetts

Tonight we suffered an absolutely brutal loss, on a dinky little flare to right field in the bottom of the thirteenth inning. I started at third base and went 1-for-4 with a walk. My base hit was a line drive right up the middle into centerfield. I also handled a few routine plays and made a true "web gem" when I dove full out and caught a line drive that would have been a sure double down the line. Although we lost, I think I put on a pretty good show for my first start with the North Shore Spirit. When you are in a utility or backup role you have to make sure you perform well every time you play, because you never know when your next start will take place. You could very well be on the bench for another seven days. Such is the life of the utility infielder.

After the game, I learned that food in Lynn is a little tough to come by late at night. We got home before midnight after the game in Brockton, which is only about a forty-five-minute drive from Lynn. While there are plenty of bars and taverns around here that are open late after games, they don't serve food late, just drinks. There are also plenty of fast food places to get late night eats, but the cuisine at Burger King, McDonald's, and Wendy's all gets old very fast, and that's not to mention its nutritional shortcomings. I tried to find a fairly healthy alternative this evening around 11:00 P.M. and I couldn't find anything. Also, being in Massachusetts, I'm a little nervous about exploring too far from home base because all the roads are so confusing that I fear if I get lost I may never find my way back to the hotel.

July 10, 2006
Lynn, Massachusetts

We had a home game today at Fraser Field, marking the first game of a week-long homestand. We beat the Sussex (New Jersey) Skyhawks fairly easily with a score of 9-3. I didn't see any action in tonight's game, but I hope to see some action tomorrow. Tonight, our manager, John Kennedy, provided a bit of his own action by getting thrown out of game. I've only been here a week but in that short span I've already seen Kennedy get tossed out of two games and nearly a third. My sense of John is that he's a nice but occasionally gruff veteran who's been around the game all his life and doesn't have any tolerance or patience anymore for missed calls. During the games, he rarely speaks and never sits down. He always stands in the corner of the dugout and sometimes he'll even light up a few heaters (cigarettes). Above all, John doesn't seem to have much faith in the umps to make good calls.

Likewise, it appears that the Can-Am umpires don't have much of a tolerance for Kennedy, either, as they usually eject him rather quickly whenever he starts to argue. Kennedy doesn't say much on the bench, but when he starts going face-to-face with the men in blue, everyone in the grandstand can hear exactly what Kennedy is saying and, as you might imagine, most of it is not appropriate for the kids in the crowd. As a result, in order to keep things G-rated, the P.A. system starts blaring music in order to drown out Kennedy's observations and opinions about the umpiring crew.

As Kennedy can attest, there is a real art to making arguing look good. Kennedy has had years of experience and he is a fun arguer to watch. He is very animated and enthusiastic. As they say, he usually gets his nickel's worth before he's banished to the showers.

• • •

One of the highlights of my first year of pro ball was playing against the Orangeburg (South Carolina) Cardinals. No, the team wasn't particularly special, but their manager was. Jimmy Piersall, the fiery former American League All-Star, was the manager of that ballclub in 1973. And it seemed like Jimmy went out of his way to put on a creative performance for the fans who showed up in Orangeburg's tired old ballpark.

One time, just before the game was to begin and the umps and managers met at home plate to exchange lineup cards, Piersall came bolting out of the Cardinals' dugout and sprinted to home plate. But instead of slowing down, he simply slid into home! I don't recall if that earned him an early trip to the showers, but clearly Jimmy seemed to enjoy being given the thumb. I remember another time when he was so angry about a disputed play that he drop-kicked a batter's helmet about forty yards. That got him booted as well.

But Piersall, despite being a showman and being good for baseball, was also a very personable and wonderful guy. Just a lot of fun to be around, unless you were an umpire.

P.S. There was a catcher on that Orangeburg team who got a front-row seat to Piersall's antics. The catcher's name was Randy Poffo, a pretty good-hitting receiver. Poffo didn't make it to the majors in baseball, but he sure did in pro wrestling. You may have heard of him by his professional name: "The Macho Man" Randy Savage.

July 11, 2006
Lynn, Massachusetts

We had another home game tonight against Sussex. These games are extremely important because in addition to there being an automatic bid to the playoffs on the line, I've also heard rumors that the players might receive an extra $500 bonus in cash from our team owner. I would love to make some extra money just for winning a few more games.

I arrived at the field today around 3:00 P.M., but shortly after the skies opened up and it rained like I have never seen it rain before. It poured for about five straight hours and completely drenched everything in sight. The field was flooded. The roads were flooded. The entire North Shore was flooded. The roads were so bad that one of my teammates got his car caught in the middle of a four-foot puddle and had to hop out and literally push his Volkswagen through the water to get it to higher ground.

Tomorrow is the last day of the first half of the season and, because of tonight's wash-out, we have a double header now slated against Sussex. If we win both games we are pretty much guaranteed to finish the first half of the season in first place. Needless to say, I'm looking forward to winning two.

July 12, 2006
Lynn, Massachusetts
The first half of the double header started at 12:00 P.M. this afternoon. I hadn't played this early in the day since extended spring training back in Tucson, which now seems like years ago, and I have to admit it felt a bit weird playing in real sunshine rather than under the lights. We arrived at the field around 9:30 A.M. but because of more foul weather we didn't leave until around midnight. Fortunately we won both games and clinched the first half of the season, but the tarp must have been pulled on and off the field at least fifteen times throughout the two games. It was unreal. There were monsoon-like conditions in Lynn, but we played through it. Clearly, the powers-that-be wanted to get these games in, no matter what.

And then it happened again.

When the double header finally came to an end, and all of us were celebrating in the clubhouse, having just clinched the first-half pennant, John Kennedy called me into his office. He matter-of-factly sat me down, got to the point, and told me that he had to release me. He explained that he didn't want to and that the move was, in his words, "complete bullshit" —but that the Spirit owner wanted to pick up a power-hitting, veteran infielder and they needed my spot on the roster to make room for him.

As you might imagine, this turn of events took me by complete surprise. It all seemed ridiculous and I couldn't believe it was happening yet again!

I'm certainly upset about getting released again but not nearly as upset as I was back in Bristol. This time around I'm more embarrassed, because I can't even imagine how I'm going to tell my friends and supporters that I have been released again. I can just imagine their reaction: "Wow, Wolff, you must really be terrible! Who gets released twice in less than a month!"

Welcome to minor league baseball, or more precisely, welcome to independent ball. These owners must work under the assumption that there is always somebody better to pick up or to trade for, and it's the young guys like me who usually get pushed around. I mean, a couple of weeks ago, John Kennedy couldn't wait to sign me and sing my praises. And here, just two weeks later, the team owner is telling the veteran manager to let me go so he can sign some hot-shot slugger. Can you believe it? As badly as I feel for myself, I feel even more embarrassed for Kennedy. Here's a well-respected baseball lifer who is being ordered around by some deep-pocketed owner who probably never even played pro ball.

And the worst part is that I played well here in the limited opportunities I got.

• • •

Now, this one is hard to believe. But in a way, it isn't.

As noted earlier, independent teams are all about winning, and winning right now. Affiliated teams are more about developing players over time. To indy owners, there's always the feeling that there's a better player right over the horizon to be signed. The reality is, of course, that the better players are still playing in organized ball, and are not looking for jobs in independent ball.

Take a look at the transactions column for any indy league and you'll find that each day somebody is getting released, somebody is getting traded, and somebody is getting signed. It's really just a turnstile of talent.

John had noted that when the Spirit had first signed him, another player had to be let go. Sure enough, the player who took John's place on the Spirit lasted about a week before he, too, was let go. As it turned out, the player the Spirit had picked up was a youngster out of Chicago named Blake Whealy. Whealy was originally drafted by the Mets and had a few good years in Class A ball. He was then picked up by the White Sox and sent to Kannapolis—Class A ball again. Apparently, Whealy lasted only a week or two with the Sox before they let him go. Whealy was then signed by the Spirit when they let John go. He got only a grand total of ten at-bats before the Spirit went on to pick up John's former college teammate, Morgan Brown. In other words, don't think for a second that John was the only victim of these indy teams and their mercurial mindsets.

I can just imagine what John Kennedy must have gone through with this merry-go-round approach to putting a roster together. Sure enough, when the Spirit didn't win the championship this summer, Kennedy was let go as well. Apparently, the veteran skipper was let go after not bringing home the Can-Am championship even though North Shore's season record was light years better than every other team in the league. And if you were to look at the roster of players who started the season with the Spirit and compared it to the roster that ended the season, you would think you were looking at two completely different ballclubs.

One of the reasons for this is that since the Can-Am League runs a little longer than the American Association, the United League, the Golden League, and some other independent leagues, the management of the North Shore team scoured all these leagues for their all-stars and then signed them the week before the playoffs in an attempt to secure the championship. It was like something out of the movie Slapshot *when the Chiefs play for the league championship against a hodge-podge team full of old veteran goons from different leagues or prisons.*

To me, what North Shore didn't take into account is that the sabermetric approach of simply looking at batting averages and runs produced doesn't help in the playoffs. They ended up losing on some costly defensive errors. I guess that's a little bit of poetic justice. But that's why baseball is a strange game. Sometimes the numbers don't tell the whole story.

The other thing to keep in mind is that (just as in the affiliated minor leagues) occasionally players who are having good years (especially pitchers) can be picked up at any time and have their contracts purchased by affiliated teams. I think two of the better North Shore pitchers were purchased in the middle of the season (one was Ryan Bicondoa, who was signed by the Chicago Cubs). It is an interesting balance of wanting your players to do well but at the same time wanting to keep your good players around to win the championship. There were a lot of other North Shore players who ended up having their contracts purchased after the season, too, like catcher Alex Trezza (Colorado Rockies) and third baseman J.D. Reininger (Washington Nationals).

July 13, 2006
Lynn, Massachusetts

I slept in this morning at the team hotel, packed up my stuff and took my time driving back to New York. En route I started working the cell phone again, making calls to other teams in the Can-Am League. One team showed immediate interest: the New Jersey Jackals, which happens to one of the Spirit's main rivals.

However, they explained that they couldn't legally sign me until I cleared waivers. That takes about forty-eight hours. I'll clear waivers on Saturday afternoon at 12:00 P.M., and then the Jackals can call me back and decide if they want to offer me a contract. I really hope they sign me so I can continue playing this summer. In addition, the Jackals are in second place in the league right now, which means that I can continue playing for a good team.

• • •

This would all be quite comical, except that it's real and it's happening to my son.

I mean, I can just imagine what kind of clubhouse ribbing a ballplayer would get if his teammates heard about this: "Hey, John, let me get this straight … you got a total of seven at-bats with the White Sox … and they released you … and then you got five at-bats with the Spirit, and they released you … man, those must've been some pretty ugly at-bats!"

But on the serious side, what's extraordinary is John's determination to keep at this. There was never a moment of self-doubt or self-pity through any of this. He just wants a chance to play. As John says, "Getting a job in the real world will happen soon enough. Right now, I want to give pro baseball my best shot … and that hasn't happened yet."

July 14, 2006
Armonk, New York

This morning I woke up back in my own bed in Armonk. For a twenty-two-year-old, it felt strange to be back home. I should be out somewhere else, playing ball. Where? I don't know. But I know there's no pro ball in the tiny town of Armonk.

Today is also my dad's birthday, and to celebrate we took some batting practice together at my old high school field. Even though I play baseball every day, it's still enjoyable to work out with my father on an empty and dusty field with no fans in the stands. Just a bucket of balls, a hot sun, and Dad throwing batting practice.

It reminds me of how much I still really love to play this game. What can I say? It's fun. Plus I really have gotten pretty darn good at hitting a baseball over the years, and I know my dad loves watching me hit just as much as I love hitting the balls over the fence at Byram Hills High School. In the meantime, tomorrow is Saturday, and I'm hoping that the Jackals will get back to me by the time I finish eating lunch or sleeping in—depending on whichever comes first.

July 15, 2006
Armonk, New York

I got the proverbial good news and bad news from the New Jersey Jackals today. The good news is that they told me they wanted to sign me. The bad news is that they can't do that today because they're on the road and they can't make room for me on the roster until they get back to New Jersey. In other words, they can't release a player while they're on a road trip.

That makes sense to me and I look forward to playing close to home over in Montclair, New Jersey. It's only about a forty-five-minute ride from Armonk. Unfortunately the Jackals, like the Spirit, want to use me in a utility role to spot some of their veteran infielders. It's not exactly what I wanted, but at the end of the day I'm just happy to be a part of a professional roster. And if I seize the opportunities I get, who knows? Maybe I can play my way into a spot in the regular starting lineup.

These past few days at home have given me a chance to eat healthy, relax, take batting practice, and allow my body to recover from an already long season with still plenty of games to go. Of course, there's also the emotional strain of the game and of constantly being shipped around the country, playing different roles. It takes a little while to get over being released or traded and to understand that you didn't do anything wrong but that you are instead just a small part of a large business or corporation. And as that small part you are subject to whatever the corporation feels is necessary to do at any given time. That's a challenging concept to get used to.

July 16, 2006
Armonk, New York

I took a round of batting practice this morning with Dad. I noticed when I got back from the workout that I had a message on my phone from the Kalamazoo Kings, an indy team in the Frontier League. They told me they needed a shortstop right away and that they wanted me to be their starting shortstop as soon as I made it out to Kalamazoo, Michigan, the hometown of Derek Jeter. When I called back I explained that I had a job already lined up with the Jackals and was possibly talking to some other teams as well. But the Kalamazoo manager, Fran Riordan, urged me to come play and I just couldn't turn down a guaranteed starting job—especially with a good team that's contending for the playoffs.

I must confess that I know next to nothing about the Frontier League, except that, unlike the Can-Am League, it's a league for mostly younger players—guys in their early twenties. But the lure of a starting position was what really intrigued me.

I called the Jackals' manager, Joe Calfapietra, right away and explained my situation to him. As you might imagine, Joe wasn't too happy to hear that I wouldn't be joining his ballclub, but deep down in my heart I knew that the opportunity to be a starting shortstop with this other team would be a much more enjoyable experience than riding the bench for the Jackals would be. To me, the fun of baseball is in the actual playing, and after being bounced around in Lynn and in Bristol I desperately want the opportunity to be able to play somewhere every day. I haven't been a starter since extended spring training, so I'm extremely excited to get out to Kalamazoo and play. The only downside is that I'll have to drive all the way out there. It's about a twelve-hour drive. Brutal!

• • •

The roller coaster of pro ball continues. I'm quite sure that John had no idea what was in store for him when he left for Tucson back in early March. It's been an amazing few months.

But I do want to take a moment to personally salute Joe Calfapietra. He couldn't have been more gracious than he was when John told him he wanted to go play for Kalamazoo. Joe was disappointed and probably a bit frustrated with John's decision, but to his everlasting credit, Joe was even in his temperament and understood why John was so eager to play every day.

Thanks, Joe. My son owes you one.

July 17, 2006
Armonk, New York

I told the Kalamazoo Kings I'd be joining them in Michigan. I hope I didn't burn any bridges with Joe Calfapietra and the Jackals because it might be a nice place to play in a future season. But the offer from Kalamazoo was just too good to turn down.

On a side note, I heard that two players from the Great Falls White Sox, Pedro Moreno and Christian Acosta, got released a few days ago. Acosta got released on his birthday. Ouch. In addition, Bristol is having an absolutely terrible season. Last time I checked, their infielders were making all sorts of errors, they weren't hitting at all, and the team was in dead last place in the Appy League. Perhaps getting released was a blessing in disguise.

July 18, 2006
Armonk, New York

My old high school girlfriend called me out of the blue today and wanted to get together. I had nothing better to do, so I invited her out to dinner and we enjoyed some nice French cuisine. The date was surprisingly awkward yet romantic.

It was a very hot midsummer night. After a thunderstorm had passed through, I felt like going for a quick swim at the local Windmill Lake, and she came with me. The air had cooled down after the rain, but the water in the pond was still very warm. It was a great midnight swim and it was a nice way to conclude my short stay in Armonk. I packed up that night, fell asleep at 2:00 A.M. and was ready to hit the road by 5:00 A.M. for Kalamazoo.

Mom and Dad didn't want me to drive alone. As a result, after some last minute discussion, Mom decided to drive to Michigan with me, watch a few games, and then fly home on Saturday. We hustled all the way, stopped only for a quick lunch and some gas, and arrived in Kalamazoo at 5:00 P.M. Not a bad ride at all.

July 19, 2006
Kalamazoo, Michigan

In case you're keeping score at home, it was twelve hours on the road—603 miles on Interstate 80 and a total of 740 miles overall from Armonk to K'zoo. Quite a haul.

When we arrived in Kalamazoo, Mom and I had dinner and then checked out the ballpark. Unlike Bristol, this one is brand new and very nice. On the other hand, it's not as big as North Shore, but overall it's fine. One curiosity, though: when you enter the ballpark you enter through right field ... and then have to walk around to the grandstand. Kind of strange, to be sure, but certainly a nice minor league park.

Around 9 P.M., I got a call from my host family here in Michigan: Ted and Louise Green. They're an older couple who live on a small farm just outside Kalamazoo. They invited me over to move my stuff in and meet the family. I stopped by for an hour and chatted for a while as Ted showed off his shotguns, hunting dogs, and his tractors out in the field. He told me that the last kid they had from the team wasn't hitting well so they made him live in the silo. Then Ted laughed, and assured me that he's sure I'll hit right away. Let's hope.

Host families like the Greens are godsends to minor league ballplayers like me because they save us big bucks. Kalamazoo is paying me only $700 a month for my services. In the Can-Am League I was making $800 a month, so you can imagine what a relief it is to not have to pay for rent or for meals.

But life in indy ball is not without its drawbacks. One of the problems with the Frontier League (and maybe indy ball in general) is that they don't pay for your transportation to get to where you'll be playing. Because of this, my first paycheck from Kalamazoo will barely cover the cost of gasoline from driving from New York to Michigan. Again, thank God for my host family.

In affiliated ball, everyone signs a regular minor league contract, which pays approximately $1,250 a month. In independent ball, though, each league has slightly different salary caps, and they pay the veteran players a lot more than they pay the rookies. A good veteran player might be able to make $3,000 a month, but he has to be really, really good to earn that kind of money.

In any event, my host "mom," Louise Green, seems very nice and outgoing. I didn't get a chance to speak with her very long but I'm sure we'll get to know each other much better as things go along. The Greens also have their niece living with them for the summer, but she seems very quiet and we didn't really speak all that much. I'm sure she's just shy.

In the meantime, I'll be keeping my mom company in the hotel for the next few nights, so I won't be really living with the Greens until the weekend. In truth, I'm a little nervous, but I'm sure the experience will provide me with some unusual and humorous stories.

• • •

Host families didn't exist when I played, but it's clearly a great way for local baseball fans to embrace one of the players. Sometimes, though, the host family's home can be tight quarters, and things can get a little cramped in a hurry. Plus, ballplayers keep bizarre hours.

I didn't know that the Kings had arranged for John to live with a host family. I do hope it works out well for John, but as his dad, I can assure you that he has never spent much, if any, time on a farm, and clearly doesn't know a shotgun from a BB gun.

Also, farm people like to go to bed early and get up with the roosters. Again, I can assure you that isn't something John is accustomed to.

Finally, in general, it's my hunch that older people on farms don't often have much in the way of air conditioning. I wonder if John checked on that as well.

July 20, 2006
Kalamazoo, Michigan

Just like that, tonight I played in my first game with the Kalamazoo Kings.

I had to be at the field today at 1:30 P.M. to fill out paperwork. The Kings want me to be their starting shortstop, and they actually traded the player that I'm replacing to the New Jersey Jackals back in the Can-Am League, so at least on paper everyone goes home happy.

I'm a little bit nervous, just like I was when I first joined the North Shore team, but that's the natural feeling to have when you're joining a new team far from home with a bunch of guys you don't know. Then again, I'm excited about the experience and I'm looking forward to having a good time out here.

I batted lead-off tonight and went 1-for-4 with a bunch of nice defensive plays at shortstop, but we lost to the Washington, Pennsylvania, Wild Things. In my first at-bat I lined out to the left fielder, but I felt good at the plate. I was facing a pretty good left-handed pitcher and I was trying to take his fastball to left field. Sure enough, in my second at-bat I hit a line drive over the shortstop's head for a single.

I felt like I was on top of the world. In two at-bats as a Kalamazoo King I hit the ball hard twice. I felt like I could do no wrong and that I was the best late-season signee ever. Unfortunately, my next two at-bats resulted in a routine ground ball to second and a fly out to the left fielder. Not a great finish to the game, but not a bad game to start my career as a King.

I did mess up a steal sign tonight, which was stupid of me. But since it's only my first game, maybe the manager, Fran Riordan, will cut me a break.

• • •

Playing in front of a big crowd and having your name announced as the starting shortstop and lead-off batter typifies the pure excitement and lure of playing in the minors. It's just what John had hoped for. True, he's playing for an indy team in Kalamazoo instead of for the Bristol White Sox, but at the end of the day, he's doing what he's always wanted to do.

You really can't ask for more than that.

July 21, 2006
Kalamazoo, Michigan

We had another home game tonight, and I was excited to go out and do my part to help get our team back on track. Unfortunately, as luck would have it, we didn't win and I didn't have much of a game, either. My first impression of the Kalamazoo Kings' organization is that it is full of very kind people and some pretty impressive players as well. The veteran players on the team caught my eye from the first day in batting practice. I remember watching outfielder Pete Pirman stroke home run after home run in batting practice only to later learn that he was the Frontier League MVP the previous year. Pirman not only has put up great numbers in his career, but he is also pretty close to being a five-tool player. I don't know why he isn't playing in Class AA somewhere with an affiliated team. I know he was drafted by the Detroit Tigers a few years back (he's now twenty-seven years old). However, when I asked why the Tigers let him go he told me that they liked some high school outfield prospect better. Some kid named Curtis Granderson. I guess when they are right, they are right.

Another Kings' player who caught my eye right away was a centerfielder named Ian Church. A few players told me to keep my eye out for Church because he was leading the Frontier League in home runs by a wide margin. (He ended up finishing the season with thirty-one, twelve more than anyone else in independent ball. Impressive.)

I was sitting at my locker, looking across the clubhouse at the locker with the name "Church" above it. I watched player after player walk into the locker room, waiting for a glimpse of this monster of a human being who blasts home run after home run—the six-four, 240 pound power hitter who eats fastballs for breakfast. However, the monster known as Ian Church never arrived. I finally asked one of guys with a locker near mine, Kyle Kmiecik, saying, "Hey, Kyle, who's that guy taking everything out of Church's locker?" Kyle started to chuckle and said, "That's Ian Church." I couldn't believe my eyes. Ian was not the monster of a man that I expected, but actually somewhat on the small side. I would estimate he's about five-ten, 170 pounds or so. I looked at Kyle and said, "That little guy is leading all of independent ball in home runs?" Kyle looked at me and nodded. "Just wait until batting practice. He'll put on a show."

But during batting practice all Ian Church did was hit line drive after line drive through the four hole into right field. Ian hits from the right side and just took a very relaxed batting practice, going with the pitch the opposite way. In truth, I wasn't all that impressed. What I didn't realize, however, is that Ian, who is twenty-six years old, has a plan when he hits. He has a plan for batting practice. He does what he wants with the ball. In batting practice he goes the opposite way. In the game, he can pull the ball at will and put it over the fence almost any time he wants. He is probably one of the smartest hitters I have ever played with. He reminds me of a former teammate in the ACBL named Jordan Foster. Foster had a great approach just like Church and was drafted out of Lamar University in Texas by the Detroit Tigers. After playing a year or two of affiliated ball, he now plays in the American Association and hits .350 or better every year. Just like Church, Foster was such a good hitter that he could actually set the pitchers up to throw him the pitch he wanted.

I remember sitting in the dugout with Jordan before one of his at-bats and he would say, "Hey, Wolffman, watch this. I'm going to go up there and the pitcher is going to throw me a first pitch curveball. I'm going to swing so hard that I'll probably fall over and look foolish on the pitch. He will then throw me the same crappy curveball and I'll hit a double or a home run." Sure enough, Foster would do that all the time and it would work. His first swing would be deliberately embarrassing—and then he would hit an absolute mammoth home run or a double in the gap somewhere. Now that's controlling the game.

Compared to the Can-Am League, the players in the Frontier League are supposed to be a little bit younger and less experienced. For the most part, that's true. However, this Kalamazoo team had a good number of players with a few years of experience in independent ball. Casey Baker and Justin Carroll, for example, both played a few years in the veteran Northern League, and you could just tell that these guys were on a higher level with their ability to play the game. They might be a little bit older and their bodies a little bit worn down from years of playing ball, but they know how to play the game on a very high level, mentally.

Casey Baker, as a hitter, has magical hands. If you were to pass by him on the street, however, you'd probably assume he's just a regular Joe. What people don't realize is that not only is Casey Baker in the best physical shape on the team, he was also a world-class martial artist. Casey is very much at home in the batter's box, and although he doesn't hit for too much power, he always seems to hit line drives. I saw him go 7-for-7 one day in River City, Missouri, with seven blistering line drives. They just couldn't get him out.

• • •

That Pete Pirman story reminded me of when I was playing in the Tigers' organization. When I got my contract for my third year of ball, I recall being disappointed that I was sent a contract for Class A ball, not AA. I spoke with Hoot Evers, who was the gruff head of player development.

"Mr. Evers," I remember saying, "I'm just curious … how far do you

think I'm going to go in this game?" It was a question that was rarely asked by a minor leaguer, but hey, I figured, I was twenty-three or so, and I wanted to get a sense of how the front office viewed me.

Evers thought for a moment, and then said, "Honestly, we see you as perhaps making it to the show as a utility infielder."

Instead of being thrilled of being looked upon some one who might actually get to the big leagues, I was angered. "A utility infielder?" I asked.

"Yes. You see, we have a youngster in Rookie ball that we like an awful lot as a second baseman."

"Rookie ball?"

"Yes, we think this Lou Whitaker has a real chance to become a star second baseman for us."

Again, understand this was 1975. Whitaker was just another kid in the low minors. Or at least that's how I viewed him.

I gathered up my courage. "Well, Mr. Evers" I said. "With all due respect, I've seen Whitaker play in spring training, and I don't think he can carry my jock."

Evers laughed and said, "Well, thank you for your evaluation, Rick, but we'll see how things develop."

And just as Curtis Granderson has become a star for the Tigers, so did Lou Whitaker. For about twenty years at second base.

July 22, 2006
Kalamazoo, Michigan

Same story tonight. Another loss. It appears that our entire team is slumping. We went from the hottest hitting team in the league to the coldest in no time. Myself included. I just need to relax, keep playing good defense, and work my way out of this minor slump one day at a time. I'm sure I'm pressing too hard to make a good impression, and as a result I'm not waiting long enough on the pitch. It's a common problem and I'm sure I'll be able to correct it.

• • •

Remember those discussions about making adjustments at the plate? That's what John has to keep on doing. I don't care what league you play in—whether at the big league level or in Rookie ball, it's always a game of continuous adjustments.

Sunday July 23, 2006
Kalamazoo, Michigan
Tonight was yet another tough loss for the Kings. That's five losses in a row now, if you're counting. The entire team is having a rough time getting anything started offensively. I had a hit tonight, and hopefully that'll serve as a starting point for me to break out and start ripping again. When this type of thing happens, I know from experience that it's important for me not to try to overdo it, but rather to just take it slow and get one hit at a time. Sometimes I try to do too much, when in fact I should just stay within myself and play my game.

Defensively, I'm doing fine. I'm making all the routine plays at shortstop, and occasionally making an outstanding one. But offensively, this is hard to figure. Apparently the Kings are known in the league for being one of the stronger offensive powerhouses, but right now nobody is hitting well. As for me, I'm hovering around the .270 mark.

Off the field, my living situation with my host family is a lot different than what I was accustomed to in North Shore and Tucson. This is the first time I have ever lived with another family in this kind of setting. As mentioned before, the Greens live about thirty to forty minutes down the highway in a cozy farmhouse surrounded by about twenty acres of corn. They have the barn, the silo, the huge tractors and everything else that one might hope to find on a typical farm in Michigan.

And that's the problem—it's a farm! There's no Internet, no cable television, no DVD player, limited cell phone service, no air conditioning, and no restaurants within walking distance to go to for some late night grub. For a relatively spoiled kid like myself who was raised in the suburbs of New York City, I feel like I've stepped back into a quieter, gentler era. Still, the Greens are extremely nice to me and take great care of me even though I think we all know that it is a slightly bizarre arrangement.

I live in a small room up in their attic in a tight double bed that my feet hang off of. There is one light, a fan, and only two electrical outlets, which means that I could charge my cell phone with in the light or with a breeze, but not both. I also feel badly when I occasionally get a late dinner with my teammates after games in Kalamazoo and then don't return to the Greens' until around two or three in the morning. In order to get to the attic I have to walk through their bedroom, and I think I wake them up almost every night. I have to walk through their bedroom to get to the bathroom, too. That turned out to be rather awkward for me the night I accidentally clogged their toilet—the only toilet in the house.

July 24, 2006
Rockford, Illinois

I got a call today from my ex-girlfriend from college, who said that she came home from her world trip early because she was sad and lonely and missed me. I didn't take her all that seriously on the phone because I haven't really been thinking about her for quite some time. But through my experience as a pro ballplayer I have myself become familiar with the loneliness of being on the road and away from familiar surroundings. I guess we'll see if she actually wants to come out to Michigan to visit me. That might mean something more than a phone call. But I'm not holding my breath.

In the meantime, we have a game tonight and I have to continue to plug away and keep hitting the ball hard. I could very well be hitting over .300 right now, but it seems like every time I hit a hard line drive it's gobbled up by a diving outfielder. I just have to keep seeing the ball and putting it in play. Just hit the ball hard. That's all I can control. What happens to it after I hit it is up to fate.

In any event, I took another 0-for-3 tonight. I hit the ball hard twice out of three times, though, one being a line out to shortstop. I think I need to sit back and continue to practice trusting my hands, but I haven't seemed to find my rhythm just quite yet. It's very easy to get down on yourself and get frustrated, but the best way to get out of a tough time at the plate is to stay positive and keep working hard. That seems like the only solution I have. Or at least it's the only solution I can come up with right now.

My old college roommate, Chris Catizone, lives near Rockford, Illinois, so he came to the game tonight and we had dinner afterwards. It was great to see him and to catch up on all the stories that I missed while I was away playing ball. It sounded like everyone had a real fun time spring semester at school while I was balling it up. Sometimes I lament the fact that I won't have a senior spring semester in college, but I wouldn't trade this baseball experience for anything in the world, despite its ups and downs.

We're currently on a nine day road trip, which is taking us all over Michigan, Illinois, and Missouri. This is our longest road trip of the season and definitely the longest road trip of my short career. I must confess that it's certainly different to be living in and out of hotels every three days and going on long bus rides in the middle of the night as we travel from one town to the next. Some of the longer drives begin after the game and last nine or ten hours; as a result, we don't arrive at our destination until the next morning. Those drives are especially tough when you are a rookie (like me) because you have to share a seat with someone else and it's very hard to get comfortable. I did discover that there's a little spot way in the back of the bus where you can lay down and get somewhat comfortable, though. It is not great, but it's better than being cramped in a seat next to a snoring teammate.

Another thing about my new team is that everyone loves to wager on stupid nonsense, just to help pass the time. On every bus ride we'll have random lotteries, and every game the pitchers will pick a batter to have a good game and they'll earn money from that if they pick correctly. In fact, we were losing so many games in a row that even Fran Riordan said that he would give fifty dollars to a pitcher who had a good start or a good relief appearance, and to any batter who had any two-out RBIs in the upcoming game. That's a pretty nice incentive if you ask me. I think only the pitcher actually got paid, though, because I know I had some two-out RBIs and I didn't see any cash.

By the way, this is one for the record books. One of my roommates on the road has two cell phones. One cell phone is for his girlfriend back at home, and the other is for all the girls he meets on the road. He seems to have girls in each town we travel to and they call him on his "special" line. Amazing.

This is an education I could never get at Harvard.

. . .

I'll say this about those long overnight bus rides. The average fan has no idea that ballplayers have to sleep on buses in order to get to the next town. Even when you're in your early twenties, it's hard to get any real rest or sleep on a bus.

In fact, I vividly recall that we would always make a dinner/ breakfast stop at one of the truck stops off the interstate. Sleepy-eyed ballplayers would straggle off the bus at two or three in the morning, sit at the counter, and have to decide whether to order a hamburger and fries for dinner or have a breakfast of eggs and cereal. In other words, dinner blended into breakfast.

But the bottom line was, no matter what you ordered, you had to eat.

Because once you got back on the bus, you most likely had another four or five hours to go before arriving at the next town, and the bus driver wasn't going to make any more stops. So if you missed that pit stop at two in the morning, you were going to be famished for the rest of the trip. And don't forget—you have a game coming up in twelve hours.

July 25, 2006
Rockford, Illinois

After a few recent contests in which it didn't seem like anything was dropping in for me, I finally had a game where everything did tonight. I went 3-for-4 with a walk, and the one out I made was a bullet that almost took the pitcher's glove off. All I have to do now is continue this pattern for the next forty games and I'll be very happy.

One feature of minor league ballparks is that they're all different in their own ways. For example, the Rockford facility appears to be brand-new, with a flashy big scoreboard in left field and nice blue seating in the grandstand. However, the actual infield itself is quite hard and rocky. Bad hops are a common occurrence here, and every ground ball poses the very real threat of smoking an unwitting infielder in the chops.

The Rockford dugouts are clean and new, but here's something different: the clubhouse was apparently just an afterthought, as it's located behind the outfield fence. I can only assume that the people who built the ballpark must have run out of money before the clubhouse was built. As a result, it's just a trailer. And of course, the showers don't work. Some of the guys were telling me that on a previous visit to Rockford, they had to play a double header in ninety-degree heat. When the second game was over, they had to hit the road for a ten-hour trip. Can you imagine what it must have been like to be on that bus? I mean, the guys didn't even have a place to shower.

Like all minor league franchises, all these ballparks hold various promotions to put people in the stands. There are Diamond Digs, Beer Batters, K-men, RBI guys, and other such nonsense that excite the crowd, and all of these promotions correlate to some kind of special deal on food or beer. Sometimes the gimmick is to pick on an opposing player; that is, if this visiting Kalamazoo King strikes out during this at-bat, then you're entitled to a free bag of popcorn or peanuts or whatever. I will say this: I've noticed that our player Ray Gill always seems to be the guy the other teams pick on, probably because he tends to strike out a lot. I haven't discussed this with him, but I imagine Ray's aware that he's become quite a popular fellow in these road ballparks.

. . .

It's true. Every minor league ballpark has its own "charm," for lack of a better word. I recall playing in Wausau, Wisconsin. It had been a beautiful sunny day and as the sun set, it was gorgeous. The problem was that the ballpark had been designed so that the setting sun was directly in centerfield, right in the batter's eyes.

I can personally attest to how difficult and dangerous this was. I know that in some ballparks they will actually call for a "sun delay" while the sunsets stop the game temporarily, just like a rain delay. But on this evening in 1974, the opposing pitcher, Jerry Garvin of the Wisconsin Rapids Twins, struck out something like six or seven of us in a row. Garvin was good, sure, but his success that day was due more to the fact that none of us could see the pitch coming out of the sun, which was right behind Garvin's back.

Then there was the time one of our pitchers was so angry for being taken out of a game in Charleston, South Carolina, that he went into the clubhouse and kicked the metallic wall so hard that the building collapsed. He wasn't hurt, but it sure was embarrassing.

July 26, 2006
Windy City, Illinois

We lost another game tonight and it's becoming clear to me that our pitchers are having a difficult time. We lost our top starter to injury and, unfortunately, our other pitchers just can't seem to keep the opposing batters off the bases. Even worse, the teams we are losing to aren't particularly good hitting teams, but they've been beating up on our pitchers quite consistently. This is, of course, not a good formula for winning.

After the game tonight, I felt like just going home, ordering a pizza and relaxing in my hotel room. However, some of the Kings' veterans called my room and told me it was time for me to come out with them. Apparently, they knew some local girls with cars and they took us to a local bar that had karaoke on Wednesday nights. We had a good time (even though the girls were a little weird) and I even sang some Prince on the karaoke stage. I think I did a pretty good job and showed some real enthusiasm, but my voice might not be well suited for Prince's vocals.

The Windy City ballpark is a little bit nicer than Rockford's. The infield is much softer and the overnight rain we got certainly helped keep it that way. The dugouts are spacious and the clubhouse is large, clean, and built underneath the stadium. Plus the showers worked. The air conditioning in the clubhouse was on at full blast, though, so it felt like walking into a refrigerator. We would be sweating in the one hundred degree weather and then come into what felt like a forty degree clubhouse. It was quite a shock to the system, but I guess it was better than no air conditioning at all.

Showers in the minor leagues come in many different styles and forms. Most of the time you are lucky if the clubhouse even has a shower. However, sometimes the showers that are provided are not so nice. Everyone wears shower shoes or sandals of some sort to avoid the disgusting floors of the showers. However, in Windy City I remember that the showers did not drain very well and once everyone started to shower the water level began to rise significantly. Dirty, disgusting water was up to the players' shins and even knees for those who showered at the very end. It was disgusting, and I'm glad I got to the showers early.

Many organizations encourage their players to remain clean-shaven and clean-cut. Therefore, many clubhouses have clippers and shavers that are available before or after the game. I believe that these shavers are meant for facial hair and head-hair, but sometimes certain players will shave their chests or more with the clippers. And tonight, I was treated to the unforgettable sight of our goofy pitcher, Dan Caldwell, making his special "chest-hair and peanut butter" sandwich.

Caldwell is the son of former major league pitcher, Mike Caldwell. Dan went to North Carolina State and was apparently on track to be a high draft choice out of high school as a centerfielder. He could run, hit, throw and pretty much do it all. But in his senior year of high school he broke his leg sliding into home plate and never really regained his speed. So he turned himself into a side-arm pitcher to keep playing, and he's enjoyed a lot of success in independent ball.

Now, I should point out that I'm a bit skeptical of most stories I'm told by guys in indy ball, because they're rarely backed up by facts. I do believe Caldwell, however, because I've seen the guy take batting practice. He's clearly a pure switch hitter who can drive the ball out of the ballpark from both sides of the plate more consistently than most of the regular hitters on our team. He has a truly amazing, natural swing.

Caldwell's goofy counterpart is Cooper Eddy. Eddy is from Iowa and had a stint with the Red Sox organization. He is known for his strange hair styles and his unusual fashion sense. Cooper's incredibly outgoing and is always looking to play pranks on his teammates. And not surprisingly, his number one target is Caldwell.

One popular clubhouse prank is the dumping of a bucket of ice cold water on someone while they are taking a shower. This prank needs to be carefully executed because one person has to hold the bucket of cold water while another turns off the victim's shower at the same time, so the full effect of the cold water is felt. Another common prank is putting baby powder in a napkin, tying the napkin shut with a rubber band, and then waiting for the person who has just finished showering to walk into the clubhouse still somewhat damp. Cooper will then throw the baby powder which goes "poof" all over the person and turns them completely white. This is known as "antiquing" someone, for obvious reasons.

The prank that Caldwell played the most was truly disgusting. He would make himself a peanut butter sandwich and then shave his chest hair. He would carefully gather up the shaved hair from his chest, and then he would neatly sprinkle it on the peanut butter sandwich. One time, he gave his specially prepared sandwich to Cooper Eddy.

Cooper, being a veteran of pranks, immediately knew something was up and checked out the sandwich before he took a bite. He saw the hair, put the sandwich back together, took a bite, laughed in Caldwell's face, and then threw the sandwich in the trash. I don't know if he swallowed that original bite, and to be honest, I don't want to know.

Pranks in the minor leagues are quite common and can at times be humbling. There is nothing worse than putting on your hat or your sliding shorts only to find out five minutes later that your groin or forehead is on fire because one of your teammates put some 'red-hot' or 'tiger balm' on your gear. These powders or gels are clear and don't begin to burn immediately, but once you start sweating they can be really painful and aggravating. The only solution is to run into the shower and turn the shower on as cold as it gets. That can pose a problem, of course, if you are fully dressed in uniform.

Pranks also take place on the long twelve-hour bus rides. Learning to cope with long bus rides becomes somewhat of a skill, and the more experienced players have learned how to handle these long trips. Some players like to watch the movies provided on the bus, while others prefer to play card games like poker, casino, spades, or pluck. Some like to text or call old girlfriends or listen to their iPods. However, the one constant among most players is that the best way to make the bus rides go faster is to make sure to stock up on plenty of beverages before the bus hits the road. Right after the game the bus will usually stop at a local gas station for the players to grab Gatorade, PowerBars, and other goodies. However, the most important beverage on the bus is beer. A few of the veterans like Brad Blackwell and Pete Pirman will secure the back of the bus and bring along an enormous cooler full of beer mostly for themselves. It is a great honor and privilege to be a younger guy and be offered a beer from the Pirman/Blackwell stash. It's kind of like being accepted into an elite fraternity.

Another way to pass the time on the bus is "playing the lottery." Caldwell will collect one dollar from every player, coach, reporter, and even the bus driver, and put everyone's name into a hat. Then, he picks names from the hat, calling out the names from the front of the bus on the intercom. The last name in the hat wins the forty dollars or so. It sounds lame, but when you're on a bus for fourteen hours this game is one of the most enjoyable games around.

July 27, 2006
Windy City, Illinois
Our game tonight at Windy City was rained out, so we'll play a double header tomorrow.

I'll say this about rain-outs. In independent ball, the front office will wait as long as they possibly can to call the game off, because they don't want to lose that revenue from the gate. But in organized ball, if it rains even a little bit, the game will be called off because management doesn't want to run the risk of injuring any of their big money players.

As a result, with the Kings we will wait and wait—from 2:00 P.M. until 10:00 P.M. if necessary—doing nothing until a final decision is made. It is, of course, during these lengthy rain delays in which many card games are played and many tarp slides take place.

I remember talking for a quite a while on the bench tonight with various teammates about the staff at many of these ballparks. We were watching the "Diamond Girls" take care of business in the stands during the rain delay. None of us could possibly imagine letting his daughter work in this kind of minor league environment. Of course these girls are all underage and they have to wear uniforms designed to show off their bodies. Now, we weren't complaining at all, but it just seems like an environment I wouldn't want my sister working in. A large amount of lonely, horny ballplayers and a bunch of attractive, underage girls makes for a dangerous combination. I can see how problems can develop.

• • •

Rainouts are a mixed blessing. On one hand, they give you a day off to heal from a variety of bumps and bruises, as well as a psychological day off from the daily stress of trying to get a hit or two. Unlike the majors, where off-days are built into the schedule automatically, in the minors there are very few, if any, off-days. An off-day is considered a lost revenue day.

But waiting for a rain out to be called can be very tough. Time seems to stand still. You have to hang out in the clubhouse, because you never know whether the game is going to be called or not. You just can't sit at home.

Bottom line? It's boring.

July 28, 2006
Windy City, Illinois

We won both halves of our double header today against the Windy City Thunderbolts and left the ballpark around midnight for a six hour bus ride to St. Louis, Missouri. As noted before, the new guys (like me) have to share seats on the bus, and of course it's impossible to get any quality sleep or rest. When we arrived at the hotel at 5:00 A.M., I was so overtired that I couldn't get to sleep right away. It was bizarre. It took me a while to convince my body that it was time to try and sleep again. I recall studying biorhythms in college, about how the body sets its own timer. And I can't even imagine what I've done to that inner clock of mine, except to screw it up big time.

Oh yeah. I went 3-for-6 in the double header today with some nice plays at shortstop. A good day at the ballpark all around. It definitely made the six hour trek to Missouri a bit more bearable.

July 29, 2006
River City, Missouri

Can you believe it? We were rained out again in River City, which a suburb of St. Louis. Once again we had to wait for hours in the clubhouse until the final decision was made not to play.

The rain-out did give me plenty of time to scout out the ballpark here, which is beautiful, except for the clubhouses. The locker rooms are literally trailers that we all have to squeeze into, with old broken lockers and chairs and no showers. We didn't even have any laundry machines, so we had to wear our dirty clothes from yesterday's games. I can't understand how they can spend millions of dollars on these stadiums, make them beautiful, and then not have enough money to build nice clubhouses. I guess the only people the minor league owners care about keeping comfortable are the paying customers.

July 30, 2006
River City, Missouri

Yesterday's rain-out meant a double header today at River City. We always play two seven-inning games on double header days instead of the standard nine-inning game. There was a Diamond Dig promotion slated for last night, so that was pushed back to tonight as well. Here's how it works: some local jeweler donates a nice diamond ring or bracelet or something of value, and it's buried somewhere in the infield. At the appropriate moment, eager fans are dispatched to find the loot. I didn't know what to expect at first, but I have to admit that it was really funny seeing a bunch of middle-aged women armed with spoons digging up the infield looking for buried treasure. It was minor league baseball at its very best.

This road trip hasn't been too bad overall, though we picked up three new pitchers along the way. That means some of our other pitchers will most likely be getting released when we get back to

Kalamazoo. It also means that I'm now sharing a hotel room with two guys instead of just outfielder Jared Johnson, as you can now add pitcher Eli Rose to our rooming mix.

There's a fancy seafood grille next to the hotel where we're staying, and some teammates and I went down to get the Sunday brunch. However, when my two roommates found out it would cost about twenty bucks they bailed on me, noting that the fare was a bit steep. I decided I wanted a good breakfast, so I ate in the grille all by myself.

The waitress who had seen the other guys get up from the table and leave felt badly for me that I was eating by myself and, much to my surprise, gave me my brunch for free. She then left a note instead of the check saying, "Tell your friends what they missed for bailing on you. I'm a cool waitress (smiley face)." That was a very nice thing for her to do.

But back to baseball. Unfortunately, the free brunch was the high point of my day. I racked up a 0-for-7 during the double header, and, to top things off, missed a key bunt sign.

In short, I now want to kill myself. I hate this game. Just when things seem to start going in the right direction, I suffer through a horrible day like this.

· · ·

One stifling Sunday afternoon in August in Charleston, South Carolina, I was playing a double header and working on an oh-fer day (as in 0-for-7). The darn thing is you try just as hard when you go for 0-for-7 as when you get two or three hits, but all that anyone cares about are the hits. Nobody cares that you tried hard. All that matters are the results.

In any event, I came up to bat late in the second game with the Charleston Pirates up by one run. This was a team that featured Willie Randolph, Mitchell Page, Lafayette Currance, Steve Nicosia, and Miguel Dilone—all of whom went onto have fine careers in the big leagues. In any event, I came to bat with the tying run on second base, and on an 0-2 count, I drilled a line drive towards left center. I remember being elated with the thought of at least driving in the tying run on this one hundred degree day, and salvaging a hit and a key RBI. I was thinking all of this just as the Charleston shortstop leapt high into the air and speared my line drive.

It was the third out. Rally over. Game over. No hit. No RBI. A complete 0-for-8 day.

It was a long, long hot bus ride back to Anderson.

July 31, 2006
River City, Missouri

About three hours into the drive home from River City our bus started to gently swerve back and forth across the interstate. We were the only vehicle on the road and I started to get a little worried that perhaps Leonard, our bus driver, was starting to nod off at the wheel. Curiously, no one else on the bus seemed to be too concerned, so I decided to ask some of the veterans if I should be worried or perhaps if I should try to keep our driver awake.

The older players in the back of the bus who were playing cards all looked up, gauged the swerving, and then said in unison, "Ah, c'mon, Wolffy ... Leonard's doing pretty good tonight. Usually he's much worse."

I looked at the guys with a face that must have shown shock and fear and they all started to laugh. "Look at the rookie! He still values his life!" They all started cracking up and continued to play cards while the bus continued to weave all over the road. I just sat back down in my seat, closed my eyes, and hoped that Leonard would "lock it up" and "keep 'er straight" for the next six hours.

Luckily, he did.

AUGUST

MY SECOND FAMILY, 800 MILES FROM HOME

August 1, 2006
Kalamazoo, Michigan
As I expected, when we got back to the clubhouse after our eight hour bus ride, sure enough one of our pitchers got released. How cruel is that? You're sitting on that stinking bus for eight hours, eager to get home, and then when you finally get there the manager calls you into his office and says, "Pack up your stuff—you're done here." That's a tough way to start one's day. Unfortunately, that's the reality of independent baseball.

Today we have a much needed and desired off-day. After that nerve-racking bus ride I think everyone just wants to go home and pass out for the rest of the week. I didn't arrive back at the farm until around 8:00 A.M. because I was so tired that I got lost on Michigan Route 43. But once I finally got to bed, I passed out until 3:00 P.M. or so.

August 3, 2006
Kalamazoo, Michigan
I slugged my first home run in the Frontier League tonight, against the Gateway Grizzlies. I turned on a low, inside fast ball and pounded it over the right centerfield fence into the party deck in the stadium.

I'll just say that I very much enjoyed trotting around the bases and I told myself that I would like to do it again sometime soon.

• • •

I was actually sitting at home, listening to the call of the Kings' game on the Internet. As the Kings' broadcaster, Mike Levine, described John's at-bat, I simply stopped what I was doing and listened with full attention. And when he said that the ball was "gone ... long gone for a Kings' home run," I ran into the kitchen and got Trish.

"John just hit a home run!" I screamed, "Come listen!"

And sure enough, the Kings broadcaster was describing the line shot John had just hit in full detail.

We couldn't have been happier for John. It was just a purely magical moment!

August 4, 2006
Kalamazoo, Michigan

We played Gateway again tonight, and sure enough I almost hit another ball out of the park. This time, a left-handed pitcher threw me a high, hanging curveball and I hammered it off the right-centerfield wall for a triple.

I missed putting it out of the ballpark by only a few feet. It would have been pretty cool to hit two home runs in consecutive games, but believe me, I was happy with the triple.

We had a midnight bus ride after the game tonight to Evansville, Indiana. Midnight bus rides are, of course, never fun, but since we have a whole bunch of new players I'm not really considered a "new" guy anymore; I now get two seats to myself. No more sharing. That may sound stupid and silly but when you have to sit in the same cramped spot for eight hours space is at a premium, and the more room you have to spread out, the better.

• • •

In 1974, when we took ten hour all-night bus rides to various Midwest League ballparks, some of my teammates would climb up into the overhead luggage above the seats in order to get some leg room. They'd take pillows with them, climb up, and stretch out up there.

It probably wasn't the safest thing to do, especially if they fell asleep and accidentally rolled out of the compartment and onto the seats and floor below. But I did notice that the guys who did this tended to do it all the time when we had all-nighters. So, at least for them, it worked.

August 5, 2006
Evansville, Indiana

We're playing a three-game series here in Evansville, the hometown of Yankee legend Don Mattingly. Fran Riordan told me that I'd have fun playing at this ballpark because it's very old and historic, not to mention that it always draws huge crowds. What he didn't tell me was this was the very same ballpark featured in the movie *A League of Their Own*. This field was where the Racine Belles used to play (or at least did so in the movie), and playing at the field feels like being a part of that movie, only without all the women ballplayers.

. . .

I don't seem to recall playing in any historic ballparks or ballparks made famous by Hollywood. But now that I think of it, I remember that the old ballpark in Charleston, South Carolina, had a most unusual feature in that when you got in the batter's box from the right side, the left field foul line was in perfect alignment with a stoplight suspended outside the ballpark at a nearby intersection. The umps would go over the ground rules and tell the managers that they (the umps) would use the hanging stoplight to help them gauge whether balls were fair or foul.

It was funny. I remember hitting a long drive down the line which hooked just foul, and the home plate ump called it foul. I said to him, "Was that ball really foul ... or did you call it foul simply because the stop light was red when the ball went past it? I mean, if the light had been green, would you have called it fair?"

He just smirked at me.

August 6, 2006
Evansville, Indiana
Tonight at the ballpark the home team had a special, between-innings feature known as the Zooperstars. In short, a few performers dress up as different zoo animals/famous players like Shark McGwire, Harry Canary, Clammy Sosa, and other baseball personalities. I must admit, it was pretty funny seeing Shark McGwire pretend to

eat one of our players, and also seeing them do some strange dances throughout the course of the game.

Unfortunately, those were the only laughs I got that night as I went 0-for-3.

On a different note, I've recently learned that our skipper, Fran Riordan, has had quite a history in professional baseball. Although he never played affiliated ball, he played for almost ten years in independent ball before becoming a field manager. He's in his early thirties and is still in good playing shape. I've been told that every once in a while he'll take batting practice and put on quite a show. He was a big power-hitter in his day and I'm sure he'd still be one of the best hitters in independent ball if he chose to keep playing.

Our pitching coach, Joe Thomas, is a former left-handed pitcher who played many years of affiliated ball. I believe he played as high as AA with both the Twins and Red Sox. He is truly one of the nicest and funniest guys that I've encountered in pro ball thus far. Some of the veterans bust Joe's chops, claiming that he doesn't swing his arms when he walks—like a gorilla or something. Joe usually laughs it off and is pretty quick at getting back at the other guys. The other thing about Joe is that he throws the best left-handed batting practice that I've ever seen. He could be a major league batting practice pitcher. I wish I could say the same for Fran. Fran's batting practice from the right side is sometimes frightening.

August 7, 2006
Evansville, Indiana
We had an early game today before our long bus ride back to Kalamazoo. We won the game, earning a sweep on the road, so spirits

were up on the bus. And it wasn't a midnight ride, so I actually had a chance to get a good night's sleep when I got back to the farm.

Unfortunately, the bus didn't get back home until 2:00 A.M. and when we did arrive back in the Kings' parking lot, I discovered that my car had a flat tire. Great—just great. I didn't feel like changing a flat at that hour so I decided to just pack it in and sleep in the Kings' clubhouse on one of the large couches. Maybe that wasn't the best decision I've ever made in my life, but it was better than worrying about changing a tire in the middle of the night.

The couch in the clubhouse was surprisingly comfortable, but I heard some creepy noises throughout the night that really started to worry me. I tried to fall asleep as quickly as possible, and eventually I managed to pass out. I was awoken in the morning around 9:00 A.M. by our assistant general manager, who looked at me as though I were a complete fool.

I think he was right.

August 8, 2006
Kalamazoo, Michigan
We played a home game versus first-place Chillicothe tonight, which meant I got to play against my buddies, Luke Bargainier and Adrian Cantu. Luke, Adrian, and I had been teammates on the Stamford Robins a couple of summers ago. Adrian was a star slugger at Lamar University, and Luke was also headed to Lamar after a stellar junior college career. But Luke decided to sign with the Astros' organization instead, played a couple of years for them, and was now playing for Chillicothe. It's amazing how small the world of pro baseball is.

Anyway, it was great fun to play against Luke and Adrian and to catch up with them while they're in town.

• • •

One of the great by-products of playing pro ball is that you really do make friends for life. Long after the final stats are put into the book, ballplayers tend to stay in touch with their teammates and competitors. It's like being part of a closed, tight-knit fraternity.

I finished playing pro ball in the mid-1970s. But during my two full years in the minors, I got to know players like Joe McIlvaine, Ron Leflore, Willie Randolph, Brian Doyle, Mike Hargrove, Jim Leyland, George Hart, Bryan Lambe, Gene Spatz, Greg Kuhl, Moe Hill, and dozens more that I could list here. Of course, some of these guys went on to become big league stars or even GMs. But at the time, we were all just Class A players, all trying to keep our hopes alive to keep playing ball and somehow survive.

Over the years, in the quirky way that life is, sometimes your paths intersect. McIlvaine went onto become the GM of the Mets and Padres. Jim Leyland, of course, always dreamed of becoming a major league manager, even though he never got to the bigs as a player. I got to work with Mike Hargrove when he was managing the Indians in the 90s and I was serving as the team's roving sports psychology coach. In other words, baseball may be a funny game, but it's a funny game in a small world.

August 9, 2006
Kalamazoo, Michigan

To me, playing for an indy team is somewhat like being cast in a reality television competition. That is, it's full of drama, stresses, and unexpected twists and turns. And by the end of the day, the weakest links are always being told, "goodbye."

For example, we signed a new outfielder just three days ago. He took a few rounds of batting practice yesterday and today, but he didn't exhibit a good swing. Sure enough, he was released after tonight's game.

That's it. Goodbye. Nice knowing you.

No one except for a few select players really have job security in independent ball. Every day you can check the transactions and see how many different players are getting released, traded, or signed. It's truly amazing, and at times frightening, how players just come and go.

That's really the main difference between affiliated baseball and independent baseball. Affiliated baseball is focused on finding young talent and developing that talent even though the young players may struggle at first. For example, a player hitting .180 in affiliated ball might live to see another season because he is young and the organization feels that he has a good approach and will get better in the next few years. On the other hand, a player hitting .180 in independent ball will inevitably be released unless he can produce some better numbers and do it fast.

With independent ball, winning is what puts fans in the stands and makes the ballclubs money. They don't care about developing talent. They care about immediate production. And that's a big, big difference from affiliated baseball. In fact, let me take a moment to give you a more detailed analysis—at least from my perspective—of how the minor league classifications break down these days.

For example, it's getting harder and harder to determine what each classification really means. As you know, in affiliated pro ball, the levels range from the major leagues to AAA, AA, high A, low A, short season A, and Rookie ball, theoretically in that order.

In the past, it used to be fairly easy to interpret how a player was progressing based on what level he was playing at. For example, if a player was in AAA he was really close to getting to the big leagues. However, in today's game the system doesn't really appear to work in the same way anymore. In fact, AAA has generally turned from being a breeding ground for up-and-coming prospects to more of a safe haven for ex-major leaguers who had good careers in the big leagues, are a bit older, but still want to keep playing. Most of the players in AAA probably won't make it back in the big leagues, but they can still make a good living playing there and can serve as an insurance policy should a major leaguer come down with an injury.

These days, the true young prospects and future superstars are found more often than not in AA. In fact, some of the best prospects will make the jump from AA straight to the big leagues and skip AAA entirely. Other exceptional prospects may jump from Class A straight to the big leagues.

However, being promoted from one level to the next is as difficult as getting drafted. As you might imagine, the jump from AA to the big leagues is huge. But the jump from Class A ball to AA might be even bigger. Here's what the veterans tell me: in AA, the pitchers have much more consistency. They all throw strikes, both with their fast ball and their breaking stuff. They rarely pitch themselves into trouble by issuing walks. Hitters in Class AA can all hit fastballs, even ones clocked at ninety miles per hour. They know that, and also know that the pitchers don't want to throw them fastballs for that very reason.

As noted, everyone in Class A ball wants to get to AA because that's where you become a major league prospect. But few players in A ball or below are legitimate prospects. Some guys are viewed as "organizational prospects" who the front office knows will never make it to the big leagues as players but are considered good people and good players who may one day become coaches or front office hires. Organizational prospects usually end up playing a number of years in A ball but never reach the AA plateau. That doesn't mean that one day they won't make it to the major leagues as a coach, though. A classic example would be Jim Leyland, who was a catcher in the low minors with the Tigers. Detroit didn't see Jim as a major league catcher, but they did value him as a potential coach or a manager. Today a three-time manager of the year at the major league level, Leyland has certainly lived up to the Tigers' evaluation.

There are two levels of Class A ball—high A and low A. For the most part these two levels are similar, with the players being a bit more polished in high A. In recent years, organizations have been putting a lot of their top pitching prospects in high A before they go on to AA, thereby skipping low A. Therefore, batters who do well in high A are almost certain to move up to AA because they've been facing the top pitching prospects in the country. Players who are placed in low A usually still have to prove themselves in high A before moving up to AA.

Finally, at the bottom of the ladder are the short season Class A teams like the Bristol White Sox. Many fans make the mistake of assuming that players in the short season teams must not be very good, which may have been true some time ago, but is not anymore.

There have been quite a few players who have gone straight to the big leagues from a short season team. Three who come to mind right away are pitchers Boone Logan (Chicago White Sox), Joe Smith (New York Mets), and Huston Street (Oakland Athletics). They all made the leap all the way from the "bottom" to the top. It is no surprise that these three players are pitchers. Pitchers with great stuff can advance up the ladder quickly if they can consistently locate their pitches and get outs. Some position players have been known to go straight to the big leagues out of high school, college or after a year in the minor leagues, but this is very rare. Ozzie Smith only played sixty-eight games in the minors, but he was an outstanding player. John Olerud (Toronto Blue Jays) and Dave Winfield (San Diego Padres) both went straight to the big leagues out of college. The list continues, but the one ingredient all of these players share is exceptional talent. In recent years there haven't been too many position players that have been able to make this huge jump.

The most challenging part of Rookie ball is, well, getting out of Rookie ball. At the professional level everyone is good at playing the game. The key to getting out of Rookie ball is to find some way to differentiate yourself from all the other guys. Some guys have great speed, some have great power, some throw 100 miles per hour, others switch-hit, and some literally never misplay a ground ball. Others just seem to do everything well.

The bottom line is that getting out of Rookie ball is one of the toughest things to do in minor league baseball. But once you do get out, you have immediately added instant and noted value to yourself as a pro player.

August 10, 2006
Kalamazoo, Michigan
We lost another tough one to Chillicothe tonight, and our frustration as a team is mounting. If we don't start winning more games (and fast) Chillicothe is going to run away with this thing.

. . .

Traditionally, by mid-August, when every day brings soaring heat and humidity, everybody's nerves begin to fray. Pitchers' arms wilt; batters find their bats becoming heavier by the day. And to top it off, when the wins start to become fewer and fewer, it just brings out the worst in everybody.

There's no real cure for this kind of slump. You just hope for better luck, maybe even a rain-out, so you can get a day to rest. Otherwise, you just have to tough it out as best as you can.

August 11, 2006
Traverse City, Michigan
We're in Traverse City, Michigan, for a weekend series against the Beach Bums (yes, that's really the team's nickname).

Stephen Young is the second baseman for Traverse City, and he played at Princeton before he was drafted by the Detroit Tigers, so I know him fairly well. Like seemingly everybody else in this league, Young played a year or two in organized ball before being let go, and he's still chasing the dream here in indy ball. Steve's a good guy, and I've enjoyed chatting with him a few times on second base during the games. We'd talk about Ivy League baseball, which must seem like a different lifetime ago to Steve. It sure does to me.

By the way, Traverse City is also a beautiful place to play. It features a brand new ballpark right on the beach near Lake Michigan. We played in front of about 7,000 fans tonight, and it was great. The stadium design is very cool, also. Try to imagine this: the ballpark is designed as a fancy beach club, with cabanas and lounge chairs all around the park. Everything is done in a first-class way all the way down to the huge scoreboard and video screen. Yeah, it's different, but it's really a great place to play. From what I can tell, of all the towns and ballparks in the Frontier League, this seems to be the premier spot. A new and different ballpark in a great little town, with big crowds every night. It's no wonder Stephen Young seems so happy here.

August 12, 2006
Traverse City, Michigan
We lost a heart-breaker today to the Beach Bums.

We desperately needed to sweep this series against Traverse City, so this loss hurts us big time in the standings. Our starting pitching just can't seem to straighten itself out. We're giving up runs all over the place, and even worse, our hitters are pressing to try and score even more runs. Overall, it's a bad combination for everyone.

August 13, 2006
Traverse City, Michigan
We absolutely needed a win tonight, but once again Traverse City got the best of us and we lost. We're not mathematically eliminated

from the playoffs quite yet, but we need to get hot over the next few weeks if we are to make up the ground we've lost to Chillicothe and Traverse City. Unfortunately, I don't know if we have the pitching to win ten games in a row or something amazing like that, but who knows—maybe if our pitching comes up big we can make a late-season push.

August 15, 2006
Florence, Kentucky

Yesterday was our last off-day of the season, at least until the playoffs. I didn't do anything all that exciting except sleep in, do some laundry, lift some weights, and then pack up for our midnight bus ride to northern Kentucky.

I did want to go out to the tavern in town before the bus ride with some of the guys, but when I was packing up my stuff and getting ready to leave, my host family's dog, Snickers, ran out the door and took off into the 20 acres of corn they have in their back yard. I felt bad leaving them to search for their dog alone in the dark so I decided to stick around for a while and help them find him. After about an hour of walking around the corn fields Snickers was discovered in a local swamp, grabbed, and brought back to the house. I then took off and got on the midnight bus to Florence, Kentucky, which was scheduled to arrive at 5:30 A.M.

That's right. 5:30 A.M.

The hotel where we're staying in Florence is seriously run down and is the first hotel that really makes me think of crappy minor league living. The hotel looks nice enough in the front, but when you drive around back to where our rooms are, you see all the dirt, grime, holes in the walls, and strewn garbage all over the place. It's not exactly the Ritz Carlton.

. . .

These last couple of weeks sound like real torture. The Kings are seemingly in free fall, and regardless of what Fran Riordan does, there doesn't seem to be any change in their predicament. There are very few more difficult challenges in baseball than to be on a team that is spiraling out of the pennant race.

August 15, 2006
Florence, Kentucky

We played a night game tonight against the Florence Freedom. They are in fifth place in our division, behind us, but because our division is so strong, they're still a pretty good club. Our record is so good that we would be in first place by four games if we were in the other division, but instead we're in fourth place in our division, five games back from a playoff spot.

A strange thing happened during tonight's game. I wasn't feeling well all game, but in a long season that's a relatively common occurrence. During a long season you're forced to play through pain, fatigue, sickness, and just generally not feeling great. However, last night I was feeling unusually lousy and it got worse and worse every inning until I couldn't take it anymore in the top of the ninth.

My spot wasn't up in the lineup for another six batters and I could barely move. I was dizzy, had stomach cramps, and finally ran up to the trainer, told him that I was falling apart and to please tell the manager that he might have to pinch hit for me. Even worse, the visitors' clubhouse at the stadium in Florence is very far from the field and I couldn't make it all the way there. So I dashed up into the stands, in full uniform, and just ran into the public rest rooms in the ballpark. Not to be too graphic, but whatever it was that I ate that day came out of me in that moment in both directions. I don't think I need to give any more details. Suffice it to say that it was pretty disgusting.

After yet another disappointing loss, I slowly walked back to the clubhouse feeling a little better and I was very embarrassed to tell my teammates what had happened. Pete Pirman asked me how I was feeling and I told him that I felt nauseous and sick. I told him that it might be food poisoning or something. But when he heard that he just said, "Oh, food poisoning? I thought that you got sick watching us play." We did not play a very good game as a team, so maybe it was a combination of both.

• • •

Sometimes, the combination of fast food, crazy sleeping hours, life on the road, and pressure to perform all add up and shut down your digestive system. I don't think there's a pro player around who hasn't suffered the same malaise that John had to endure. I know I did on occasion, and as a result I always made it a point never to drink the local tap water from a restaurant or diner whenever we were on the road. There is just too much to risk, especially if the bathroom is a long sprint away from the dugout.

August 16, 2006
Florence, Kentucky

The ballpark here in Florence is nice, but the infield surface is not all that great. I've had to field several bad hops. The park's also got a strange design, because the clubhouse and locker rooms are a good walk from the field. The seats are also colored in bright yellow and bright red, with some blue ones mixed in as well. In the evening the seats are not all that noticed, but in the bright afternoon sun, the seats that are not filled are very in-your-face and bright. The yellow and red seats make the stadium seem even hotter than it actually is, and I don't like it. I much prefer dull colored seats. Oh well.

My roommate, Jared Johnson, has his girlfriend in town for the next few days, so they got a separate room in our hotel. Ballplayers have a lot of down time when we're not at the ballpark, and being away from home for so long can get lonely, especially when you don't have a roommate. It's nice to have someone to get breakfast and lunch with or just to watch television with. When you're by yourself it can get unusually quiet.

We also lost the game today, 1-0. I was 0-for-2 with two line drive outs and a walk. It's astonishing that we couldn't even scratch out one run. If we fall completely out of the playoff race, which is the direction we appear to be headed, this could be a very long August.

Also a medical note. During the game tonight I was playing shortstop and my good friend Kyle Kmiecik was playing second base. A ground ball was hit up the middle with a baserunner on second base. We both knew we had to knock the ball down in order to prevent the runner from scoring, even though we probably wouldn't get the out at first. So we were both running full speed towards the ball and we both dove for it at the same time. Kyle ended up catching the ball and saving the run but in doing so he dove on top of me and partially dislocated my shoulder.

I wanted to say something about my injured shoulder to Fran Riordan, but I couldn't say anything because we really didn't have anyone else who could play shortstop. But I also knew that my left shoulder was not good. Just lifting my glove was painful and swinging the bat, I sensed, would probably be torture. I'm one of those guys who doesn't want to come out of the lineup for any kind of reason, but I worried that if I remained in the game in the condition I was in I might do more harm than good. Still, I gutted it out and finished the game.

We'll see how my shoulder feels tomorrow.

August 17, 2006
Florence, Kentucky

Believe it or not, but after all of these losses I can't wait for our long bus ride back to Kalamazoo after tonight's game. The bus rides have turned into an entertaining combination of movie time, drinking time, card playing time, sleeping time, and hoping we don't crash the bus time. I've explored almost every random song on my iPod during these long and boring bus rides, but reading is nearly impossible because of how dark it is on the bus.

The last day of a road trip is always the worst because the hotel's housekeeping staff kicks you out of your room at the crack of dawn. It feels like you just put your head on the pillow when you hear them tapping on the door, telling you to get out so they can clean the room.

We get a little bit of meal money when we are on the road, but without a car, it's difficult to find good places to eat. I have been surviving on the delicious and extensive offerings of Domino's, Burger King, McDonald's, Wendy's, and all the other various fast food and pizza delivery options. I can't wait to get back home or even back to school so I can return to a halfway decent diet.

As we travel around the Midwest I have noticed that I enjoy eating a late breakfast before I head to the field. As my roommate will confirm, I have a tendency to order French toast, eggs, and bacon. It is one of my favorite morning meals and because I eat it so often I have had the opportunity to sample various types of French toast served from all sorts of restaurants. The restaurants all have different textures and different flavors which depend on the type of bread they use to make the French toast and how crispy they make it. So far I have enjoyed the French toast at Burger King, Shoney's, Mabel's, Cottage Café, Theo and Stacy's, Lume's, Bob Evans, Denny's, the Greens', and many more that I can't think of at the moment. But I'll say that it's the little diner in Kalamazoo—Theo and Stacy's—that takes the award for best French toast. They make the very best by far.

• • •

Just a quick culinary note. When I played in Anderson, South Carolina, I remember discovering the pure joy of eating fried chicken at a chain restaurant called Church's. It was so good and tasty that to this very day, I still crave it.

And then, the following year in Clinton, Iowa, they had an A & W Root Beer drive-in restaurant in the middle of town. Their cheeseburgers and root beer floats were outstanding!

It's amazing that I can recall these kinds of memories some three decades later.

August 18, 2006
Kalamazoo Michigan

I still have a slow leak in one of my tires, so you can imagine how much fun it will be to arrive back in Kalamazoo at six in the morning and not be able to drive home to my bed. Looks like another overnight stay in the Kalamazoo Chateau clubhouse. Even though the couch is comfortable, there are no blankets, it's freezing cold, and there are always random beeping noises in the middle of the night that either keep me awake or freak me out because I'm absolutely convinced someone (or something) is moving around somewhere in the shadows. I would much rather go back to my attic in the Greens' house and sleep there even though I don't fit in my bed and there is no television or air conditioning.

I'm not complaining, I just find my housing situation enjoyably comical.

Here's a note. When I signed my contract to come play for the Kalamazoo Kings, the general manager explained that they have a testing policy regarding steroids and drugs. I have not been tested yet, however, and I have not heard about anyone else being tested either. We were tested routinely with the White Sox, and I will say that some of the players in the independent leagues are built a bit differently than the guys I saw in affiliated ball. I have a feeling that the drug testing program may be a bit too expensive for the independent leagues to afford on a regular basis.

August 19, 2006
Kalamazoo, Michigan

We're in the midst of a six-game homestand, with the Rockford Riverhawks in town now. They're a scrappy team, and I though it was interesting to learn that their second baseman, Brad Dutton, is from Brisbane, Australia. I was chatting with him at second base during tonight's game and he told me that he lives in Australia in the off-season.

Sometimes I feel like *I'm* far from home here in Kalamazoo. I can't imagine how far from home Dutton must feel, especially after a tough game.

On another note, the Kings have been coming up with some interesting game promotions lately. For example, on Saturday nights they've been giving away a car. Usually it's just an old Buick or beat-up Saturn, but hell, it's still a free car.

They'll pick four or five "lucky" fans from the stands to come down to the infield where the car is parked, with all its doors open. Music is then played and the people have to walk around the car until the music stops. Once the music stops it becomes a mad scramble (like musical chairs) to find a seat in the car. During each round, one of the doors is closed and the competition gets more and more fierce. When it finally gets down to the last round (one door open, two people circling the car) you know something bad is going to happen. The people always get a little too serious and when the music stops all you see is aggressive pushing and shoving, fingers closed in the door, heads smashed, arms slammed, people fighting with each other on the seat in the car. It's just a mess.

It's like watching a train wreck. You know it's going to be gruesome, but you can't look away.

I just hope I never need a car that badly.

August 20, 2006
Kalamazoo, Michigan

Out of the blue, I decided to call Nick Leyva today to see how he's doing and to chat for a little while. We haven't spoken since I was released. Cuz was happy to hear from me and told me that he was getting updates on me from Josh Morgan and was glad to hear that I was doing well and having fun. He also told me to call him after the season is over to discuss the possibility of getting back into affiliated ball. He sounded like he could help me out because he has so many contacts in the world of baseball. I'll be sure to call him and I hope that we can work something out. Getting invited back into affiliated ball is definitely one of my off-season goals.

August 21, 2006
Kalamazoo, Michigan

We won the first game of our series against the Windy City Thunderbolts tonight. I noticed my friend from Princeton University, Adam Balkan, was released by this team and then picked up by the Evansville team, but unfortunately he didn't last very long over there and was released a week later by the Otters. Adam's a fine player and had a great college career at Princeton, but just like I did, he's getting a taste of what life in the minor leagues is all about.

I also noticed that an old friend from the White Sox, catcher Charlie Lisk, was picked up by the Windy City team and is playing well for them. Charlie was released in spring training by the Sox this past year and has since bounced around from the Marlins' organization to the Northern League and now to the Frontier League. We grabbed dinner after the game and laughed about all the different teams and organizations we have each played for over the past few months.

August 22, 2006
Kalamazoo, Michigan

We lost tonight's game to Windy City and I was given the night off. I made a few bad base-running blunders last night and I guess I'm being benched for messing up. Fran said that I wasn't being punished and that he just wanted to "mix things up" a little bit. Adam Leavitt played shortstop tonight in my place. Technically, he's the backup second baseman, but he does a good job bouncing around the middle infield.

I don't know if I really believe that but one of the things that's not really discussed too much in the open is the constant paranoia in minor league ball. Players are always wondering what their managers are thinking and how can they stay on the good side of their boss. Errors and batting slumps are part of the game, but the question is—how many errors and hitless games can you endure before you lose the support of the manager?

• • •

This is really the pits for John. It's late in the season, the team is dropping out of contention, and he's playing hurt with a bad shoulder. Clearly

Fran is evaluating John and his teammates as to who he wants to bring back for next year. There's no need to sugarcoat this: it's is a bad time to be hurting and not be in the lineup.

August 23, 2006
Kalamazoo, Michigan

Yet another horrible loss tonight. It is fairly safe to say that it would take some kind of baseball miracle for us to get back into the playoff race at this point. Our record isn't terrible, but we are not playing well as a team, whereas the teams ahead of us are playing great. I had the night off again tonight and was watching from the bench when our starting catcher hurt his side swinging too hard at a pitch. Trevor Eastman, our backup and bullpen catcher was put in the game, and we needed someone to catch in the bullpen. Because there are so few players on the roster, I was the only logical player to go down and catch, so I geared up and headed on down to the bullpen. As it would turn out, the Thunderbolts put up seven runs in one inning and knocked out four of our pitchers, so I was working hard in the bullpen catching and warming up our staff. I missed a few sliders and fastballs in the dirt, but I eventually got the hang of it as time went on. It was surprisingly fun for a night, but surely not something I would want to do every day. You've got to be nuts to be a catcher.

• • •

I'm glad that John was able to help out in the bullpen. But I'm doubly glad that he came to the realization that being a catcher is a very risky proposition. For all the bumps, bruises, and jolts that catchers are forced to endure on a daily basis, I personally would much prefer to play infield.

I'm happy that John feels the same way, even though they say that catching is the fastest route to the majors.

August 24, 2006
Washington, Pennsylvania

We arrived in Washington, Pennsylvania, early this morning around 7:00 or 8:00 A.M. It was a long bus ride, so when we finally arrived at the Red Roof Inn near the ballpark I hopped into bed and slept until 2:00 P.M. These bus rides are starting to get a little old and boring. They're somewhat fun for the first four hours or so, when we're watching movies and telling stories, but then you get tired and it's impossible to get comfortable. Your muscles start to get tight, cramp up, and all you want to do is find a bed—but you have to stay on the bus for another six hours. Torture.

The season is likely going to come down to the last few series and we'll need to win about nine games in a row to make the playoffs. It's not impossible, but I don't know if our pitching staff is deep enough to carry us through that many games without making too many costly mistakes. It's crucial that the team stays mentally focused through the next dozen games or so if we want to make the postseason.

August 25, 2006
Washington, Pennsylvania

I wasn't in the lineup again tonight and we got smoked by the Wild Things. They are a team built on speed and they do a very good job of getting on base and making other teams make mistakes. I asked my manager why I wasn't playing every day, since for the past week or so I've been sitting against righties and playing against lefties. Fran really didn't give me an explanation, only that he's going with his hunches.

I have a funny feeling that Fran might be trying to keep my at-bats under 150 so that I can qualify as a rookie again next year in this league. Second-year rookies are a hot commodity and that would make it easy for me to find a job again in this league or somewhere else if I needed to. At least, that's the positive spin I'm putting on this situation.

Unfortunately, my shoulder still hasn't rebounded back to full strength since that collision. Fran, who throws batting practice before the games, must be noticing that I'm not driving the ball into the gaps like I was two weeks ago. In truth, my shoulder just isn't supplying the power like it was before I got hurt.

• • •

Getting hurt is part of any ballplayer's everyday fear. But getting hit by a pitch, spiked on a pivot at second, or getting a strawberry on one's butt from sliding on hard dirt is just the price you pay. Ballplayers learn to live with these aches and pains and move on.

But it's a little different when your arm, shoulder or knee isn't working properly. Bumps and bruises are annoying, but you can play through them. When your shoulder isn't giving you enough strength or power, then you have a real concern.

Of course, players don't like to ask out of the lineup. Managers don't want to hear bad news, especially on a team that's struggling big time like the Kings are, especially when the roster is thin to begin with. But in talking with John, it's clear that his shoulder is not even close to being one hundred percent, and I'm sure Fran has noticed that as well. I wouldn't be surprised if John ends up being done for the season. If you can't swing the bat with real authority, then all you're really doing is hurting the team.

August 26 2006

Washington, Pennsylvania

Midnight bus ride back to Kalamazoo. Fran has been in a bad mood recently, and rightfully so. We just keep losing and losing. What had seemed to be a fairly strong club now has degenerated into a team with poor pitching and a lackluster offense. We're just marching toward the end now, as we have very little chance of making the playoffs.

At this point in the season everybody gets annoyed and irritated over the smallest things. It is a scary time of year because you never know who is going to freak out and get upset. The coaching staff, the front office people, even the other players are all depressed and just waiting for the season to end. It's a terrible way to spend the last few weeks of an otherwise good summer, but that's just the reality of our situation right now.

August 29, 2006
Kalamazoo, Michigan

We just finished a three-game homestand against Traverse City, and unfortunately, it's only been more of the same disappointment. What little pitching we have left is now in tatters, our hitting has all but dried up, and our desperate hopes of turning the last few weeks around are now gone. We're simply playing out the string now, and it's not a good feeling.

Of course, our failure is nobody's fault in particular. Baseball isn't a game of pointing fingers. It's just that we had some key injuries along the way, some hits didn't fall in for us, and because of that, things just didn't come together for us this year. You also have to give some credit to our opponents. Some of these teams seized on their strengths, such as aggressive base running, or a solid and dependable bullpen, and flat out beat us. In this game, you always feel worse when you didn't play up to your potential, but you feel differently when your opponent beats you by playing up to theirs.

● ● ●

This is the reality of all sporting endeavors. At the end of the long, hot season, only one team emerges as the champion. Everybody else goes home unhappy because they didn't win. That's just how it is in sports.

But John has learned a valuable lesson in his stint with the Kings. Because you play so many games in pro ball, it's the team that's the most consistent over time that more often than not ends up as the champion. There are very few exceptions to this rule in baseball. Teams which have

players who execute, make the plays in the field, get the timely hits, and
who throw strikes invariably end up in the winner's column.

August 30, 2006
O'Fallon, Missouri

As I feared, my shoulder still isn't getting better. When I take batting practice, I can no longer summon any kind of power behind the ball. I'm dragging the bat through the hitting zone and because of it I'm just not doing the team any good offensively.

As a result, I finally decided to suck it up and talk with Fran. I asked him to shut me down for the rest of the season. I hated like hell to make this request, especially because the team is struggling so badly, but deep down I know that I just can't get the job done in my current injured state. He must sense this as well, because he's been throwing batting practice and he must see that my power has suddenly disappeared.

Much to his credit, Fran understood entirely, and since we were no longer in the playoff hunt he agreed that it was fruitless to keep playing me. It was clear to him and to me that since I hurt my shoulder ten or so days ago, my batting average has plummeted. It's like going up to the plate with a rubber baseball bat. Even if I do hit the ball solidly, the ball just isn't going to go anywhere.

• • •

I know John well enough that the very last thing he'd ever want to do
is voluntarily take himself out of the lineup, but after listening to him
describe his loss of power, I had to agree with him that he was being

selfish if he continued to keep playing. Here was a player who just hit his first home run and triple in back-to-back games a few weeks ago, and had been cruising along at a .270 clip when he either dislocated or hyperextended his shoulder. Since that day, he hasn't been able to hit a single ball hard because he can't generate any bat speed.

If the Kings were still battling for a playoff spot, I might have asked John to keep fighting through the pain because even if he couldn't hit, he could at least help out on defense, or maybe put some bunts down for hits. But with Kalamazoo officially eliminated from the playoff chase, it seems silly to risk any more personal injury.

August 31, 2006
O'Fallon, Missouri

Here's something I hadn't seen before in baseball. While playing at River City, one of the Rascals' better hitters slid into home plate and didn't get up immediately. When he finally arose, he limped awkwardly off the field to the clubhouse.

We all just assumed he had hurt his leg or something, but we later learned that when he collided with our catcher at home plate, he ended up "having an accident" in his pants and had to leave the game. Now that's embarrassing, not to mention bizarre.

I just hope he had an extra pair of pants.

Also, River City doesn't have any showers in their trailers either, so imagine what it might have been like if this player had been on the visiting side and had to take that long bus ride home without showering.

On second thought, you're probably better off not imagining that.

SEVEN

SEPTEMBER

BACK TO SCHOOL?

September 4, 2006
Kalamazoo, Michigan

We played our last game of the season tonight, and my bittersweet month with the Kings has come to a close. I haven't played over the last few games because of my shoulder, and I must confess that I feel somewhat sheepish about it. But my shoulder definitely needs rest and rehab and I just can't contribute anything offensively in this condition.

As tired as I am, both physically and emotionally, from this long season, I'm still somewhat disappointed that it's coming to an end, though.

For the record, we went 1-and-2 against the league-leading Chillicothe Paints in our final series. It was a frustrating way to end the season, but before the last game, the Frontier League Commissioner, Bill Lee, was on hand to give out the league MVP award to none other than my good friend and teammate Ian Church.

Ian Church fully deserved the award, having had a stellar year. He hit better than .330 and smacked 31 home runs. I believe he hit ten home runs more than anyone else in the league.

After the game we had a team party at the stadium that started around midnight and went very late into the night. In truth, some guys were sad that the season was over but others were actually quite glad to be done with it since we had fallen out of playoff contention quite some time ago. When the players know that there's no chance of making the playoffs, it's hard to stay motivated.

We had plenty of beer at the party and everyone was on hand. I even had a chance to have a few beers with Bill Lee, the commissioner of the Frontier League—who happens to be a great guy. It was quite a scene under the ballpark lights: guys were driving around in golf carts, singing over the loudspeaker, hitting on the front office personnel, and telling stories from the long season we had just finished up. Everyone was trying their best to enjoy their last moments together as Kalamazoo Kings.

Everyone in baseball knows that rosters change dramatically in the off-season, so it's understood that this might be one of the last times we would ever see our good friends and teammates together. At around four or five in the morning I decided to get a ride home from Kyle Kmiecik and ended up passed out on his couch. The next morning I returned to my home with the Greens, packed up my stuff, said my goodbyes, and headed out on my twelve hour journey back to Armonk.

There were a few things that I wanted to learn from the Greens before I left, but I never was able to find a good time. For example, I wanted to learn how to ride the tractor, shoot different kinds of guns, and change the oil in my car. These were things that the Greens could do, but we never were on the same schedule. Despite the tight quarters, I became good friends with the Greens and I thank them for their kind hospitality.

I was only in Kalamazoo for about a month, but it felt like

a long, long time to me. I was fortunate enough to make what I expect to be some lasting friendships in my short stay with the Kings and I made sure to give those guys big hugs and to get their e-mail addresses and cell phone numbers so that I could make sure to keep in touch with them. Of course, on any team you can't really be best friends with everyone, but I made sure to give everyone a hand shake and wish them all the best of luck. Fran Riordan and Joe Thomas both gave me big hugs and we wished each other the best of luck in the future even though, deep down, it was kind of a bittersweet farewell. When you and your team go through a disappointing season, the goodbyes never seem to be as sincere as when you have a great season together. I guess that's one of the hard realities of professional sports.

September 5, 2006
Somewhere on the Interstate Heading East

As soon as the car was packed and cruising down the open road, it suddenly dawned upon me that I would only be home in Armonk for a day or so before I had to return to Cambridge for my last semester of college. I missed college quite a bit during my year away playing ball and I must confess that I'm very excited to be heading back, even though the majority of my friends and classmates have graduated and are no longer on campus.

This made me realize that I'll be living with another new crop of people—in fact, a whole new team. I'll be living with several members of the Harvard mens' ice hockey team this fall and although we know each other cordially, we have never been roommates. Now,

I'm sure to some folks the idea of living with a bunch of goon hockey players hardly seems ideal, but trust me—a semester living with nine hockey players and other friends will certainly be a fun experience for me.

Despite being excited about meeting my new roommates, I've also begun to reflect on the completed season and my very unorthodox first year of professional baseball. The first thought I had was, "Do I even want to play again next year?" I mean, I had a pretty unusual summer full of ups and downs. I have grown a lot as a person because of the experiences, but is the game still fun?

After thinking about it for a long, long time on the interstate heading home, I decided that I do still love to play baseball and that I definitely want to play again next year. Now, that's easier said than done. I don't know where it will be, but I'm eager to give pro ball another shot.

In truth, at this stage in my career, I can look in a mirror with a smile and accept the fact that I may never make it to the big leagues. For many players, that is a very difficult thing to come to grips with, but I'm okay with it. I'm proud of myself for being able to play this game professionally, even if it's at a low A or independent level, and I know that I'll always love this game, even if I never make it to "the show."

There is another side of this coin, too—as in, why is a kid with a Harvard education still pursuing a career in minor league baseball? When is it time to "grow up" and get a real career? The truth is, I don't know. All I know is that I just can't imagine my life without sports. I remind myself that I was a hard-core baseball player long before I was a Harvard graduate and I hope that one day I can somehow combine my education and sports background into something I will enjoy doing off the field.

Evaluating my first season from a statistical perspective, let's see. They did actually keep game stats in extended spring training, and I believe I was hitting .296 in well over one hundred at-bats in Tucson before we broke camp for Bristol. I also recall having a good number of RBIs and stolen bases, plus I only made one error at second base the whole time I was out there. All in all, I had a solid, if not extraordinary, extended spring. And then, before I hurt my shoulder in Kalamazoo, I was hitting around .270 with a double, triple, and a homerun in about sixty at-bats. After the injury my average dropped to .207, though, mostly because I lost the ability to drive the ball with any authority. It was a terrible way for me to end my first season in pro ball.

Everything was going so well for me in Kalamazoo. I was hitting consistently and playing solid defense at shortstop, and when the injury happened, I was just furious with the world. After a tumultuous spring and summer, I finally had landed a starting job. I was doing well and earning my keep. All my hard work was starting to pay off, and getting injured at the end of the year served to sour all the positive effort that I had put into the season somewhat. It just didn't seem fair, but I guess that's why they say there's always next year.

Looking ahead, I just hope that I can still keep a job in pro ball. The reality of minor league baseball is that it helps quite a bit to have some decent stats to put on your baseball resume when you contact new teams over the winter. These days, in the era of *Moneyball* and laptop scouting, a player's stats brand him more than ever. But the problem—at least for real baseball people—is that stats can be misleading. When you get only one hundred at-bats, a couple of bloop hits here and there, a couple of line drives that aren't caught—your batting average quickly goes from a so-so .240 to a stellar .290. That's just the way it is in baseball.

The truth is that the ballplayers themselves know the difference. When you watch your teammates day after day in batting practice and in games, you gradually get a full sense of which guys really punish the ball on a routine basis, and which guys are just hoping for a slap hit here and there. As a player, you don't need to check out the stats; you know which guys are prospects and which guys are suspects from what you see with your own eyes.

That being said, I came out of extended spring training having put up good, solid numbers. Everybody recognized that. For me, it solidified my sense of self-confidence that I can make the plays, hit a ninety plus mile-per-hour pitch on a line, and run the bases with skill. Those same skills carried me right through into Kalamazoo, where I was doing great until I injured my shoulder.

Above all, I know that, whatever the future may bring, I acquitted myself as a pro ballplayer. Remember, my dream ever since I was a little kid was to someday play pro ball. Well, that dream came true. And for that opportunity, I'll be eternally grateful.

• • •

I explained to John a long time ago that while the dream of playing pro ball is a wonderful and romantic fantasy for millions of aspiring ballplayers, the harsh reality is that minor league ball is a demanding, difficult, and at times, brutal way of trying to make a living. Ballplayers get cut, seemingly for no reason at all. Others just give up, pack up their bags, and go home. Injuries are commonplace. New signees arrive unannounced, oftentimes to take your job in the starting lineup.

Plus there are the games themselves. Long, long road trips. Lousy rooming accommodations. Bad food. And the ease with which you can slide into a devastating batting slump before you know it. No matter how much you may try to will yourself to get a hit, it just isn't that easy. Look, if you can, at the stats of any minor league team in class A ball. You'll be stunned and amazed at how many of these kids hit less than .200 for the year. Also look at the infielders and how many errors they commit. You'll be astonished.

But despite all of these hardships, it's still a rare, rare achievement to become a pro ballplayer. And as I've told John, no matter where you go or what you do for the rest of your life, you will never, ever, forget how special it was to have been a pro.

Very few of us ever see our dreams come true. For John—and myself—we have been doubly blessed.

EPILOGUE

Fall 2006
Cambridge, Massachusetts

I'm now back in school, fully transformed into a student again and finishing up my last semester here at Harvard. As noted before, I'm living with a bunch of hockey players, which is great, since most of them want to finish up in school and then go out and chase their own professional dreams, just as I have.

In terms of next spring, I've decided that I definitely want to get back into affiliated baseball. Indy ball was fine, but ultimately for those teams, it's all about winning—and I still want to be viewed more as a developing prospect. As a result, I'm working the phones and e-mails on a daily basis, in the fervent hope that some kindly scout or generous front office person somewhere will give me another chance.

But so far, though, no luck. It's just as competitive as ever to get signed these days, and again, with everybody in baseball being online, it's too easy to check out my stats and simply say, "Well, this Wolff is a college kid, and his numbers weren't outstanding, so why should we give him a contract when there are other ballplayers who haven't had a chance yet?"

I fully understand and accept that, but it doesn't deter me from making the rounds. Some of the baseball front office people take my calls, are friendly over the phone, and say that they'll see what they can do. Others, though, are gruff, and basically hang up on me. And others I leave voicemails that are never replied to.

As a result, I'm caught in a kind of baseball purgatory. That is, I feel that my skills have improved dramatically over the past year, and that I'm now ready to play the best baseball of my life. But I can't find a job in affiliated ball. I've even offered to pay my way down to spring training, or to go to tryout camps in Florida or Arizona, but alas, no dice. As a result, I keep working every day on my swing, my fielding, and my running, but deep in the back of my mind I know that this may be all for naught—that the clock is ticking on my career, and that time is running out.

But that's okay. I still hope for that call saying, "Sure, John, come on down to spring training," but even if it doesn't come, I'll still love the game and be grateful for the lessons it has taught me. The game is part of who I am, and has been so for as long as I can remember.

I'm a ballplayer—a pro ballplayer. And in the end, the realization of that dream should be enough for a lifetime.

EDITOR'S NOTE

In January 2007, John got a call and worked out for the New York Mets' regional scout Larry Izzo. A veteran scout, Izzo had seen John play several years ago during the summer and apparently liked John enough to ask him to fill out a follow-up card for him. Now that John is a free agent, he asked Larry to take a look and see what he thought. Thanks to a good rehab program at the Harvard strength and conditioning center, John's injured shoulder from last August in Kalamazoo had sufficiently healed during the fall semester; he had now returned to full strength again.

Izzo worked John out at an indoor baseball facility on Long Island and gave a glowing report to the Mets' front office, and within days, John signed a contract to report to the Mets' minor league facility for spring training in March 2007.

John was overjoyed.

His dream continues.

WHERE ARE THEY NOW?

As noted, the one constant in pro baseball is change. And a lot has happened since 2006. Here's a brief recap of some of my buddies from that year and what happened to them in 2007:

Casey Baker played the 2006 season with the Kalamazoo Kings. He surpassed the league's age limit and decided to retire. Status: Retired.

Adam Balkan played the 2006 season with the Windy City Thunderbolts and the Evansville Otters. He played in the Can-Am League for the 2007 season. Status: Active.

Luke Bargainier played the 2006 season with the Chillicothe Paints and was traded in the off-season to the Bradenton Juice of the South Coast League. Status: Active.

Jojo Batten was drafted in the thirty-fifth round by the Arizona Diamondbacks in the 2004 draft. He played the 2007 season in Yakima (short season A). Status: Active.

Brad Blackwell was drafted by the New York Yankees in the twelfth round in 2003. He played the 2006 season with the Kalamazoo Kings. Status: Active.

Chris Brennan was signed as an undrafted free agent by the White Sox in 2005. He played two seasons in Great Falls and decided to retire. Status: Retired.

Dan Caldwell played the 2006 and 2007 seasons with the Kalamazoo Kings. Status: Active.

Adrian Cantu played the 2006 and 2007 seasons with the Chillicothe Paints. Status: Active.

Justin Carroll played the 2006 season with the Kalamazoo Kings. He was signed by the American Association for the 2007 season. Status: Active.

Marcos Causey was drafted by the White Sox in the thirty-fifth round of the 2005 draft. He was drafted out of South Florida Community College and played two years in Bristol. He was released after the 2006 season. Status: Released/Retired.

Ian Church played the 2006 season with the Kalamazoo Kings and was the Frontier League MVP. Signed by the St. Louis Cardinals and played the 2007 season in the Florida State League (high A). Status: Active.

Marquise Cody was signed by the White Sox as an undrafted free agent in 2006. He was assigned to Bristol for the 2006 season but was released halfway through. He decided to retire. Status: Released/Retired.

Kyle Collina was signed as an undrafted free agent by the Cleveland Indians out of Lehigh University. He played the 2007 season with the Kinston Indians (high A). Status: Active.

Lester Contreras was drafted in the fourteenth round by the Arizona Diamondbacks in the 2004 draft. Played the 2006 season with the Yakima Bears and was released in the off-season. Status: Released.

Vic Davilla went from being the premier hitter for the North Shore Spirit to being the manager of the team.

Mike DeCarlo was signed by the Arizona Diamondbacks out the College of William and Mary. He played two years with the Diamondbacks and had a call-up to AAA. In 2006, he spent the year at Yakima (short season A). Status: Active.

Matt Dugan was signed as an undrafted free agent by the White Sox in 2006. He received an invite to spring training but was released during camp. Status: Released/ Retired.

Brad Dutton played the 2006 and 2007 seasons in Rockford. Status: Active.

Trevor Eastman played the 2006 and 2007 seasons with the Kalamazoo Kings. Status: Active.

Cooper Eddy played the 2006 and 2007 seasons with the Kalamazoo Kings. Status: Active.

Justin Edwards was selected in the third round of the 2006 draft by the White Sox. He played the 2007 season with Kannapolis. Status: Active.

Matt Enuco was drafted in the thirty-sixth round by the White Sox in the 2006 draft. Played the 2006 season in Bristol and was released in the spring training 2007. Status: Released/Retired.

Enrique Escolano was selected by the White Sox in the thirty-eighth round in the 2005 draft. He played the 2006 season in Bristol and was released in extended spring in 2007. Status: Released.

Jeury Espinal was signed as an undrafted free agent by the White Sox in 2006 out of the Dominican Republic. He was released in spring training in 2007 after playing one season in Bristol. Status: Released.

Raleigh Evans was a twenty-first round pick by the White Sox in the 2005 draft out of Lake City Community College. He played two seasons in Bristol and was released in the middle of the 2006 season. Status: Released/Retired.

Zak Farkes was drafted in the thirty-ninth round by the Boston Red Sox out of Harvard in 2004. In 2007 he played for the Lancaster Jethawks (high A) in the California League. Status: Active.

Jordan Foster played the 2006 and 2007 seasons in the American Association for Fort Worth. Status: Active.

Stefan Gartrell was selected in the thirty-first round of the 2006 draft by the White Sox. He played the 2007 season in Kannapolis (A). Status: Active.

Kent Gerst – was selected in the eighth round of the 2006 draft by the White Sox. He played the 2007 season in Bristol. Status: Active.

Trey Hendricks – was drafted in the twenty-fourth round by the Diamondbacks out of Harvard in 2004. He played a few years with the Diamondbacks and reached the high A level before being released after the 2006 season. He signed a contract with the Frontier League for the 2007 season. Status: Active.

Jake Jean – was signed as an undrafted free agent by the White Sox. He played the 2007 season in Great Falls. Status: Active.

Brandon Johnson – was a forty-fourth round pick by the White Sox in the 2003 draft. He attended Crowder College and has progressed up the ladder. He played in Bristol in 2004, Great Falls in 2005, Kannapolis in 2006, and Winston-Salem in 2007. Status: Active.

Jared Johnson – played the 2006 season with the Kalamazoo Kings and was released in the off-season. Status: Released/Retired.

Josh Klimkiewicz – played the 2006 season in the American Association with El Paso, then decided to retire. Status: Retired.

Kyle Kmiecik – played the 2006 and 2007 seasons with the Kalamazoo Kings. Status: Active.

Charlie Lisk – is currently playing in the San Diego Padres' organization at Lake Elsinore (high A). Status: Active.

Donny Lucy – was a second round pick by the White Sox in 2004 out of Stanford University. He continues to be a top catching prospect for the White Sox. He played the 2006 season with the Birmingham Barons (AA) and the 2007 season with the Charlotte Knights (AAA). Status: Active.

Scott Madsen – was signed as an undrafted free agent by the White Sox in 2006. He played the 2007 season in Kannapolis (A). Status: Active.

Anthony Manuel – was selected in the forty-fifth round by the New York Mets in 2005. He played the 2006 season in Hagerstown (A). He decided to retire during spring training 2007. Status: Retired.

Ryan McCarthy – was a ninth round draft choice out of UCLA and has played a number of years in the White Sox organization. In 2007 he played in the Carolina League (high A) for the Winstom-Salem Warthogs. Status: Active.

Andy Mead – was drafted in the fortieth round by the White Sox in the 2006 draft. He played the 2007 season in Great Falls. Status: Active.

Josh Morgan – was drafted by the White Sox in the twentieth round in 2005. He is one of the few players to be drafted four times in his career. He was drafted by the Chicago Cubs, the Kansas City Royals, and twice by the Chicago White Sox. He was drafted out of the University of South Alabama and played two years in Bristol before having labrum surgery. He rehabbed in extended spring training and was assigned to Great Falls for the 2007 season. Status: Active.

Tim Murphey – was drafted in the seventh round by the White Sox in 2004 out of high school in Georgia. He was released by the White Sox in 2007 and finished the season playing for the New Jersey Jackals of the Can-Am League. Status: Active.

Matt Nachreiner – was drafted by the White Sox in the fifth round in 2003 out of high school in Texas. He asked for his release after spring training in 2006, received his release, and retired. Status: Released/Retired.

Pete Pirman – played the 2006 season with the Kalamazoo Kings of the Frontier League. He surpassed the age limit for that league (twenty-seven) and was signed by the Northern League. Status: Active.

J.D. Reininger – played the 2006 season with the North Shore Spirit and was signed by the Washington Nationals. He played the 2007 season in Hagerstown in the South Atlantic League (A). Status: Active.

Manny Rodriguez – was signed by the White Sox in 2000 out of Panama. He played the 2006 season in Kannapolis and was then released. Status: Released/Retired.

Eli Rose – played the 2006 season with the Kalamazoo Kings and was released in the off-season. Status: Released/Retired.

Chris Rowan – played the 2006 season with the North Shore Spirit and decided to retire in the off-season. Status: Retired.

Dustin Shafer - was a forty-third round pick of the White Sox in 2003 and played a couple of years in Bristol for the organization before he was released in spring training 2006. Status: Released/Retired.

Matt Sharp – was signed as an undrafted free agent by the White Sox in 2005. He played two years in Great Falls, Montana. In 2007, he played in Kannapolis (A) and Winston-Salem (high A). He attended UCLA. Status: Active.

Colt Smith – was signed as an undrafted free agent by the White Sox and played Bristol. He was released in the off-season. Status: Released.

Sean Smith – was a fifteenth round pick by the Pittsburgh Pirates in 2000. He was selected by the White Sox in the Rule 5 minor league draft in 2004. He played the 2006 season in Winston-Salem (high A) and played the 2007 season in AA with the Birmingham Barons. Status: Active.

Steve Squires – was a forty-ninth round pick in the 2005 draft by the White Sox. He was released in spring training 2006 after playing the previous summer in Bristol. He ended up signing with the Kalamazoo Kings in late August. He was released by the Kings at the end of the season. Status: Released/Retired.

Travis Tully – was a twenty-first round pick by the Arizona Diamondbacks in 2005 out of the University of Houston. He played the 2006 season in Yakima (short season A) and was released. Status: Released/Retired.

Justin Upton – was the first overall pick in the 2005 draft by the Arizona Diamondbacks. He played the 2006 season for the South Bend Silverhawks (A) after being in extended spring for a short period of time. In 2007 he started off in high A but was then called up to the major leagues. Status: Active.

Balthazar Valdez –played the 2006 season in Bristol and was released in the off-season. Status: Released.

Nick Walters – was drafted by the White Sox in the thirty-first round in 2004. He played two seasons with the White Sox and was released. In 2007 he was signed by the Oakland Athletics and played the 2007 season in Stockton (high A). Status: Active.

Alex Trezza – played the 2006 season with the North Shore Spirit and was signed by the Colorado Rockies. He was released by the Rockies in spring training 2007. He re-signed with the North Shore Spirit for the 2007 season. Status: Active.

Alex Woodson – was selected in the sixteenth round by the White Sox in 2005. He played two seasons in Bristol and then played the 2007 season in Great Falls, Montana. Status: Active.

Stephen Young – played the 2006 and 2007 seasons with the Traverse City Beach Bums. Status: Active.

ACKNOWLEDGMENTS

On the baseball side ...

There are literally dozens of people who helped me make my dream come true, and I fear that I might leave some names out. Forgive me if I do that, because I am indebted to all of you.

Dan Gray, Charlie Conway, Mike DeAngelo, Craig Fitzgerald, Dan Perlmutter, Tim Mullen, Mark Kilgallon, Angelo Centrone, Anthony Yacco, Scott Lucas, Joe Stancati, Phil Schnorr, Vic Candelaria, Eric Brown, Matt Hyde, Jeff Friedman, Mike Freire, Jack Dunnigan, Dan Pill, Dick Caswell, Willie Mack, Brian Collins, Ian Church, Greg Delmonico, Larry Izzo, John Tumminia, Al Goldis, Rob Nelson, Joe Grillo, Rick Bentzen, Scott Cooper, Aaron Barth, John Thomas, John Ryan, David Altchek, Barry Heyden, Keith Williamson, Bryan McGrane, Nick Cetrulo, Tony Biagioli,

Chris Catizone, Mike Stoll, Dane Skillrud, Martey Dodoo, Charlie French, John Freese, Dylan Reese, Ryan Maki, Steve Mandes, John Cosgrove, Brendan Byrne, Kevin Du, Brian Barnhill, Justin Tobe, Scott Richardson, and of course, my mom, dad, sisters Alyssa and Samantha, and my grandparents, Bob and Jane Wolff.

These people were all there rooting for me, and I'll never forget their kindness.

On the publishing side ...

Mark Weinstein, who did a brilliant job in editorially guiding us through this most unique publishing experience, Ken Samelson (who came up with the idea for this book), Bill Wolfsthal for steering all of the wonderful promotion and marketing, Scott Cooper for his outstanding publicity efforts, and of course my dad, who is somewhat familiar with the book publishing process.